Golden Nuggets

EXPERIENCES IN THE OLD SOUTH

DR. JAMES A. FRANKLIN SR.

PAGE PUBLISHING, INC.
Conneaut Lake, PA

First originally published by Page Publishing 2020

ISBN 978-1-6624-0941-7 (pbk)
ISBN 978-1-6624-0942-4 (digital)

Printed in the United States of America

This book is dedicated to my parents, Moses and Rosa Cunningham Franklin. They had twelve children, William, Robert, Aldine, Edward, Benjamin, Juanita, John Thomas, Roosevelt, Joe Louis, Rubenia, Lillian, and Albert. They also raised four grandchildren, Greta, Thaddeus, Ethel, and Jonathan. It is also dedicated to my children, James Jr., SoMonike, and Jamel; and to all of those persons on whose shoulders I stand. This book is also dedicated to the memory of Mrs. Clara Wright Franklin.

This book is dedicated to my parents, Moses and Rosa Cunningham Franklin. They had twelve children, William, Robert, Aldine, Edward, Benjamin, Juanita, John Thomas, Roosevelt, Joe Louis, Rubenia, Lillian, and Albert. They also raised four grandchildren, Greta, Thaddeus, Ethel, and Jonathan. It is also dedicated to my children, James Jr., SoMonike, and Jamel; and to all of those persons on whose shoulders I stand. This book is also dedicated to the memory of Mrs. Clara Wright Franklin.

Contents

Introduction

Introduction

THIS STORY BEGINS in McCormick, South Carolina. McCormick is the largest town in McCormick County, which is located on the Savannah River. The Savannah River separates the State of South Carolina from the State of Georgia.

McCormick was formed from several surrounding counties. Gold was discovered in McCormick County in the mid-1800s. The Dorn family began mining gold in the 1850s. When my family came along in the early 1900s, my father remembers Dorn mining as having occurred in and around Dorn's Alley, which was owned by the Dorn family. Although he didn't remember the early history of the Dorn family, he did remember Mr. Gary Dorn and Mr. Jennings Dorn, with the company being named M. G. and J. J. Dorn. My father was Moses Franklin, and my mother was Rosa Franklin. They had twelve children. I am the youngest of the twelve. I used to tease my father and mother that I was glad that they went to bed one more time.

Dorn's Alley consisted of mill houses and was located a couple of hundred yards from downtown McCormick. The roads through Dorn's Alley were dirt roads. The house where I was born and lived in Dorn's Alley was surrounded by three former mines. We used to play in two of them. The legend in Dorn's Alley was that one of the mines ran underground from Dorn's Alley to Dean's Alley, about a mile in length.

The current McCormick County Library was built over a former Dorn mine in Dorn's Alley. People used to also live in houses at that same location. Therefore, I have chosen to name this book *Golden Nuggets: Experiences in the Old South.*

Much of the Dorn business operated in, near, or around Dorn's Alley. In the 1950s, the Dorn horse stables and barns were destroyed by fire. Unfortunately, several horses and one mule were killed in the fire.

This huge operation was in the center of Dorn's Alley. Three houses were also located around this establishment. My house was located two houses from the stables. When the fire alarm was sounded, folks from all around came into Dorn's Alley. At the time, my father was uptown at the Buzzard's Roost. As he was coming into Dorn's Alley, he told others around him that the flames were coming from his house, and he asked his buddies to go on since it was his house that was in flames. Back in those days, all shanty or frame houses that caught fire, burned completely. Fortunately, it was not his house. By the way, the Buzzard's Roost was located near the entrance to the Dorn Building supply building and right at the railroad tracks. This was where the black men of Dorn's Alley and from other areas would sit after a day's work and especially on Saturdays and Sundays, after church. No, these were not lazy men, but men who needed a place to chill and talk. These were the days of no televisions, very few radios, no sports teams, no video games or other technology, no electricity, no running water, no indoor plumbing, no refrigerators, or other conveniences.

Mr. Thomas Russell McAbee had married Ms. Cornelia Dorn, one of the daughters of the Dorn brothers. The McAbee's had a son named Jennings Gary McAbee. We met him one day as we (a couple of black kids from Dorn's Alley) were walking through Dorn Company property. To go downtown from Dorn's Alley, we had to walk through the company lumberyard. This shortened the trip to downtown. We befriended Jennings and started to play with each other every day, except on Sundays. He was the only white friend that the black boys had to visit Dorn's Alley on a regular basis. A story about Jennings appears later in the manuscript.

The location of the current post office is on the property where the Dorn Company Lumber Shed was located. At that site was also located a blacksmith shop, which was operated by Mr. Jonah Talbert and later by Mr. Charlie Grant. Mr. Gary Dorn (M. G.) also had an office which was located at the end of the lumber shed. The post office area near the railroad tracks is where Mr. Thomas Russell McAbee managed the M. G. and J. J. Dorn Building Supply Company. This is also where the main offices of the company were located. Adjoining the supply building was the cotton storage warehouse. Dorn's Alley and the Dorn Company were interconnected.

The Dorn Company sponsored a fireworks display every Christmas in Dorn's Alley. This was for all the black workers and families of the Dorn Company. I am putting companies here because the Dorn empire included farms, timber, pulpwood, cotton ginning, cottonseed sales, a large planer or sawmill, the local bank (Dorn Banking Company), etc. At the end of each fireworks display, all the workers were given a large bag of fruit and candy to take home for Christmas.

I knew Mr. Gary Dorn during the later part of his life. He always welcomed the children from Dorn's Alley to his office when he was able to come to his office. When I knew him, he was wheelchair bound. When the children would visit him, he would always give us chewing gum and candy as parting gifts. We really missed his talks and gifts when he was no longer able to come to his office as his health declined.

Sometimes he would reminisce about his company. My father's work life had been with the company. His comments about the company and Mr. Dorn were very interesting to an adolescent. The Dorn Company had huge timber, pulpwood, sawmill, cotton ginning, cottonseed oil, building supply, banking, and farming enterprises. Some Dorn family members were also involved in petroleum enterprises and operated a service station (gasoline station).

Mr. Luther Rankin assisted in the operation of the Dorn sawmill (planer). Mr. Jennings Franklin, a very nice white gentleman who lived in a community adjoining Dorn's Alley, assisted in the management of the Dorn Farms and forests. Mr. Harvey Sanders managed the lumberyard and coordinated repairs to Dorn properties. His brother, Mr. Jamie Sanders, was head of the Dorn Banking Company. I am sure that there were other managers, which my father did not discuss.

The McCormick Grammar School was located near the entrance to Dorn's Alley. The white kids had a different school year than the black kids back in those days. This was due to the fact that the black kids worked on farms, including some farms owned by the Dorn family, especially their cotton farms. We were not expected to start school until after most of the harvesting had been completed.

When the school year started for black kids, some of us could not attend because all the cotton had not been picked. When we were not in school, we could always hear the white kids playing at the McCormick Grammar School.

As a kid, I watched them tear down the McCormick Grammar School building. The bricks to the building were cleaned and hauled away. I never knew what happened to the old bricks.

Having no television, families in Dorn's Alley had a lot of quality family time. My mother would tell stories, we would sing and read the Bible, and there were always chores to do. Without electricity, there was always something to do. Chopping/cutting wood always kept the boys busy. Ironing was a chore for my mother and my sisters. The irons had to be heated on the stove in a continuous fashion. Washing clothes was a daily activity because you had to wash by hand using a rubboard. We had no automation. Everything was hand driven.

As I look back on those days and our visits to Mr. Gary Dorn's office, I felt that he might have wanted to do something about our plight, but at his age and disability, he might not have known exactly how to do so. I was never turned away from his office.

In addition to an in-depth look at Dorn's Alley and its surroundings, this document will look at a number of characteristics about my hometown of McCormick, South Carolina. Of particular importance, it will address one of the most successful organizations which helped black male youth back in the day and how we may use part of the ideals from that organization today.

It will also cover some of the characteristics of a typical Southern black community and some highlights and challenges which the black community faced. Further, the project will address a couple of black heroes of the old South, black patriotism to the United States, and the positive way of how black and white children associated in the Old South.

Dorn's Alley

Dorn's Alley

THIS IS A story of a boy who was born and grew up in the Old South. The Old South period of my growth was just before the end of World War II. I was born on a cold day in February in McCormick, South Carolina. The place where I was born was Dorn's Alley, which was located about five hundred feet from the beginning of Main Street. Our houses would be what one would call shanty buildings. The houses had two to three rooms, including a kitchen. When you would enter the house from the front porch, which all of us had, some with a swing; you would enter one of the bedrooms.

The bedrooms had a fireplace, with chimney access. The one chimney would serve two fireplaces, back to back, in two different rooms.

I was one of twelve children who were born in this wooden-framed building. I was the last born to my mother, Rosa, and to my father, Moses. It was a house that had cracks in the walls, cracks that were welcomed during the summer months but would cause you to freeze your behinds off in the winter months. We covered the cracks with old newspapers. Yes, newspapers! As a kid, I would watch my mother take some Argo starch, change it to liquid form, and brush one side of the newspaper, give it to the children, and we would paste the paper over the cracks in the walls.

No, I never thought that we were poor because all black people lived in the same kind of house. By today's standards, we would be poorer than dirt. Did I mention that we didn't know what lawns were because our yards were just plain dirt? We didn't mow our lawns, but we swept the yards with limbs from the trees which were tied together to form a kind of broom. The "brooms" were tied together with a piece of cloth which had been torn from a sheet which was no longer of any use on a bed, because of the holes and slits resulting from long wear.

When late spring arrived, we would punch holes in the wallpaper to receive some comfort from the wind, which would occasionally blow, only to play papier-mâché all over again, when winter would come.

I learned that I had two brothers who served in the United States Navy during the war. They almost lost their lives as the ship on which they served was bombed by the Japanese during the war. Luckily, the side of the ship where they were assigned did not receive the initial strike of the bombs, and they were spared.

This small Southern town of McCormick is located in the Upper Savannah area of the State of South Carolina. It is located near the Savannah River. It is the county seat of McCormick County. The county is bordered by Edgefield County, Greenwood County, Abbeville County, and the Savannah River.

During my time as a youth, McCormick was a very bustling little town with farming, sawmills, and some factories as the town's major enterprises. United States Highway 378 made McCormick a much-visited town as tourists traveled from Columbia, South Carolina, to Atlanta, Georgia, the most direct route at the time. Highway 378 traveled from east to west. The most popular highway through McCormick from north to south, was Highway 28, which connected Greenville, South Carolina, to Augusta, Georgia. Like most small towns, motels were scattered about, and service stations or gasoline stations were plentiful.

Again, my house was in Dorn's Alley. This wooden frame structure had four rooms, three bedrooms, and a kitchen. We did not have the luxury of a living room, family room, dining room, den, parlor, etc. The tin top on the house would let you know when it was raining. This rustic house was one of nine houses located in Dorn's Alley. All of these houses were owned by the company, M. G. and J. J. Dorn, two brothers who became very wealthy with the gold and other resources discovered in McCormick County in the nineteenth century. M. G. and J. J. Dorn operated sawmills and a large planer where timber was processed into lumber. The company also acquired and farmed thousands of acres in the county by direct operation or through sharecroppers. Also, the company operated a cotton gin, a seed mill and a large hardware and supply store and sold finished lumber from its warehouse. When the market changed, the company phased out its farming operations and set thousands of acres in pine trees where cotton and other crops once grew. My father worked for M. G. and J. J. Dorn most of his productive life.

A tragedy occurred at the main planer operation when my father got caught in the belt operation as he was trying to correct the course of some lumber. He received severe burns on his left hand and left arm. Hospital care did not exist in McCormick County. The nearest burn unit for black people in the late 1940s was in Columbia, South Carolina. My mother and father traveled to Columbia on several occasions for treatment. On one trip to Columbia, they took me with them. We traveled by Greyhound Bus. When we got to Columbia, I had to use the restroom. There were no restrooms for coloreds, so my mother and father walked me for several blocks to the South Carolina State Hospital on Bull Street. They were told that coloreds could use the facilities at the State Hospital. The guards would only allow me to go to the restroom. I was scared because I had to go inside where the patients were. As I look back, I think that this was a "trick" by the guards to see if the clients would bother or scare me. They must have laughed as I exited the place because I had peed on myself. Boy, was I scared!

There was no such thing as job site injury protections, OSHA, disability benefits, sick leave, annual leave, etc. The company did make an effort to help my father and returned him to work at another job site within the company. He became a night watchman at the planer, where he was the primary operator before his injury.

Most of the men who lived in Dorn's Alley worked for M. G. and J. J. Dorn. The rent for each house was $7 per month. This was in the early 1950s. For the most part, the company kept up the houses: new boards for any which needed repairing or replacing, new screen doors when needed, and painted or replaced the tin roofs when needed. The company also provided three faucets for the residents of Dorn's Alley. These water faucets, or spigots, were located at certain points in Dorn's Alley. Although the families were not assigned a certain faucet from which to get water, we simply used the one closest to our house.

The houses had no electricity and no running water until the late 1950s. One challenge in the wintertime was the freezing up of the water faucets, which was quite often in January and February. The families had to get together to make fire around the base of the faucets to unthaw the frozen pipes. No, there were no cut off valves, nor could we let the water slowly run all night to keep from freezing. We tried that and were often accused of wasting water. For a long time, we had no water bill from the company. At the time, we did not know what an energy bill was.

In the houses of Dorn's Alley, each bedroom had a fireplace, and each kitchen had a wood-burning stove. The fireplaces were used to keep us warm and often to cook food. We used cast iron skillets or frying pans to cook certain foods in the fireplace. These food items included eggs, bacon, hoecake, cornbread, and biscuits. The word *hoecake* comes from having to use the blade of the hoe, in early times, to cook bread. The trend continued in Dorn's Alley, without the hoe, but the word *hoecake* stuck with the practice. In some Native American cultures, this is called fry bread.

As cooking stoves became more affordable, families purchased these stoves for their homes. These stoves had four "eyes" and an oven. These were wood-burning stoves. Wood had to be precut for the stoves and fireplaces, or cut at the individual homes for use by the cooking stove or fireplaces. The cooking stove had a stovepipe, which went through the roof of the house. The stove had a draft, which was used to control the airflow. The stovepipe was a cylindrical unit that was clamped together into the round shape. It was made of tin. Most of the fireplaces and stovepipes would need attention because of wear over the years. Most of the homes that caught fire had fires that started around the chimney or stovepipe areas.

An unfortunate incident happened to my sister, Lillian. As a small child, around four years old, Lillian was playing around the fireplace. The fireplace was an open flame. Lillian lost her balance and fell into the flames. My brother, eight-year-old Joe Louis, who was nearby, pulled our sister from the flames. This happened at night in the winter of 1946. There were no medical facilities in McCormick, and none close by for burn victims. Back in those days, the black community had a number of "healers." My father knew of an elderly black man whose services he sought for my sister who suffered what would be called second- and third-degree burns today. She had burns about her face, head, and arms. My sister was near death. My father brought the elderly man to the house. When he observed my sister, he asked that my sister be left alone with him so that he could pray for her.

When I asked what he did, it was described to me as some type of exorcism being performed. Did he have any herbs? No one could tell me. He stayed with my sister all night long. I was told that the next morning, the elderly man's suit was soaking wet. He simply told my parents that she would be alright now. Even though my sister lived, she would carry the scars of that day all her life.

None of the homes in Dorn's Alley had electricity. At night, we used kerosene lamps to see by. These lamps were made of clear glass, with kerosene in the bottom of the lamps. The lamps had a wick, which was a thick piece of slow-burning fabric with the bottom in the base where the kerosene was located and the top exposed to being lit. The kerosene would slowly be drawn from the base to provide the accelerant to fire up the wick when lit. As the kerosene was exhausted or the wick burned out, they had to be replaced. The wick could be raised or lowered with a crank on the side of the lamp. Kerosene lamps made it hard to study, and we often suffered from eye strain. As the kerosene burned, soot would build up on the inside of the globe. When this happened, the globes had to be washed.

Kerosene was also used to start fires in the fireplaces and in the cooking stoves. You had to be careful doing this because the kerosene would often cause a small explosion, especially when thrust into a fireplace or stove, which may still have some fire in them.

Since we had no electricity, we had no refrigeration. Houses in Dorn's Alley had iceboxes. This was usually a white insulated cabinet, with four legs. It was called an icebox because it had a top compartment for the storage of ice. Wrapped meats and other perishables could be placed in the upper compartment with the ice. Other less-susceptible perishables could be placed on the lower shelves. In the summertime, the ice could last for up to twenty-four hours, if the size of the ice was large enough to last a day. Each icebox had a drip tray to catch the water from the melting ice. The tray had to be emptied often so the dripping water did not "spoil" other items in the icebox. We had to go to the icehouse each day to purchase ice.

We were lucky that Dorn's Alley was located several blocks (across the railroad tracks) from the icehouse. As you can imagine, some of the ice melted on the way home. More rural homes depended upon the iceman. The iceman peddled ice around the town and county on the back of a pickup truck. Heavy canvas covered the ice to keep it from melting. The iceman sold ice from ten cents up, based on the size of the ice needed. The ice came in three-hundred-pound blocks. The ice pick was used to split the ice into two one-hundred-fifty-pound sizes. The ice hooks were used to handle the ice and to measure according to price. If the house did not have a container for the ice, the iceman would use ice string to tie around the ice so that the purchaser could carry the ice into the house.

Without any running water, we had no restrooms. We had an outdoor toilet. The outdoor toilet existed at every house in Dorn's Alley. It was also called the privy or outhouse. This unit was constructed of wood with a sloping roof and a single front door. There were air openings at the top and bottom of the structure. These structures were formed over a hole in the ground, usually six feet deep. The inside floor of the privy was usually made of concrete because the privy had to be moved to another location once the hole was almost filled with waste. The movers of these privies had to have some skill since rollers had to be used to move them and privy "boxes" had to be constructed to go into the newly constructed holes.

Dr. C. H. Workman

There were very few black medical doctors in South Carolina in the 1940s and 1950s. Of course, there were none in my small hometown of McCormick. My mother had twelve children, all delivered by white doctors or white midwives. The doctor who delivered me was Dr. Claude H. Workman. As was customary in those days, Dr. Workman came to my mother's house to deliver me, since delivering me in his office was out of the question. There was no space in his office where this service could be provided for black women. His small office did include a clinic for white patients. There was a black hospital in Greenwood, South Carolina, twenty-three miles away, but Dr. Workman was not on staff there, and pregnancies were not thought to be something that needed hospital care. Quite frankly, most black babies were delivered by midwives, females who knew something about delivering babies. All midwives did have knowledge of lubricating the vagina opening, contractions, pushing by the expectant mother, blood flow, and cutting the umbilical cord. They also knew that any severe complications would call for the services of a medical professional. Of course, back in those days, a newborn baby could be lost during childbirth. Occasionally, the mother would be lost during childbirth.

By the way, Dr. Workman's motto was "The true aim of life is service." What a fitting motto for any human being. And how true for a country doctor who delivered over four thousand babies, performed over one thousand five hundred tonsillectomies, made over forty to fifty house calls a day, and often working for seventy-two hours straight without sleep. What a life for a physician!

Dorn's Alley Life

There was a railroad track that bordered Dorn's Alley. As a kid, we would play on the tracks and on the coal shoot. We did not realize the danger of what we were doing. The coal shoot was located near the end of Dorn's Alley. Coal was used to power the trains. The coal shoot was on a separate track high above the train tracks. The train would enter the coal shoot, which dropped coal near the engine of the train. Obviously, there was some spillover of the coal to the ground below. The residents in Dorn's Alley, who had coal-operated heaters were given permission to pick up any spillover coal. This worked out fine until some none Dorn's Alley residents decided to get coal from the shoot rather than spillover coal. This ended spillover collections by Dorn's Alley residents. Coal heat back in the day to the poor families of Dorn's Alley was like pure joy. The coal gave off a lot of heat and lasted a long time during those cold winter months. We could also buy a load of coal from local vendors, but most residents had to buy on credit.

Early morning trains hauled a lot of coal. During this time, the whole alley neighborhood would shake. Usually, it was near the hour of 3:00 a.m. I was told by my father that it was train number 192. It was a heavy freight train that was carrying coal to the Savannah River site. This site was commonly called the bombing plant, where bombs were made for the military. He also said that some of the coal was taken to the Clarks Hill Dam, which generated electricity. My father and I used to talk about this particular train because of the noise that it made while everyone was sleeping. Obviously, over the years, we became used to the noise. In the summertime, when we had visitors from the North, it was a shock to these visitors as they tried to sleep.

We lived in a tin-top house. In the late 1950s, white night riders would come through Dorn's Alley and throw rocks on top of our houses. Rocks on a tin-top house in the "dead of the night" made a lot of noise.

Naturally, this practice kept everyone awake. When this was reported to police, their response was that it would be hard to catch such persons unless the police camped out in Dorn's Alley. The sad part was that only one policeman worked at night in those days in McCormick, and he didn't leave the main part of town. When we suggested to our fathers that we wait on them some nights, they said no. They felt that this would only make the problem worse. After several weeks, the rock throwing stopped.

Church life was very important to the residents of Dorn's Alley. During the 1950s, each church had regular services at least once a month with Sunday school being held every Sunday. Sunday school usually started at 10:00 a.m. and regular church services beginning at 11:00 a.m. On the Sunday of regular church services, a Sunday night service was also held.

Getting to church was a chore for many since no family in Dorn's Alley had a car at the time. Residents had to walk to church or ride in the family's wagon. My family was a member of the Bethany Missionary Baptist Church, with the exception of my father. He was a member of the Ebenezer African Methodist Episcopal (AME) Church. The two churches were located on opposite ends of the town of McCormick. Other residents in Dorn's Alley were members of one of these two churches or another church, namely, Zion AME Church, Mt. Moriah Baptist Church, Springfield AME Church, or Shiloh AME Church.

In addition to Sunday school and regular church services, special programs were held at the churches. Most churches had revival services twice a year (spring and fall). Other programs included church anniversaries, choir anniversaries, twelve tribes' programs, missionary programs, pastor's anniversaries, an Easter program, a Christmas program, and watch night services.

We got electricity in our house during the mid-1950s. Mr. James Thomas Wideman wired our house for $40. We got a refrigerator in 1957 and a television in 1958. Before going to church on Sunday morning, we looked at the Parade of Quartets Program on Channel Six in Augusta, Georgia. It was hosted by Mr. Steve Manderson, who happened to be a white male. At the time, it was an all-black parade of quartets from the two-state areas of South Carolina and Georgia. Each group would have fifteen minutes or less, depending upon the number of groups Mr. Manderson had scheduled for that Sunday. It

was not prerecorded. This program lasted four hours, eight to twelve. I thought that it was fascinating, but we had to go to church.

My mother had twelve children, although not all twelve were home at the same time. Her way of keeping up with us as we walked the two miles to church was to keep all of us walking in front of her. She would also have a switch when she thought one was needed.

The black church did not have much money to pay the preacher. Part of his appreciation was shown by a family hosting the pastor at their home. He was fed and made comfortable as he waited to preach that Sunday night. This practice was passed around to the different families in the church.

During the week, most families had Bible study, sang spirituals, and had family prayer. Grace at meals was a requirement.

Games were made up by the children in Dorn's Alley. Toys were usually made by the boys. Toys such as slingshots, bows and arrows, and pop guns were made. Marbles were purchased. Hopscotch was prominent all over Dorn's Alley. The girls usually did jump rope, played house, and played with dolls. Climbing trees was most enjoyed by boys. Both boys and girls played with Western Flyer wagons, played tag, played softball, and played hide and seek. All boys played basketball and football, while some girls played basketball. Older boys played baseball.

There were basketball goals everywhere: on trees, on posts, and on our homes. The "goal" was usually an old peach basket with the bottom cut out and nailed to the tree or post or to the back of a house. This was the most active game in Dorn's Alley.

Older boys also pitched horseshoes. We got used horseshoes from the blacksmith shop near our homes. These were discarded shoes left when the blacksmith put new shoes on the mules and horses. Older boys and adult men also played checkers. Adult men played such card games as bid whist, tonk, dirty hearts, spades, blackjack, and poker. Families played bingo. Girls also played with Old Maid cards and a game called jackstones. The billy bat was a game played by boys and girls. This was a handheld "bat" with a rubber ball attached with an elastic band. The ball was hit by the bat using one hand. The person with the most successful hits without missing the bat won the game.

There were two old mines where we played. We didn't realize the danger at the time. There were also two small branches, which had vines around them. The boys would often swing on the vines and fall into the branch water. This was a lot of fun. It was a boys-only activity.

Very few families in Dorn's Alley had a radio in the 1950s. Those who did listened to WLAC radio in Nashville, Tennessee. WLAC played music that appealed to black audiences. They could only get this station at night. Purchasing records thorough the mail was popular during the 1950s for those who had electricity and a record player. Ernie's Record Shop of Nashville, Tennessee, and Randy's Record Shop of Gallatin, Tennessee, were the main sources of record purchases by mail as advertised on WLAC. During the day, Waymon White and Mal Cook would broadcast from a station in Augusta, Georgia, where the famous musician James Brown grew up.

To support the beauty shop appearance, most females in Dorn's Alley got their "hair done" at home. Every house had straightening combs. These combs, made of heavy metal, were put on the hot stove, and used to straighten or press the hair. Sections of the hair were greased (Royal Crown Hair Grease was the most popular and least expensive with Hoyt Sullivan's Hair Grease coming in second), and the hot combs were passed through the hair. The comb was also used to help to style the hair. Rollers were made at home. They were made using Granny's old stocking parts and joining them with small pieces of paper, usually brown paper. The small stockings/hairpieces were used as a twist to curl the hair. After several hours or overnight, the hairpieces were removed, thereby creating the curls.

The boys in Dorn's Alley got their hair cut at Mr. Elmer Mims's House. His son, Elmer Jr., had picked up barbering skills from a relative. He cut the hair of the boys who lived in Dorn's Alley. He only charged ten cents.

To further amuse themselves, the boys in Dorn's Alley caught flying June bugs. A string was tied around the leg of these green June bugs, and the boys would let them fly around to see how high the bugs would fly without releasing the bug. At night, the boys and girls caught lightning bugs, or fireflies. These little bugs would give off light. We would put them in a sealed jar as they flew around, giving off light at night.

Food and Eating Habits in Dorn's Alley

The families in Dorn's Alley were poor families, although we didn't know what poor was since everybody was poor. To make ends meet, the families in Dorn's Alley used different practices. In today's families, usually three meals are eaten each day. In Dorn's Alley, we usually had two meals a day.

Unlike today, most of the families in Dorn's Alley had a garden. This was the prime source of food for Dorn's Alley families. In each garden was a variety of vegetables to include tomatoes, corn, collards, butter beans, peas, string beans, okra, salad greens, sweet potatoes, watermelons, cantaloupes, etc. These items were picked from the garden as needed. Some were canned in Mason jars to be consumed during the winter months. Fruit tree items were gathered or purchased to be consumed and canned for the winter. These fruit items included pears, peaches, blackberries, muscadines, scuperdines, and plums. Pears, peaches, blackberries, and plums were also used to make jelly and preserves, which were also used during the winter.

There were a few large families in Dorn's Alley. Mothers had to find a way to stretch the use of food. Most popular were rice and grits. Both were cheap by back in the day standards. The use of rice created the bog, a lot of rice with a little chicken or with a little pork could go a long way. A can of tomatoes mixed with rice could feed a family. The use of grits along with a can of sardines, a can of mackerel, or a cheap mullet fish could go a long way. The use of flour and meal helped to fill many stomachs with a variety of breads, such as biscuits, hoecakes, fry bread, cornbread, and corn muffins. Mothers could also take flour, mix it with a can of salmon, and feed a crew of people with twenty-five salmon croquettes. The cheap desserts were Jell-O and tea cakes.

Families could usually make it during the growing season. It was the off-season when families experienced a lack of food. This is why canning was so important.

To have meat during the year, most families in Dorn's Alley had a hog. A pig (young hog) was purchased during the spring. The animal was raised in a hog pen. The hog pen was constructed of wood and wire. The hogs ate from a hog trough. The trough was made of rustic wood in the form of a V. Old tires were cut in half and used to water the hogs. The hogs were fed with slop (food wastes from the house), with corn, and sometimes with store-bought feed.

Sometimes during the fall, a fattening pen was constructed within the hog pen. The purpose of the fattening pen was to get the hog ready for slaughter by restricting his movement thereby causing the hog to gain weight. The fattening pen was constructed with a wood floor and made into a small area of the hog pen.

Hog slaughtering was a neighborhood adventure of slaughter, preparation, and sharing. Mr. Elmer Mims was the chief of the slaughter operation. Everybody else did as he directed. All the neighbors gathered at water faucet number 2. Wood was gathered, washpots were assembled, a slaughter table was brought to the sight, knives were sharpened, and water for boiling was readily available at the site. Only one hog was slaughtered at a time. The hog was killed at the site with a gun or hit in the head using the blunt part of an ax. The throat of the hog was immediately cut.

The hog was put on the slaughter table with hot boiling water from the washpot being used to scrape all the hair from the hog's body. Once the hair had been removed, the hog was cut so that the inside organs could be removed. The inside organs were separated or cut up into different parts (e.g., liver and intestines). The remainder was cut up into hams, shoulders, feet, legs, head, ribs, back, etc. All the hog was used, with the exception of intestinal waste and the hair.

Meat scraps were made into sausage, seasoned, and put into hog casing (hog intestines) or put into store-bought casing. Fat scraps were boiled into crackling, with the grease from the scraps being used to make lye soap. The hog's skin was used to make fatback. Fatback became known as the poor man's steak. In later 1950s, bologna became the poor man's steak. The hooves from the hog were boiled and used to make medicinal compounds. The hog's head was used to make hog's head cheese or souse meat. Families shared their harvest.

The liver of the hog was used to make liver pudding. The blood of the hog was often caught as the hog bled. The blood was used to make blood pudding. To make liver pudding was common with all hogs. Blood pudding was only used by families who wanted something different and daring. Poverty will often drive families on how they use meat and meat products available to them. Both puddings were rich in vitamins, minerals, and proteins. When properly prepared, the puddings could be sliced or made into a type of sausage. Items, such as rice, bread, oatmeal, barley, onions, cumin, and meat scraps were used to make the puddings solid.

We had no freezers since we did not have electricity. Each family had a smokehouse, or two or more families shared a smokehouse. Salt was used to preserve the meat, and most of the meat was stored in a smokehouse. A smokehouse was constructed of rough lumber and completed sealed with boards over boards. No light was to enter the smokehouse. The door to the smokehouse was heavily constructed with rough lumber. Smoke was created by building a smoldering fire in the middle of the smokehouse, thereby smoking the meat to preserve it. The meat in a smokehouse was hung from the ceiling of the smokehouse.

Most of the families in Dorn's Alley had a chicken house. The chickens were used to feed families and for the laying of eggs. Each family had at least one rooster. Baby chicks were born in the chicken house. They were raised to be fryers or to be hens (to lay eggs and to give rise to new chicks). Some families purchased baby chicks from the hardware store. When a chicken was needed for Sunday dinner, a chicken was caught. Wringing the neck of the chicken or the use of an ax to cut off the head of the chicken was used to slaughter the chicken.

As with the hog, hot boiling water was used to clean the feathers off the chicken. As with today's food trends, fried chicken was most popular in Dorn's Alley. However, the baked chicken could be used to feed more family members. The baked chicken was also used to make chicken soup. When things got really tough, it was not uncommon for a child to steal one or more eggs from a neighbor's chicken house.

Wild game was also used to supplement the meals of families in Dorn's Alley. Each family had at least one rabbit box, which was used to entice a rabbit to enter the box only to be caught inside. Possums,

deer, squirrels, coons, and quail were part of the family table. This made hunting a very popular past time.

Fish was very popular with the families in Dorn's Alley. Every family had one or more fishing rods, fishing limbs, or fishing canes. No one had a boat. There were creeks and rivers all over McCormick County. Fish bait (worms) was plentiful. Dorn's Alley residents would catch bream, bass, catfish, and other types of fish.

Water, Kool-Aid, and tea were the drinks used in Dorn's Alley. Occasionally, for special occasions, a store-bought soda, pop, or drink would be purchased. Sometimes milk was purchased from Mrs. Jennings Franklin, a white lady who had a milk cow and lived at the adjoining community to Dorn's Alley. Sometimes a family may have been able to purchase store-bought milk.

Dorn's Alley Families during the Late 1940s and 1950s

Mr. Willie Crawford and Mrs. Mattie Sue Crawford
Children: Willie "Billy," "Honey Bunch," and "Sister"

Mrs. Ida Crawford

Mr. Ossie Adams and Mrs. Lillie Ree Adams
Children: Ossie Jr., Rebecca, Patricia, Craig, Jimmy, Brenda, Ruby, and Catherine

Mr. Neal Callaham and Mrs. Jean Worthy Callaham
Child: Jean

Mr. Walter "Tell" Callaham and Mrs. Ethel Callaham
Children: Neal, J. T., Walter, Mildred, Donald, Belinda, and Neraldine

Mr. Willie Belcher and Mrs. Annie Ruth Belcher
Mrs. Kittie Belcher

Mrs. Bell Mars

Mr. Elmer and Mrs. Annie Lee Mims
Children: Elmer Jr. and George

Mr. and Mrs. Sugar Moore
Children: Ed, Mary, Martha, and Flora

Mrs. Lillie Adams
Children: Lucy, Charles, Boot, Ruth, and Willie

Ms. Lucy Adams
Children: Bobby Lee Holloway and Cora Mae Moore
Cora's Child: Marie

Mr. Moses Franklin and Mrs. Rosa Franklin
Children: William, Benjamin, Patricia, Edward, Robert Lee, Juanita, John Thomas, Roosevelt, Joe Louis, Rubenia, Lillian, and James Albert (the author)
Rubenia and Raiford Chamberlain's children: Greta and Thaddeus
Lillian and John Moore's child: Nancy
John and Rodessa Franklin's children: Ethel and Jonathan

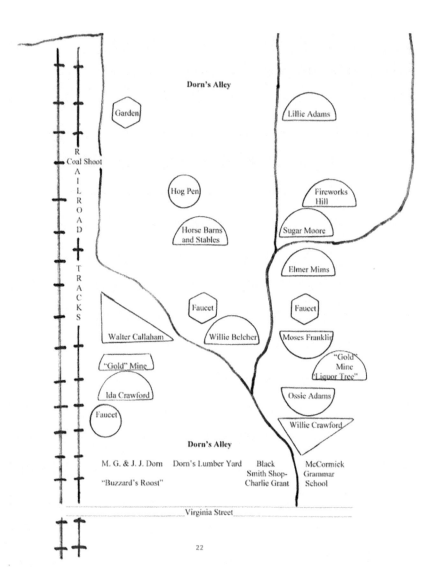

Dorn's Alley

Garden

Lillie Adams

R
Coal Shoot
A
I
L
R
O
A
D

T
R
A
C
K
S

Hog Pen

Fireworks
Hill

Horse Barns
and Stables

Sugar Moore

Elmer Mims

Faucet

Faucet

Walter Callaham

Willie Belcher

Moses Franklin

"Gold"
Mine
"Liquor Tree"

"Gold" Mine

Ida Crawford

Ossie Adams

Faucet

Willie Crawford

Dorn's Alley

M. G. & J. J. Dorn   Dorn's Lumber Yard   Black
                                                    Smith Shop-
"Buzzard's Roost"   Charlie Grant

McCormick
Grammar
School

Virginia Street

22

Dorn's Alley Liquor Tree

Many of the black men who drank alcoholic beverages would come into Dorn's Alley and drank at the liquor tree. The liquor tree was a large oak tree that was surrounded by large hedge bushes and near an old "gold" mine. The area was located about seventy-five feet from our house. The large hedge bushes prevented the men from being seen.

It was illegal to drink liquor on the streets of McCormick, and most of the black men, including those who drank, did not have cars. When they got their spirits, they were not in the habit of walking long distances to consume their products. The liquor tree in Dorn's Alley was the choice location. After all, Dorn's Alley was the choice location since it was the closest black community to downtown McCormick. Main Street was about one hundred fifty feet, and the closest liquor store (Bussey's Liquor Store) was only about two hundred feet away.

Although some women drank, it was taboo for them to drink at home or even away from home. Since most black men did not have a car or a driver's license, naturally just about all black women had neither. Most black communities had a bootleg house. Oftentimes black women would sneak off to a bootleg house during the day when their husbands were working. Most black women who did work had domestic jobs working in the homes of white citizens and got off work before their husbands. This is when the sneaking usually occurred. Most bootleg houses were operated by women, so these women kept their drinking a "secret." No ladies ever visited the liquor tree.

Some of the men would drive their wagons to town on Saturdays, park them at the blacksmith shop, do their drinking at the liquor tree, and drive their wagons home. Also, while at the blacksmith shop, their mules could be fed, given water, give their "horseshoes" and hooves some attention, etc. Any needed repairs to the wagon or its wheels could also be made while the owner/operator hung out at the liquor tree.

During the late 1950s, bottle collectors would collect empty bottles, which were deposited at the liquor tree. It was easier to use these half-pint and pint empty liquor bottles to sell bootleg whiskey rather than the Mason jars which had been used at the bootleg houses.

Rubbing alcohol drinks were also popular at the liquor tree. These drinks were a mixture of 50 percent rubbing alcohol and 50 percent water. This was a cheap but dangerous mix to use to get high. Bay rum hair tonic was available and drank at the liquor tree. A dangerous incident happened at the liquor tree one day. A consumer acted in a crazed condition, shaking, foaming at the mouth, and eyes "turning back into his head." The police were called. The man's hands and legs were put into cuffs. He was taken to the mental hospital in Columbia, about seventy-eight miles away. I later learned that he might have been hallucinating (e.g., seeing snakes) and experiencing the shakes or DTs (delirium tremens), a condition almost unknown to McCormick officials at the time. I also later learned that some of these men might have had severe drinking problems to the extent of being addicted to alcoholic beverages and would consume any substance with alcohol. By the way, this visit to address an emergency is the only time that I remember the police visiting the liquor tree.

Growing Up

One remarkable thing about growing up in McCormick is that more than 90 percent of all black men worked, although most occupations were limited to sawmills, working in pulpwood, working as farm-workers, and working on the railroad or in janitorial services. A few black men were considered as tradesmen, i.e., carpenters, electricians, brick masons, and other construction workers. Nonetheless, almost every black man had a job. As such, this transcended to their children. Their sons were brought up with a strong work ethic. Every son was expected to find and to hold a job. By the age of ten, most black boys had a job working on a farm or in a store, delivering papers, working in the peach field or peach-packing house, shining shoes, and mowing the lawns of white citizens, to name a few. Most black families did not have lawns. Our yards were usually Johnson grass and weeds. We used a sling blade and a manually push rotating grass cutter for any greenery in our yards. Our yards usually did not have any vegetation, other that leaves and other debris. We maintained our yards with tree branches, usually tied together, using a cloth strip (or sash). We used such to sweep the yard, not to mow the lawn.

My Uncle, Jonah

My uncle, Mr. Jonah Talbert, taught me how to plow a mule. I learned early on that plowing a mule was not to be my profession. The work was long, and the hours were hard. I could not get used to "Gee" and "Hah," and I don't think that the mule that I was plowing could get used to my temperament. You could not choose when the mule went to the restroom, and you had to watch where you stepped. I remember one time when one of the plow handles broke. It was then that I learned that I could curse at the age of thirteen.

Local author Mr. Bobby Edmonds wrote of Uncle Jonah in his book *The Making of McCormick County*. He identifies my uncle as an African American storyteller who attracted audiences of white boys from the white school during their lunch break. The school was located across the dirt road from my Uncle's place of business, which was located at the entrance to Dorn's Alley, where I lived. By profession, my uncle was a blacksmith. He also owned a farm on the southwest end of the town of McCormick. He was well known as a cotton farmer.

One of the most exciting times on his farm was in the fall of the year when sweet potatoes were harvested. Uncle Jonah had several acres of sweet potatoes. His potatoes were so good until you could eat them raw. They were made more delicious when my Aunt Sally, Uncle Jonah's wife, would bake them for us to carry home across town to Dorn's Alley. The harvest from his farm was how we were paid for helping him on his farm. In addition to sweet potatoes and other vegetables, we were also able to make buttermilk from his farm. He and Aunt Sally would milk the two dairy cows, which were on his farm. Aunt Sally would churn the milk, and we would take some home. Often, Aunt Sally would let me churn the milk.

My mother was one of the greatest cooks in Dom's Alley. For instance, she would take the sweet potatoes and make sweet potato custards, sweet potato pies, sweet potato bread, or sweet potato souf-flé or just slice them and bake in butter and sugar. Sweet potato patties would come later.

I was so spoiled by sweet potatoes until my father started to plant them in our garden, which was located near the coal chute on the railroad track, which bordered Dorn's Alley.

Uncle Jonah and Aunt Sally were both preachers. They had a church on the southeast side of the town of McCormick. The name of the church was Saint Louis Church. Services were held monthly.

Uncle Jonah got to be my uncle when Aunt Sally married him. Aunt Sally was my father's sister. Her maiden name was Franklin.

Children Standing before an Outhouse in Dorn's Alley

(Thaddeus, Joey, Greta, Lois, and Nancy)

Homes in Dorn's Alley

Early Work Life

Working Odd Jobs

THE CHILDREN OF Dorn's Alley were brought up to work. As with all poor communities, every one of some size in the family had to work. It was just a natural thing. It was expected.

My first job was to throw newspapers off the back of a pickup truck. I had to get up at 4:30 a.m. each day to get on the back of the truck, which picked me up from my house. My route was finished by 6:00 a.m. This gave me time to get home to get ready for school. I had to walk two miles to school. I was ten years old.

We hired ourselves out to do yard work and other chores at white family homes. This practice was expected in McCormick. We would go to the back doors of whites in our community, then knock and ask if any work was needed at their homes. Our yard work included cutting grass. No, we did not have gas-operated lawn mowers. The rotary push mower and the sling blade were used to cut the grass. We also did pruning and raking leaves. When our work passed lunch-time, the families were nice enough to feed us something for lunch. No, we could not go into their homes. We were usually fed outside and ate on the steps or on any backyard lawn furniture, which might have been available.

If the white families liked our work, they would usually choose us as their regular yard worker. The word was passed around among the kids in Dorn's Alley that a certain house had chosen a specific child from Dorn's Alley to do their yard work. I did yard work for Mr. and Mrs. Paul Brown.

We had four major grocery stores in the 1950s. They were Ream's Supermarket, Talbert's Supermarket, Campbell's Dixie Home Store, and Well's Supermarket. A lot of white McCormick residents did not have cars back then. If they did, the husbands drove those vehicles to work. Grocery deliveries were popular. Several kids from Dorn's Alley provided bicycle deliveries of groceries all over town. These bicycles were equipped with a very large metal basket on the front and with a smaller metal basket on the back of the bicycle. Each bike had a light on the front, a reflector on the back, and a type of bell. Two of my brothers were grocery delivery boys. They worked in the stores and also delivered groceries.

My Christmas break (two weeks) was used to plant pine tree seedlings. As the M. G. and J. J. Dorn Company was phasing out much of its farming operations, the vacant land was used to plant pine trees. As you can imagine, it was pretty cold at Christmas.

Our workday began as the sun was rising and ended with the sun setting at approximately 5:45 p.m. We didn't use the words "layer up" back then, but that was what we did each day.

I got this job through my father. He and another Dorn employee (Mr. Boot Adams) were the rope casters. All the workers were spaced out along a rope, which had "flags" attached evenly along the rope. Each worker had to follow his flag. The rope casters would cast the rope forward. Each worker had a dibble, which was used to open the hole in the ground and to close the hole after planting the pine seedling. This kept the pine seedlings planted in an orderly fashion, equal vertically and horizontally.

Other odd jobs included picking peaches and working at the peach-packing houses in Johnston and Trenton, South Carolina. Mrs. Carrie Martin of Plum Branch, South Carolina, would pick up us each day and transport us to Johnson and Trenton on the back of a pickup truck. Some of us would pick peaches in the peach orchards, and others of us would work at the Boatwrights' or Holmes' Peach-Packing House. Those of us who worked at the peach-packing house had a variety of jobs: sorting the peaches to determine which peaches were solid (hard) enough to survive the trip north in a refrigerated transfer truck, put the softer peaches in bags to sell locally, operate the cooling unit where crushed ice was used to create the coldest water possible to flow over the peaches before they were put into peach baskets, and the packers and loaders who put tops on the peach baskets and loaded the baskets into the trailers of the transfer trucks. I worked at the peach-packing house and was paid twenty-five cents an hour. Those who worked in the peach orchards were paid by the number of baskets of peaches, which they picked. This work lasted two months during the summer.

In the late summer, we picked cotton and field peas. I picked cotton mainly for Mr. John Bell. He was a black man who either rented or owned a large cotton crop. This was the real sunup-to-sundown job. The most precious item that a cotton picker could have was the availability of water. In the mornings, we packed a lunch and had a jar of water. It didn't matter that we didn't have ice in the water. This was the hardest work that I ever performed as a child. When the cotton rows got low and you had to pick on your knees while dragging your cotton bag; that was a challenge. We didn't have gloves back then, so it was not unusual to have pricked hands at the end of the day.

Each cotton picker had a cotton sheet. No, it was not like a bedsheet. It was a "sheet" made of brown croker-sack-type material. As the picker would fill up his cotton sack, he would empty the cotton onto his sheet. At the end of the day, his sheet would be tied up and weighed at the assembly site. I was paid two cents a pound and very seldom picked over one hundred pounds. I don't know how our forefathers worked in the cotton fields all day. I guess they got used to this type of work.

Occasionally, the pine tree nursery in Trenton would need green pine combs from pine trees to produce new pine tree seedlings. Farm agents would get the word out that pine combs were needed. Again, the pine combs had to be green. The pine combs do not fall off the pine trees until they turn brown, so we had to climb pine trees to get green pine combs.

Even with any gloves, this was challenging. Picking was not easy. You had to grasp the pine comb and twist the comb from the limb of the pine trees. Yes, there were some pricked hands, a few occasional falls, but the money was good. We got $3 for a croker sack full of green pine combs. This only lasted a couple of weeks.

Lowe's Shoe Shop

The first significant job that I had was to work at Lowe's Shoe Shop in McCormick. The owner was Mr. Sam Lowe, a white gentleman who lived in the White Town community, located five miles southeast of the town of McCormick. He had two sons, Benny and Luther. Luther was the oldest.

I started to work in the shop as a shoeshine boy when I was in the eighth grade at Mims Elementary School. When I first started there, the cost of a shoeshine was ten cents. For mixed colored shoes, the cost of a shine was twenty-five cents because we had to use two different colors, which we could not mix together. Mr. Lowe kept a tally of the number of shines performed. At closing, Mr. Lowe gave each boy five cents for each pair of shoes shined and ten cents for mixed-colored shoes. I thought that our pay by Mr. Lowe was very fair since he bought all the shining and polishing items that we needed. Obviously, he provided the place where we worked. We also got tips from most of our customers. Most of the shines occurred on the shoeshine stands. Some shoes were brought in to be shined. There were two stands in the shop with two sides, one for whites and one for blacks. Oddly enough, we had more black customers than whites who got their shoes shined. The white stands had two seats, and the black stands had three seats. The stands for white customers were located at the front of the shop near the real large window where they could look out onto the street. The stands for black customers were located on the opposite side near the middle of the shop.

All the shoeshine boys were black. I was taught to shine shoes by two brothers, Arthur and Sylvester Jenkins. Arthur was the most patient and helpful to all new shoeshine boys. In order to shine a shoe, we had to clean the shoe. We used a cleaning solution, which was a thick liquid made from a powdered mixture and water. Along with a wire brush when needed, this mildly thick solution would clean dust, dirt, mud, and some other debris from shoes. After the solution was placed on the shoe, we wiped the solution off with a rag. This prepared the shoe for the application of shoe paste. We used a shoe paste that closely matched the color of the shoe. The most popular colors were black, brown, tan, and cordovan.

After the paste was put all over the shoe with a small round brush, the first of up to three brushes were used to brush the polish into the shoe. The first brush was used to brush the heaviest of the polish. By the time the second brush was being used, you could see the shine coming through. We continued to with the second brush, and sometimes the third brush until a gloss was accomplished. A shoeshine rag or cloth was used to get maximum shine.

The shoeshine rag was made of heavy cotton fabric with a smooth side and a less smooth side with some cotton protruding from the cloth. The less smooth side was used to really shine the shoe. The cloth was approximately eighteen to twenty-four inches long. The color was white or off-white. The width of the cloth was approximately four to five inches wide. The use of the cloth really put the real shine on the shoe. We rolled the cloth up approximately two to three inches on each end for each hand. We then stroked the cloth across the shoe in a fast motion. The fast motion was needed to make the rag pop. This came about with the rhythm made by the talents of the shoeshine boy as he stroked the toes of the shoes and pulled the rag off to make several types of pops. A pop was also generated when the back of the shoe was stroked. The popping of the rag was a show within the shop. Usually the better the show, the more tip each shine boy got.

Most customers liked a spit shine. Yes, we spit on shoes. As time passed, we were asked to use water. Between the use of the rag, the spit, and the heat generated on the shoe, a sharp glow, or major shine with rays seemingly coming from the shoe was created. This was especially true for the front of the shoe. The more talented shoeshine boy could make the whole shoe shine. It was always complimentary when a customer would say, "I can see myself in my shoes."

In addition to the shine, some customers wanted the soles of their shoes to stand out. We cleaned their soles with saddle soap. We then used sole dressing. This was a liquid substance that gave a glassy tone to the soles. This solution was applied to the sole, heel, and to the thread of the shoe, which existed between the sole and the main body of the shoe. The application of the sole dressing cost an extra five cents.

Another paste that we used was neutral paste. As the color implies, it was a clear paste that could be used on any smooth shoe. We often used the neutral paste to improve the finish to a shined shoe, often using it instead of spit.

Some shoes had to be polished with liquid polish, especially suede and all-white shoes. Some shoes were two-toned shoes. Most two-toned shoes were either black-and-white or brown-and-white. Some customers wanted their polished shoes to shine. We could do this after the shoes dried, use a very light coat of neutral polish, take our rags, and shine the polished shoes. We shined a lot of boots and ladies' shoes too. Boots were twenty-five cents and ladies' shoes cost the same as men's shoes, ten cents.

No, we didn't always get a tip, but the better the shine and the more entertaining the shoeshine boy, the greater the tip. Usually, the tip was five cents to ten cents.

Most of our customers loved to get their shoes shined. Sure, they looked better. I think that many of them felt better. It was quite common to come to town to get your hair cut and to get your shoes shined every Saturday. The barbershop for whites was located on Main Street, and the barbershop for blacks was located on the back of the Main Street Alley. The shoe shop where I worked was among the businesses which separated Main Street from the Main Street Alley. The shop was next door to Banks Restaurant. Whites went into the front for service, and blacks went around to the back to be served.

Another thing that I liked about Mr. Lowe was his sense of fairness. Customers were served on a first-come, first-served basis. You did not have to stop shining a black person's shoes and go to shine the shoes of a white person who came in after a black person.

This practice held true for the shoeshine boys. The shoeshine boys received customers as they came into the shop. Whoever got to the customer first got the shine. Over time, some customers had favorite shoeshine boys. We all knew that so there was no rush to get to those customers.

We also got customers from outside the shop. We would stand in front of the shop. Some customers would be coming to the shop, and others would not. We would use the common (we didn't know it then) sales pitch: "Shine, shine." We would be asking the people if they wanted a shine. The shoeshine boys worked on Saturdays. Usually, the number of shoeshine boys were five. The hours were from 8:00 a.m. until 8:00 p.m.

We got along quite well with Mr. Lowe. He was a nice man by preintegration standards. He was always cordial and asked about our families. He had a bench for us when we were not busy. He also sold shoes. He would let us have shoes at a discount. He always wanted us to smell nice. Back in those days, poor boys only had a Saturday night bath. At other times, we "washed off." When we would come to the shop on Saturdays, Mr. Lowe had a deodorant waiting for us. We called the small room the Mum room because he would have Mum deodorant waiting for us at the shop.

His boys were pleasant. Benny was the most welcoming of the two sons. When Luther got to be sixteen, he called all the black shoeshine boys to the back of the shop. He asked, "Isn't about time that you all called me Mister?" Of course we did not answer. We only smiled to ourselves. Sure, we talked about it later. No, we did not call him Mister during the time that I was there.

Working on Saturdays

Working at the shoe shop gave us the opportunity to see a lot of action. We saw arguments each Saturday. We saw fights almost every Saturday. During most of my five years at the shoe shop, we had only white policemen. During my last year there, a black person was hired, Mr. Agg Zimmerman. Though he was a type of policeman with a policeman's uniform, he was not allowed to carry a gun. Also, he could arrest only black people. When a white person acted up, he had to go to a telephone and call a white policeman.

Black people would always be embarrassed when they were arrested, usually for being drunk or in a fight situation. The white policeman would grab the black person in the back center of his pants, jack him up, and march him straight down Main Street to the jailhouse.

The Saturday mornings always started off good in the area of Lowe's Shoe Shop, but with all the drinking of beer, wine, and whiskey, which occurred during the day, things really started to deteriorate in the early afternoon. One Saturday afternoon, I saw Mrs. Louise Dennis really cut a dude up pretty bad. Blood was everywhere. This occurred between Banks Restaurant and Bussey's Liquor Store. I understand that the dude had threatened Mrs. Dennis.

Working at the Icehouse

In addition to working at Lowe's Shoe Shop, I also ran an icehouse for Mr. Roy Tompkins in the summertime. We sold ice at a penny a pound. The ice came in three-hundred-pound blocks. I had to open the icehouse no later than 4:30 a.m. It was necessary to be there that early for the men who were loggers and pulpwood workers. These men liked to be in the woods when the sun came up so that they could cut wood when it was coolest. Some people traveling stopped in as well to fill their coolers. The stores in those days did not have bags of ice, nor did they have ice makers. If you wanted ice, you had to go to the icehouse.

The original icehouse in my hometown had been operated by Mr. Bully Singletary, a black man. The type of structure of his icehouse was of thick rustic boards with no lights or electricity. The thickness of the boards and the type of board kept the ice as long as anything back in those days. After Mr. Singletary stopped selling ice, Mr. Gunsey Kelly took over the icehouse. Mr. Singletary, Mr. Kelly, and Mr. Tompkins were all black men.

When Mr. Tompkins went into the ice business, I was in the eleventh grade. This was my last summer home before going to college. I sold ice during the week and worked at the shoe shop on Saturdays. Mr. Tompkins sold ice at his icehouse on the weekends. Mr. Tompkins's icehouse was different from the icehouse of Mr. Kelly and Mr. Singletary. His icehouse was the latest on the scene. It was an electric free-standing building, which kept the ice-cold until it was sold. The ice still came in three-hundred-pound blocks. When a person came to buy ice, I would cut the ice straight down the middle into two one-hundred-fifty-pound pieces. The ice hooks were very important at the icehouse. They were used to handle the ice, to measure portions, and to lift the ice into tubs, ice crushers, and coolers. The ice pick was used to cut the ice, to chop the ice, and to measure smaller pieces of ice. Most people wanted their ice in blocks. Because most families still did not have refrigerators, a lot of children came to the icehouse to get a small block of ice to take home to put in the home's icebox. Even though most homes had a refrigerator by

1960, some still did not have a refrigerator. In order to carry their ice, we used ice string. Ice string was made up of several strands of fiber, which was designed specifically for ice. The smallest piece of ice which could be purchased was a ten-cent piece (ten pounds of ice). The piece was cut, a piece of ice string was tied around the ice, and the child took the ice home.

One thing that parents always told their children back then was to hurry home with the ice so that all of it would not melt by the time the child got home. Once home, the ice was put in the top area of the icebox. The icebox had a drip tray under the top of the icebox to catch the water from the ice as it melted. This prohibited the water from dripping on other foods at the bottom of the icebox. The construction of the icebox was similar to that of a refrigerator except that the icebox had no electricity. The icebox had insulation and looked attractive in a house, but its use was limited without refrigeration. Often foods would spoil in the icebox.

Some people wanted crushed ice from the icehouse. An ice crusher was available at Mr. Tompkins's icehouse because his icehouse had electricity. At Mr. Singletary's and Mr. Kelly's icehouse, the ice pick was used to break the ice into smaller pieces. The ice crusher had a large square opening at the top. The electricity operated a belt on the crusher, and the center of the crusher had a built-in ice chipper that chipped away at the block of ice at the top of the crusher. As the chipper rotated to chip up the block of ice, the pieces fell into a bottom square part of the crusher, which had an aluminum lining which caught the crushed ice. The crushed ice was put into jugs, coolers, tubs, or other types of containers, which were brought by the customers. Sometimes we would double bag brown paper bags for the crushed ice.

Mr. Tompkins had an accountability system. I reported to him every evening. During the day, he worked at a Gulf Service Station. He told me that he needed to receive from me $3 for each block of ice. This was important because he would take the difference out of my pay. Back in those days, there were no child labor laws to speak of. I started to work at 4:30 a.m. I had no breaks. I ate on the job because I had no lunch break either. I closed the icehouse at 7:00 p.m.

Sometimes I did not sell each block of ice for $3 due to waste from chipping and some melting, which occurred with the opening and closing of the icehouse door. Also, sometimes the ice did not chip as you wanted, which resulted in some waste. To help to offset these losses, which would reduce my pay, cantaloupes and watermelons were very important in McCormick during those hot summer months. A cool or cold melon seemed to be referred by local consumers. I developed a side business by allowing some patrons to put their melons in the icehouse for cooling when I had space. No, Mr. Tompkins did not know about this. He only wanted $3 for each block of ice sold. The side business earned me five cents per melon. Mr. Tompkins gave me twenty-five cents for each block of ice sold.

Where did the blocks of ice come from? They came from the ice plant in Greenwood, South Carolina. The blocks were delivered to the icehouse in McCormick by a large truck. The huge blocks of ice were covered by large canvases and tied down. There were no refrigerated trucks, or if there were, the ice plant could not afford them.

The truck would back up to the icehouse and extend out some wide, thick planks to the doorway of the icehouse. The blocks of ice would slide down the planks as they were being guided by the deliveryman with his ice hooks. I would grab the ice with my ice hooks and guide them into an organized standing position in the icehouse.

Although I would give extra special help to a lot of customers in packing their coolers, lifting their coolers into their vehicles, cleaning some of the coolers which hadn't been cleaned since the last time they were used, giving water for containers to use in barrels and kegs, etc., I never received a tip during the summer of 1960. At the shoe shop, I did receive some tips but not at the icehouse.

Merchants in My Hometown of McCormick

The Merchants in My Hometown of McCormick

MOST OF THE merchants in my hometown were friendly and cordial people. Many of them operated by the folkways and mores of the time.

Mr. R. L. Crook operated the store closest to Dorn's Alley. His was a small grocery store, but he had a bench on the front of his store. It was nice to sit on the bench in the cool of the day and enjoy a Nehi soda, which came in orange, grape, and strawberry. Lance nabs were also popular with the soda. We sometimes put Lance peanuts in the soda, which seemed to make the soda last longer for more enjoyment.

Mr. Reams operated the Reams Grocery Store. One of his sons managed the store. Mr. Reams was famous for making his own ice cream. Most grocers sold Borden's-Sanka, which later became Borden's, and Sealtest ice cream. Mr. Reams's had more flavors than other makers of ice cream, and he froze his ice cream in large square aluminum containers. His store was the third largest grocery store in McCormick behind Talbert's Supermarket and the Dixie Home Store.

The Tolbert Fashion Shop was the upscale clothing store in McCormick. This store was most popular with women and girls. He kept the females in current fashions.

Kelly's Pool Hall and Restaurant catered primarily to black customers. This was the most active place in McCormick on Saturdays. Bussey's Liquor Store was close by, and Banks Restaurant was across the alley. Liquor could be bought from the liquor store, and beer could be bought from Banks. When black patrons got their spirits and purchased a fish or chicken sandwich from Banks, laughter and goods times came to the back alley. When they finished their consumption, they went back to the pool hall. Mrs. Viola Holloway, an attractive black female, was the assistant manager of the pool hall and kept things in order.

Corley's Hardware and Supply Store was a joy when he parched his peanuts each day. The smell of peanuts roasting at his store appealed to everyone. A bag of freshly parched peanuts only cost five cents and lasted a long time. That was some good eating back in the day.

The second busiest grocery store was Mr. Dennis Talbert's Supermarket. This was where you could get freshly cut meats. This was also where most patrons went to get their hog sausage put in casings. I used to take my father's meats for sausage to Mr. Talbert, who would grind the meat together, put some seasoning in the ground meat, and then put the meat into casing. This was the best-made sausage in the world. I have never tasted any better.

Mr. Lupe and Mrs. Etta Brown operated Brown's Shell Station. I worked there for a short period on Sunday afternoons after church. Mr. Brown was known to give each customer at least three cents more in gasoline than they had purchased. He was a very nice person. Mr. Harvey Sibert managed the mechanical side of the business. He taught me how to do my job for Sunday afternoons. Mr. Sibert was off at that time.

Mr. Strom operated the Western Auto Store. Back then, you could lay away toys in his store. Bicycles, red wagons, and BB guns were most popular for boys.

Smith's 5 & 10 was the most popular store for youth. By its name, things were inexpensive. A lot of his toys and other items were made in Japan. The store's variety was attractive for youth because school supplies were readily available there.

The second most popular clothing store was Drucker's Store. Mrs. Drucker was a Jew and quite a salesperson. Although she had Mrs. Mann and others to assist her in the store, she was the best salesperson. She knew that it was her job to "make it work"—that is, your fashions of interest. She had a large variety of men's, women's, and children's clothing.

Strom's Drug Store on Main Street was operated by two brothers, Wilbur and Lawrence Strom. This was a Rexall Drug Store. Back in those days, they had some one-cent sales on several items, such as Tussy Deodorant, and ice cream, I believe that both brothers were pharmacists. Dr. Brown's office was located on the second floor of this building. You had to go into the store to go up to his office.

There was a second Strom's Drug Store. It was operated by Mr. Rudolph Strom and his son, Rudolph Jr. At the time that I knew him, he was an older gentleman. One thing that was unusual about him was that he called all black males Jack. When you would enter his store, he would say, "What's for you, Jack?" My brother-in-law said that when this happened to him. He looked around as if to see where Jack was.

Mr. Joe Hamilton's store was the favorite store for black children. He had all the candy, and you could buy as little as a penny's worth. His candy and cookies were "loose" items, and you could buy as much as you wanted. Candy, such as BB bats, tootsie rolls, banana splits, squirrel nuts, jawbreakers, kits, sugar daddies, sugar babies, chocolate-covered peanuts, hot balls, bubble gum, candy corn, etc. were sold in Mr. Hamilton's store.

Well's Grocery Store was about the same size as Tolbert's Supermarket. The most popular thing about his store was that he provided more grocery deliveries than most of the other grocery stores.

The largest grocery store was the Dixie Home Store. As such, this store was the most popular and had more brands of goods than the other stores. It was a part of a chain of grocery stores. Because it was a part of a chain, most items were less expensive than other grocery stores. When the name was changed to Winn Dixie Stores, the owner chose to go out of business rather than to sell under the new banner.

Patterson's Clothing Store was most popular among young men. He had the best variety for this age group. It was where I bought my only suit. Most of my clothing was hand me down clothes from my older brothers.

Mr. Moton Dorn sold the best hot dogs in town at his small grocery store. He also had a bench outside. His hot dogs were two for a quarter. With a five cents soda, eating was a charm, a good meal for thirty cents.

The Wholesale place was where you could buy a box of twenty-four bars of candy for ninety cents and sell them for five cents each, making a profit of thirty cents. The most popular five-cent bars were Big Time, Hollywood, Milky Way, Snickers, Hershey's, Baby Ruth, Three Musketeers, M&M's, and Pay Day.

Another small grocery store was Mr. Garland Campbell's grocery store. For us, this was the cookie store. The Johnny Cake cookie was the most popular. This was a large one cent cookie. Most cookies were at least two for a penny. The Johnny Cake was so large that you could make a sandwich with it. The most popular two-for-a-penny cookies were coconut macaroon, shortbread, gingersnaps, lemon snaps, and vanilla. The other penny cookies were vanilla crème and chocolate crème.

Black beauty was very important to women and girls back in the day. Beauty shops or salons were all over the black community. Naomi's Beauty Shop was the most upscale of them all. She operated a free-standing facility on the corner of Carolina Street in the Bottoms. Mrs. Frances Callaham also dressed hair in her home in the Bottoms. Other shops were operated by Mrs. Mary Frances Murray and Mrs. Red Gilchrist; however, most of the hairdressing, as it was called, was done in the home. All black homes had straightening combs. These were combs made of heavy metal that could be put on the top of a hot burning stove, on a hot plate, or stuck into the coals of a fire. When the hot combs were mixed with the appropriate grease, it would "straighten" or "press" the hair as it was moved slowly through the patron's hair. The hair was styled as desired. For the black guys, there were several barber establishments: Garrett's Barbershop, Talbert & Franklin Barbershop (which became Talbert's Barbershop), and Elmer Mims Jr., to name a few. Before the electric clippers, hand-operated clippers were used by the barbers. This was often with some discomfort, especially when the blades were dull.

The Nantex was a sewing plant that operated in downtown McCormick. You could look in the windows to see the operators in the summer as they worked at the sewing machines. Like so many other sewing companies, the Nantex went out of business.

Tom's Grill was operated by Mr. Thomas Kennedy. This was more popular than Banks Restaurant because it also had a pool hall and pinball machines. With the pinball machine, you could earn money from Mr. Kennedy. You could also lose a lot of money. While

Banks Restaurant was known for its fish and chicken sandwiches, Tom's had the best hamburgers and hot dogs. Blacks were served at the back of these restaurants. Tom's Grill also constructed a liquor store between the white side and the black side of his restaurant. This made it more convenient than having to walk uptown to Bussey's Liquor Store.

Mattison's Sandwich Shop was operated in the Bottoms by Mrs. Eula Mattison. She served a variety of short order sandwiches and beverages. It was a nice stopover before going to church on Sunday night at the Bethany Missionary Baptist Church. Mrs. Mattison also had a pretty daughter who operated the business. This made the sandwich shop more popular for young men.

Both motor companies (Ford and Chevrolet) had good businesses back in the day. The Chevrolet dealership was operated by the McGrath family, and the Ford dealership was operated by the Caudle family. One of the most exciting events every year was to see the new Ford or the new Chevrolet. When each new vehicle arrived, it was covered and placed in the showroom. The date of the showing was put on the window of the store. A large crowd gathered to see the unveiling of the new automobiles on the appointed dates.

Many of the grocery stores sold demeaning images of blacks on certain products. Those products included Aunt Jemima Pancake Mix, Old Black Joe Black Eyed Peas, Uncle Ben's Rice, Rastus Cream of Wheat, Little Black Crowder Peas, and Old Black Joe Grease. Today, they have spruced up, or modernized, the images on many of these products.

The jewelry store was the place for young boys who wanted to give their girlfriend a gift for Christmas. I was no different. During my four high school years, I bought a gift from the jewelry store each Christmas. It was usually a necklace, earrings, and bracelet set. They were inexpensive, and your girlfriend usually felt that she was getting a lot. She could always brag about who gave her the gift, which she usually wore only on Sundays. My biggest problem was getting my gift to my girlfriend. We had no car. I did not have a driver's license. Usually, we had to get with another driver going in our direction, give him some gas money, and hope that he would return to pick us up.

Mr. J. Fred Buzhardt Sr. was a popular attorney in McCormick. His son, J. Fred Buzhardt Jr., a McCormick High School honor student and West Point graduate, was on the staff of Senator Strom Thurmond. I knew him at the time that he worked for the senator. I was pleasantly surprised that he was from McCormick. As a matter of fact, he provided a reference for me to get a job at the United States Post Office on North Capitol Street when I needed summer work in 1961 in order to help to pay for college. I had just graduated from high school. During the summer of 1961, I was invited to visit him and Senator Thurmond since we were all from McCormick and Edgefield Counties. We often talked about the peach crop and other local happenings in the two counties. At the time, I was living with my brother Roosevelt at 533 Third Street NE, Washington, DC. I later learned that Mr. Buzhardt became a staff attorney in President Richard Nixon's administration. He became special White House counsel to the president during the Watergate investigations. He eventually left Washington and moved to Hilton Head, South Carolina. I was informed that he passed away at the young age of fifty-four on December 16, 1978. He is buried in the town where he grew up, my hometown of McCormick, South Carolina.

The movie theater operated seven days a week with a different show appearing every two or three days. Love stories, comedies, and mysteries appeared during the week. Most of the weekend movies were westerns and jungle movies. The western was the most popular movie during this period of time. The most popular jungle heroes were Gordon Scott as Tarzan and Johnny Weissmuller as Jungle Jim. Bomba and Jungle Boy were less popular. The most popular western heroes were Roy Rogers, Gene Autry, Hopalong Cassidy, Jay Silverheels, the Cisco Kid, Tim Holt and Cheetah, Dale Evans, Wild Bill Hickox, Robert Taylor, Wild Bill Elliott, Tex Ritter, Bob Steele, John Wayne, Randolph Scott, Robert Taylor, Rock Hudson, Jane Russell, Richard Widmark, William Holden, Barbara Stanwyck, Lee J. Cobb, Calamity Jane, Montgomery Cliff, Tyrone Power, Gary Cooper, Clark Gable, Annie Oakley, Dale Evans, Lash Larue, Michael Ansara, and Ward Bond. Sometimes there were double features and cartoons. Of course, the seating was segregated. Whites sat downstairs in auditorium style seats. Blacks sat in the balcony on benches in a much smaller area. In the balcony was where all the heat existed from the film operator's section and theater projections. You had to duck under the projection to get to the right side of the balcony. Both my father and my brother John were movie operators. It costs nine cents to go to the movie. It had increased to fourteen cents by the time I got out of high school. Whites paid the same price but had more comfort.

McCormick had a number of motels back in the day. Two major highways ran through McCormick, Highway 28, and Highway 378. Highway 28 ran from north to south, and Highway 378 ran from east to west. There were no Interstate Highways. Highway 378 was the main road from Columbia to Atlanta, Highway 28 was the main road from Greenville to Augusta. McCormick has always been a great fishing and boating area, so vacationers were always around along with through traffic, which needed to take a rest. The Interstate Highway System and faster highway miles reduced the traffic through small towns, thereby reducing the need for many local motels, which were in small rural towns. Both many of the motels and many of the local merchants went out of business.

In addition to several motels, the town of McCormick had two downtown hotels. They were the McCormick Hotel and the Carolina Hotel. These were two fairly large buildings with two floors. Of course, blacks were not allowed to rent rooms at these hotels. They only worked there as maids and cooks.

The Dorn Banking Company was the only bank in town at the time. It was managed by Mr. Jamie Sanders. Mrs. Wilbur Strom helped to manage the bank. My encounters with her were few, but I remember her to be a first-class lady. She presented a banking environment of class and sophistication. Many current bankers could learn a lot from her demeanor. I received my first loan from this bank. I had just graduated from college, and I needed a car for my job. My mother's influence helped me to get the loan.

Evelyn's Beauty Salon catered to white patrons. The shop was located on the front of her residence on South Main Street, just behind the Nantex. The shop had a large picture window for those curious enough to look inside. The shop lasted for decades. Although we had no contact with her, we would notice how she welcomed her patrons, always with a smile. We often passed her shop as we passed on our way to the Bottoms, where we had a lot of relatives.

Deason's Florist was located on the other side of Bethany Church on South Main Street. This was a very popular florist sitting on a hill. The family lived in a house behind the florist. Not too far from the house, Deason's Pond was located. You could fish in his pond, but you dare not try to swim. Over the years, we were run out of the pond with the threat of a shotgun.

There was another Dorn Grocery Store, which operated across from the ginhouse. This was the store where many of the ginhouse workers went to get lunch. Mrs. Dorn was a very cordial and sweet person who would always give you more than you paid for. She reminded you of Mr. Lupe Brown at his service station. She had the best hoop cheese and cold cuts in town. Her husband had a leg disability and was not as nice as Mrs. Dorn. We would always wait until he sat down before we would enter the store. We all wanted Mrs. Dorn to wait on us.

Bully Singletary's Icehouse was an adjoining business next to the Dorn Grocery Store. This was one of the few black-owned businesses in town. He sold ice by the block or crushed. The icehouse was specially constructed to keep the ice solid for as long as possible. Mr. Singletary was a very large man who could handle the three-hundred-pound blocks of ice with ease. Some vegetables were stored in the house. He would often buy a new car every few years. This was a luxury enjoyed by very few blacks in McCormick.

When Mr. Singletary decided to retire, Mr. Roy Tompkins opened up a more modem icehouse, a free-standing electric icehouse. Melting was not an issue as it had been for Mr. Singletary. Vegetables, as well as watermelons, were stored when space was available. Mr. Tompkins, also black, was very industrious in that he had other businesses: a barbecue business and also a service station.

It is rumored that a bowling alley once existed in McCormick. The site of the Nantex building is said to have been a bowling alley.

It is also rumored that a soft drink company was located in McCormick. It reportedly made the once popular drink, upper ten.

Upper ten, by its name, was a ten-ounce lemon-lime soda in what appeared to be a green bottle.

The M. G. and J. J. Dom Planer was a sawmill-type operation, which produced lumber, sawdust, blocks of wood for home consumption, etc. In terms of current recycling efforts, this planer used most of its by-products for other uses. The sawdust was shavings produced from the dressing of the lumber. This sawdust was used at the Dorn Cotton Gin. The gin was operated by a boiler. The boiler was operated by being fired up with the use of the sawdust. As the gin was operating, a fireman used a large pitchfork to feed the boiler to keep the ginhouse operating. Wagonloads of clean cotton lined up at the ginhouse. A large circular suction arm was used to remove the cotton from the wagons. The ginhouse separated the cotton from any cottonseeds, and the cotton was formed into a bale. The bales of cotton were weighed, and this is how the farmers were paid, at so much a pound. M. G. and J. J. Dom had a large number of rental houses, or shanties. They all had wood-burning stoves. The blocks, or wood waste, from the planer was sold to the occupants in the rental houses, so there was very little waste from the planer. M. G. and J. J. Dom also owned thousands of acres of land in McCormick, most of it in farmland and in timber or forests. The cotton acreage had a direct relationship with the cotton gin, and forests had a direct relationship with the planer. As a child, I planted pine seedlings on Dorn property. My father was able to get me hired during our two-week Christmas break. We layered up and got out there each day with the rising of the sun. Each worker had a seedling sack and a metal dibble. There were a line crew and flags tied to the line. You simply followed your flag by taking two steps and planting a seedling. The dibble was used to make the hole for the seedling, and the dibble was used to pack the seedling by backpacking. At the end of the day, all seedlings were in a straight line. We worked from sun to sun, and I made $5 a day. The planer was located just below the Milliken Company on South Main Street.

The South Carolina Highway Department was located across the street from the planer of the M. G. and J. J. Dorm Company and the Milliken Company. This was the place to go for all your highway needs. It also had a maintenance shed.

Some McCormick Area Businesses
During the 1950s to 1960s

Cox Furniture Store
Dorn's Lumberyard

Bully Singletary's
Icehouse
Dorn's Grocery
Wholesale Goods
Jewelry Store

Tom Minor's
Gulf Station
Charlie Grant's
Blacksmith Shop
Orange Spot
Strom's Drugs

McCormick Hotel

Carolina Hotel
Dr. C. H. Workman
Attorney J. Fred
Budzartz
B. Perrin's Station

McAbee's Building
Supply
Buck Franklin's Store

Walker's Funeral
Home
Gary Dorn's
Service Station
Roland's Truck Stop

Reams' Market
Garland Campbell's
Grocery
Talbert's Fashion
Shop
Bussey's Liquor
Banks Restaurant
Lowe's Shoe Shop

Corley's Hardware /
Smith's 5 & 10 (1)
Dermis Talbert's
Market
Faulkner Tires
McGrath Motors
Display Lot
L. Brown's Ser. Sta.

Strom's Western Auto
Strom's Furniture
Strom's Funeral
Home
Campbell's Dixie
Home Store
Drucker's Clothing /
Smith's 5 & 10 (2)
McCormick
Messenger
Wilbur & Lawrence
/ Dr. Brown's Office
Cloth Shop

Patterson's Clothing

R. L. Crook Store
Kelly's Pool Hall
and Restaurant
Franklin & Talbert's
Barbershop
Cotton Storage Bldg.
Zeke Brown's Ins.
Hugh C. Brown
Agency
Freeland's Ser. Station

US Post Office

Dorn's Grocery Store
Edmunds Store

People's Drugs
(Walgreen)
(Rexal Drugs)
Well's Grocery
Joe Hamilton's
Grocery
Claude Hughley's
Store
Dorn Banking
Company
Strom's
Drugs—Rudolph
Harvey Murray's
Station
Red & White
Supermarket
E. & J. Shoppe

Dillishaw's Grocery

Garrett's Barbershop

Garrett's Fortune
Telling
Lucille Brown's Store
Mary Frances
Murray's Beauty
Parlor
Eula Mattison's
Sandwich Shop
Sanders' Oil
Company
Dorn's Ginhouse

Bell Motel

Fred Searles's Place

Deason's Florist

McGrath Motor-
Chevy White
Hardware
Caudle Motors-Ford
Park's Cleaners
McCormick Theater

Tom's Grill
Nantex Sewing
Factory

Carolina Tool
Company
McCormick Tire
& Retreading
McCormick
Dry Cleaners
Drennan's Motel

Milliken Company

Bussey-Richardson
Cleaners

Roy Tompkins's
Icehouse

Bladon's Gro.
& Restaurant
Pruitt's Small
Engine Repair
Naomi's Beauty Salon
Garrett's Wood Yard

IGA Grocery

Evelyn's Beauty Salon

Frances Callaham's
Beauty Salon
J. W. Fooshe Oil
Company (Gulf)
Moton Dorn's
Grocery
Dorn's Cottonseeds

Oak Hill Motel
M. G. and J. J.
Dorn Inc.

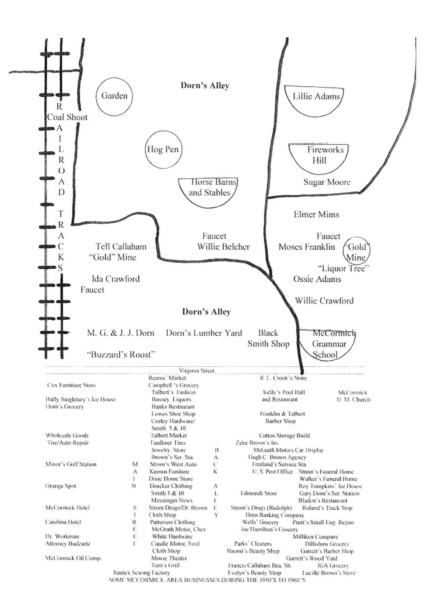

Dorn's Alley

Garden

Coal Shoot

R
A
I
L
R
O
A
D

T
R
A
C
K
S

Lillie Adams

Hog Pen

Fireworks
Hill

Horse Barns
and Stables

Sugar Moore

Elmer Mims

Tell Callaham
"Gold" Mine

Faucet
Willie Belcher

Faucet
Moses Franklin

"Gold"
Mine

"Liquor Tree"

Ida Crawford
Faucet

Ossie Adams

Willie Crawford

Dorn's Alley

M. G. & J. J. Dorn

Dorn's Lumber Yard

Black
Smith Shop

McCormick
Grammar
School

"Buzzard's Roost"

	Virginia Street			
	Reams' Market			
Cox Furniture Store	Campbell 's Grocery			
	Talbert's Fashion		Kelly's Pool Hall	McCormick
Bully Singletary's Ice House	Bussey Liquors		and Restaurant	U. M. Church
Dorn's Grocery	Banks Restaurant			
	Lowes Shoe Shop		Franklin & Talbert	
	Corley Hardware/		Barber Shop	
	Smith 5 & 10			
Wholesale Goods	Talbert Market		Cotton Storage Build.	
Tire/Auto Repair	Faulkner Tires		Zeke Brown's Ins.	
	Jewelry Store	B	McGrath Motors Car Display	
	Brown's Ser. Sta.	A	Hugh C. Brown Agency	
Minor's Gulf Station	M	Strom's West Auto	C	Freeland's Service Sta.
	A	Keown Funiture	K	U. S. Post Office	Strom's Funeral Home
	J	Dixie Home Store			Walker's Funeral Home
Orange Spot	N	Drucker Clothing	A		Roy Tompkins' Ice House
		Smith 5 & 10	L	Edmunds Store	Gary Dorn's Ser. Station
		Messenger News	L		Bladon's Restaurant
McCormick Hotel	S	Strom Drugs/Dr. Brown	E	Strom's Drugs (Rudolph)	Roland's Truck Stop
	T	Cloth Shop	Y	Dorn Banking Company	
Carolina Hotel	R	Patterson Clothing		Wells' Grocery	Pruit's Small Eng. Repair
	E	McGrath Motor, Chev		Joe Hamilton's Grocery	
Dr. Workman	E	White Hardware			Milliken Company
Attorney Budzartz	T	Caudle Motor, Ford		Parks' Cleaners	Dillishaw Grocery
		Cloth Shop		Naomi's Beauty Shop	Garrett's Barber Shop
McCormick Oil Comp.		Movie Theater			Garrett's Wood Yard
		Tom's Grill		Francis Callaham Bea. Sh.	IGA Grocery
	Nantex Sewing Factory		Evelyn's Beauty Shop	Lucille Brown's Store

SOME MCCORMICK AREA BUSINESSES DURING THE 1950'S TO 1960"S

63

Adult Sponsored Youth Organizations Foundations for the Success of Black Youth in the Old South

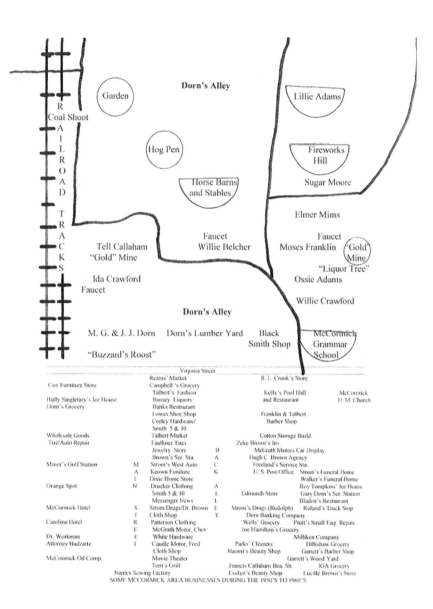

SOME MCCORMICK AREA BUSINESSES DURING THE 1950'S TO 1960'S

Adult Sponsored Youth Organizations Foundations for the Success of Black Youth in the Old South

T_ODAY'S_ PARENTS, EDUCATORS, and community leaders could borrow many of the characteristics of these black youth organizations as they guide and direct today's youth.

NFA

The New Farmers of America (NFA) was the most successful student organization for black male youth in the history of the states where the organization was located: South Carolina, Georgia, North Carolina, Virginia, Delaware, Maryland, Alabama, Florida, Kentucky, Tennessee, Arkansas, Louisiana, Missouri, Mississippi, Oklahoma, and Texas. The basic unit of the NFA was the chapter unit, which was located in black high schools in these sixteen states.

Within each state were federations of schools. A federation was composed of schools that were in close proximity to each other. Two or more federations made up a district. Two or more districts made up the state association.

The state associations were divided into sections. The three NFA sections were as follows: the Booker T. Washington Section, which included Delaware, Maryland, North Carolina, South Carolina, and Virginia; the H. O. Sargent Section, which included Alabama, Florida, Georgia, Kentucky, and Tennessee; and the Almmot Section, which included Arkansas, Louisiana, Mississippi, Missouri, Oklahoma, and Texas.

Again, the NFA was an all-Negro youth organization that was an integral part of the vocational agriculture teaching program within Negro high schools. These programs were located primarily in the Southern states, where agriculture was more prominent.

Although the study of agriculture had existed in Negro high school for several years, the NFA was started and developed to train Negro youth in the areas of character, thrift, cooperation, citizenship, scholarship, and agricultural leadership, while also studying general agriculture.

Nationally, the NFA started as a movement in Virginia in 1927. The federal government had the position of federal agent for agricultural education for Negroes, and a number of states had a teacher-trainer position at each Negro land grant college. The person who held the position of federal agent was H. O. Sargent. The teacher-trainer at Virginia State College was G. W. Owens. Other early developers included S. B. Simmons, W. T. Spanton, W. S. Davis, W. A. Ross, D. M. Clements, W. N. Elam, and J. R. Thomas.

Mr. Owens wrote the constitution for the NFA. Meanwhile, Mr. Sargent worked within the Department of Education to officially start the NFA in Negro schools.

The movement grew in interest in other states. Chapters spread all over the South, ultimately to form NFA chapters at the local and state levels. As more schools were established for Negro children with vocational agriculture programs, the NFA expanded to become a national organization in 1935. South Carolina received its state charter in 1937.

The study of vocational agriculture was designed for youth to receive training in farming, farm mechanics, farm carpentry, livestock production, and innovations in agriculture. The teacher of vocational agriculture was the key to the success of the agriculture program and to the success of the NFA chapter. Only students who were taught in the agriculture program could join the NFA. The teacher of agriculture also served as the NFA chapter advisor. Organizationally, there was a chapter NFA advisor, a federation NFA advisor, a state NFA advisor, a sectional NFA advisor, and a national NFA advisor.

The vocational agriculture program extended into the community. The agriculture teacher lived in the community and visited the homes of students enrolled in the vocational agriculture classes. Students also had to have a supervised farming program. This program or project could be a part of any phase of vocational agriculture instruction. A student might have a livestock production project, a row crop project, an agriculture mechanics project, a forestry project, etc. The student had to keep records for his project. During his visits to the students' homes, the vocational agriculture teacher would monitor the project and review the student's records. Appropriate support and advice would be given to the student.

These activities contributed to the major success of the vocational agriculture program and to the tremendous success of the NFA. We often hear of the word "mentor" today, but the NFA advisor was a mentor to youth and a friend to their families, which resulted in hard work and educational success by the students. As time passed, the vocational agriculture teacher was employed for twelve months because most farming activities occurred during the summer months.

The vocational agriculture teacher was a well-respected leader in his community. He was seen all over the community, had good public relations skills, had technical and practical knowledge, was a churchgoing Christian, and was seen as a friendly person.

Although a young organization by most standards, the NFA became involved in the war effort during the second world war. $150,000 was invested in stamps and bonds by NFA associations, chapters, and members in 1943. By 1944, more than 17,800 former NFA members were in uniform as American soldiers. Supporting these soldiers were NFA boys who invested more than $280,000 in stamps and bonds and collected over two million pounds of scrap metal for use in the war industries. By 1946, NFA members had invested more than one million dollars in war stamps and bonds. The NFA truly represented the primary aim of the organization, which was the development of agricultural leadership, cooperation, citizenship, and patriotism.

In May 1927, the State of Virginia held its first meeting at Virginia State College in Petersburg, Virginia. At this meeting, it was decided that the association would foster patriotism through the following efforts:

> To increase self-respect
> To take better care of individual health
> To beautify their homes
> To use time wisely
> To increase economic efficiency
> To provide organized rural recreational activities
> To create new interests

Reference: John Phillip Burgess, "History of the NFA in South Carolina," master's thesis, June 1956

Dr. H. O. Sargent

According to a chronology written by Dr. Ernest Norris, professor of agriculture, Prairie View A & M University, the key federal official for the development of the NFA was Dr. H. O. Sargent. Although Dr. Sargent was from Alabama, he proved to be a true friend to the NFA. He wanted the NFA to have the same recognition as the all-white Future Farmers of America. Dr. Sargent was honored with one of the new sections of the NFA being named for him, the H. O. Sargent Section. There were two other sections for the NFA: The first was the Washington Section, which was named for Dr. Booker T. Washington, a pioneer educator and founder and President of Tuskegee Institute, Tuskegee, Alabama. It was Dr. Washington who first promoted skill development for former slaves and the sons of former slaves. It was Dr. Washington who first coined the phrase "There is just as much dignity in tilling the fields as there is in writing a poem." The third section was named the Almmot Section, which was named with the first letter of the states where expansion took place.

Dr. Sargent had a host of devoted black educators who helped him along the way. There were Dr. W. W. Owens of Virginia College, Mr. S. B. Simmons of the North Carolina Department of Vocational Agriculture, Mr. Church Banks of Prairie View A. & M. College, Dr. Ernest Norris of the Kentucky State Office of Education and Prairie View A. & M, and Mr. J. R. Thomas of Virginia College.

Dr. Sargent worked tirelessly for the NFA until his untimely death in an automobile accident in 1936.

Purposes for the NFA

1. To develop competent, aggressive, agricultural, and rural leadership
2. To encourage intelligent choice of farming occupations
3. To encourage members in the development of individual farming programs
4. To encourage members to improve the home, the farm, and surroundings
5. To participate in worthy undertakings for the improvement of agriculture
6. To practice and encourage thrift
7. To develop character, train for useful citizenship, and foster patriotism
8. To participate in cooperative efforts
9. To provide and encourage the development of organized rural recreational activities
10. To strengthen the confidence of farm boys and young men in themselves and their work
11. To encourage improvement in scholarship
12. To create and nurture a love of country life

These are remarkable purposes for which numerous organizations could benefit by revising or substituting some of these purposes for their own organizations. Truly, these are some of the reasons why the NFA organization was so successful with young black males. Responsibility, the work ethic, self-esteem, belongingness, cooperation, scholarship, management, home and family life, and patriotism are common threads for the NFA.

NFA Emblem

The significance of the emblem of the NFA spoke volumes for the meaning of the NFA. The emblem had five symbols: The first symbol was the plow, representing tillage of the soil, the basis of modern agriculture. Little did non-farm-people know that there were different types of plows. Some examples were the bottom plow, moldboard plow, and turnwrest or middle burrow plow. The use of the plow started with the oxen pulling the plow, then horses and mules became more prevalent. Later, the plow became mechanized and different forms of the plow were developed. The second symbol was the owl, representing wisdom. The third symbol was the rising sun, representing progress. The fourth symbol was an open boll of cotton with two leaves attached at its base, representing important economic, agricultural interests of many members. The fifth symbol was an American eagle with a shield, arrows, and an olive branch, representing the wide scope of the organization. The emblem carried the three letters NFA and the words "vocational agriculture."

The emblem was sewn into shirts, jackets, on stationery and in other ways.

The NFA Creed

I believe in the dignity of farmwork and that I shall prosper in proportion as I learn to put knowledge and skill into the occupations of farming.

I believe that the farm boy who learns to produce better crops and better livestock and who learns to improve and beautify his home surroundings will find joy and success in meeting the challenging situations as they arise in his daily living.

I believe that rural organizations should develop their leaders from within and that the boys in rural communities should look forward to positions of leadership in the civic, social, and public life surrounding them.

I believe that the life of service is the life that counts, that happiness endures to mankind when it comes from having helped to lift the burdens of others.

I believe in the practice of cooperation in agriculture, that it will aid in bringing to the man lowest down a wealth of giving as well as receiving.

I believe that each farm boy bears the responsibility for finding and developing his talents to the end that the life of his people may thereby be enriched so that happiness and contentment will come to all.

NFA Chapter Organization

Each local chapter (at each high school) had an outline of how each meeting was to be organized and followed. There was an opening ceremony, a roll call, an order of business, a pledge of allegiance (salute), and a closing ceremony. Each chapter had a set of by-laws, which included the list of officers and their duties, a list of stations for each officer, a list of committees that were required, and other responsibilities. The local vocational agriculture teacher was the official advisor to the chapter.

The NFA chapter was not a class in school, although the members of the chapter were enrolled in vocational agriculture classes. The NFA was an extension of those classes, with NFA activities occurring in the evenings, at night, and on weekends. A requirement of the NFA was that each member had a responsibility in and for the NFA, i.e., "every member should have an opportunity to appear on at least one program during the year." The requirements for chapter meetings were as follows:

> It is carefully planned in advance of the meeting time.
> It starts and closes on time.
> It proceeds according to an established order of business.
> It is conducted according to accepted parliamentary procedure.
>> (Note: Roberts's Rules of Order by Major Henry M. Roberts and Stewart's Helps in Mastering Parliamentary Procedure by Henry Stewart were used by NFA chapters.)
> It includes well-prepared committee reports.
> It shows that each officer is familiar with his duties and responsibilities.
> It commands the interest and attention of all members.

It provides for maximum member participation and develops cooperative attitude.

It includes both business and entertainment features.

It moves along with "snap," thus preventing monotony and the wasting of time.

Such structure, discipline, and practice were the foundation for the success of numerous black males in the Old South.

Ceremonies | New Farmers of America

President: "Fellow members, join me in a salute to our flag."
(The gavel is rapped three times to call members to stand.)
All: (At salute) "I pledge allegiance to the flag of the United States of America and to the republic for which it stands, one nation under God, indivisible, with liberty and justice for all."
President: "I now declare this meeting adjourned."
(The gavel is rapped as the meeting is adjourned.)

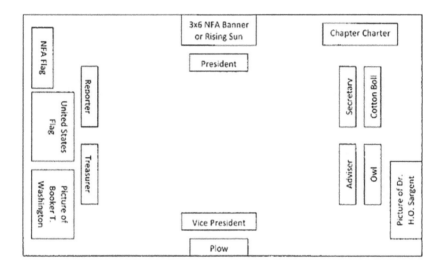

Paraphernalia

1 American flag
1 picture of rising sun, or the NFA banner
1 plow (miniature)
1 bunch of cotton balls
1 picture of Dr. H. O. Sargent
1 owl
1 gavel and block

1 official secretary's book
1 official treasurer's book
1 scrapbook
1 chapter charter
1 NFA flag
1 straight stick of native wood

New Farmers of South Carolina

The New Farmers of South Carolina was chartered with the secretary of state of the State of South Carolina on February 28, 1934. Those persons listed on the charter are Mr. Charles H. McLeod of Elloree, Mr. DeWitt T. Robinson of Orangeburg, Mr. John P. Burgess of Orangeburg, and Mr. William W. Wilkins of Orangeburg.

The purposes of the charter were as follows: (a) to create interest in the intelligent choice of the occupation of farming, (b) to strengthen the confidence of the farm boy in himself and his work, (c) to create and nurture a love of country life, (d) to encourage cooperative effort, (e) to promote thrift, (f) to promote scholarship among students of vocational agriculture, (g) to encourage recreational and educational activities for students of vocational agriculture, and (h) to advance vocational agricultural education in Negro public schools in the schools providing for such instruction. The headquarters was located at State A & M College, Orangeburg, South Carolina.

The managers were Mr. Verd Peterson of Columbia (supervisor of vocational agriculture), Mr. John P. Burgess of Orangeburg (itinerant teacher-trainer), Mr. William W. Wilkins of Orangeburg (itinerant shop teacher-trainer), Mr. DeWitt T. Robinson of Orangeburg (advisor), and Mr. Waymon Johnson of Olanta (treasurer).

NFA Chapter Officers

At the height of its existence in the State of South Carolina, there were 102 NFA chapters. As new black high schools were established, new NFA chapters were organized.

The New Farmers of America in South Carolina "faded away" with the "merger" of the New Farmers of America with the predominantly white Future Farmers of America (FFA). There was no real "merger." The NFA was simply absorbed into the FFA. Merger usually means that the two entities would negotiate the use of characteristics from each entity, which would become a part of the merger.

The NFA lost in every way. The NFA lost its name, colors, emblem, creed, by-laws, banner, charter, awards, summer camps, and catalog items, such as jackets, pocket knives, T-shirts, pencils, sport shirts, pen sets, neckties, etc. Much of the NFA leadership at the state and national levels were also lost. The fifty-three thousand former NFA members were "lost" to the FFA.

NFA Chapters in South Carolina

The NFA chapter officers were president, vice president, secretary, treasurer, reporter, watchman, parliamentarian, historian, chaplain, and the song and cheer leader. Each officer had specific duties outlined in the NFA Guide.

The NFA Guide was the official organ of the NFA organization. It was published periodically at the national level through the US Office of Education, and by the NFA.

NFA Meeting Room Organization

The NFA meeting room had a national design necessary for all meetings. Each meeting had a structure with stations for each officer. Each station was represented with some type of paraphernalia. The president was represented with a picture of the rising sun, the vice president with the plow, the secretary with a boll of cotton, the treasurer with a picture of Booker T. Washington, the reporter with flags of the United States and the NFA, and the advisor with the model of an owl.

Each NFA chapter had a gavel and block, an official secretary's book, an official treasurer's book, a copy of the by-laws, a scrapbook, the chapter charter, and a straight stick of native wood.

Each NFA member was required to possess an NFA Guide and to bring it to local meetings. An agenda and parliamentary procedures were used to conduct NFA meetings.

Important Components of the NFA Organization

One of the most important components of the NFA was news writing. Each member was taught the skills needed to write a story, especially a news story. The members were taught that "you can awaken the interest of other young men who do not belong to the NFA and the interest of other mothers and fathers through well-written stories about what the NFA is doing." The ABCs of writing were as follows: accuracy in facts, names, and dates; brevity, which is complete but does not pad; and clearness, which makes the meaning impossible to mistake. In pairs, the members critiqued each other's writing, and ultimately shared with the chapter.

NFA members also sponsored local radio programs. A special subject program was held, or radio spots, were developed for broadcast. The topics were seasonal and usually broadcast as public service information.

Each chapter had an advisor. This was the regular agriculture teacher. The advisor provided the adult leadership for the chapter and governed all activities of the local group. He also rotated as the federation advisor. Most advisors were taught listening skills, public relations skills, organizational skills, observational skills, and management skills and well versed in youth human growth and development while in college. This is one of the reasons why the agriculture major in college had more credit hours to complete than other majors.

Every NFA chapter was encouraged to establish an NFA forest. Local NFA advisors and chapter officers would make contact with local forestry landowners and ask if a portion of his/her property could be used as an NFA demonstration site. If approved, a plot of five to ten acres was selected for the project. Students were able to learn forestry management practices to include the marking of trees, pulpwood versus timber trees, proper spacing of plants, reforestation, plant diseases, thinning, marketing, etc. NFA signage was placed on the sight, and the site was able to compete with other NFA chapter sites.

Each NFA chapter had one or more community service projects. These projects included NFA food drives, NFA clothes banks,

NFA home improvement projects for the elderly or disabled, NFA school campus improvement projects, and back in the day, NFA firewood drives.

Each NFA chapter sent students to summer camp at the NFA camp. My camp was located in Orangeburg, South Carolina. My camp was called Camp PeWilBurWhitCade, named for five vocational agriculture teachers. It was a weeklong camp, which started on Sunday night and ended on Friday midday. There were structured activities for the entire day, which started at 6:00 a.m. with exercises on the center campus and ended at 10:00 p.m. with lights out. It was a barrack-type camp for sleeping with bunk-type beds. The cabins were made of wood and were not air-conditioned. We only had large fans. The showers were group showers.

Each NFA chapter had an annual audit done of their finances. This was done by the school's financial officer or school's bookkeeper.

NFA Contests

There were several contests sponsored by the NFA at all levels. One contest was public speaking. This contest was designed to develop the ability in young men to speak forcefully and effectively before any audience. Only winners of the state and sectional public speaking contests were eligible to enter the National NFA Public Speaking Contest. Another contest was the quartet contest. The purpose of this contest was to develop a greater appreciation for good music, including the Negro spirituals. The contest was designed to stimulate NFA members to sing and develop desirable musical talent among its members. This type of contest was without additional music. Another contest was the quiz contest. This contest was conducted for the purpose of stimulating a thorough study of the NFA Constitution and By-Laws, the NFA Guide, and correct parliamentary practice for NFA members. It was a most enjoyable and instructional event that supported the flow of academics for NFA members. Another contest was the talent contest. This contest was designed to encourage the use of desirable entertainment and to develop musical abilities for NFA members. This contest often included dramatic interpretations, individual singing, and individual playing of instruments. There were other contests, such as soil judging, animal judging, and other contests, as determined by the individual state associations.

These contests started at the individual chapter level with a chapter elimination. The contests and eliminations continued at the federation level, district level, state level, section level, and national level. At each level, an award was presented to the respective winners. These awards usually included a plaque and a monetary award to the winners.

A number of other awards were given to NFA members. Instead of competing against other members, these awards were awards that were earned through individual self-determination. They included the Star Superior Farmer Award, Star Modern Farmer Award, Dairy Farming Award, Farm Mechanics Award, Farm Electrification Award, Farm and Home Improvement Award, and Soil and Water Management Award. Through the use of competitive events and special recognitions, all NFA members could be recognized for out-standing efforts in the NFA organization.

Most of these contests and awards were funded by the Future Farmers of America Foundation. This foundation was established in 1944 to provide business and industrial firms, organizations, and individuals with an opportunity to support the programs of the NFA and the FFA. In 1963, there were three hundred donors who gave annually to the Future Farmers of America Foundation.

At the local level, NFA chapters often sponsored NFA sweet-heart contests. Girls Competed similarly to girls in current beauty contests. Although there were no bathing suit competitions, gowns, Bermuda shorts, talent, and poise were major components of these contests. The winners would receive a bouquet, trophy, banner, and a monetary award.

A three-judge panel judged the contest.

As mentioned earlier, some NFA chapters sponsored an NFA school forest. These forests were in different stages of development. Usually, the size of the forestry plot was from ten to twenty acres in size. NFA members used the forests for planting pine seedlings (with proper spacing), for marking trees for thinning or for marketing, to cut fire breaks in the forest, to treat trees for insect and other damages, etc. Most importantly, the teaching of reforestation was demonstrated and reemphasized. The dibble was used by NFA members to plant new trees. Each NFA school forest had a sign constructed at the site. There was also an NFA forestry judging contest.

Local Fair

The local fair was an integral part of NFA life. Often NFA members submitted a project to the fair to be judged in a fair contest. The fair in my home county was called the McCormick County Agriculture Fair. There were sectional fairs (e.g., Eastern County Agriculture Fair) and a fair at the state level (the South Carolina State Fair).

The agriculture exhibits were a focal point of these fairs, which included everything agriculture, including animals, such as beef cattle, dairy cows, horses, chickens, turkeys, hogs (swine), rabbits, birds, goats, sheep, mules, and donkeys. The fairs also included cooking projects, flowers, canning, sewing, and farm machinery and farm implements. Additionally, these fairs included harvested items, such as cotton, tobacco, com, soybeans, sweet potatoes, okra, peas, tomatoes, peaches, pears, blackberries, squash, strawberries, peanuts, and muscadines.

These exhibits received ribbons, trophies, or monetary prizes. The big draws for the agriculture fairs were amusement rides, petting zoos, and games of chance. At the fair in my hometown, we also had a colored talent show and a hoochie-coochie show. The hoochie-coochie show was composed of scantily dressed females who would come out on stage and dance to the music, with the intent to entice adults to come inside the tent for the full show.

Before integration, there was a white student day and a black student day at local fairs. At the state fair level, which lasted for two weeks in South Carolina, the first week was the white week and the second week was the black week at the state fair in Columbia, South Carolina.

The NFA members went to the State Fair in Columbia, South Carolina, each year during the Colored State Fair. The Colored State Fair followed the first week of the state fair, which was for whites only. The New Homemakers of America (NHA) traveled to Columbia on the same buses with the NFA boys. This was looked forward to by both NFA and NHA groups each year.

When students arrived at the state fairgrounds in Columbia, they went directly to the grandstands for a leadership program. The leadership program started at 9:00 a.m. The program usually concluded by 11:00 a.m. The buses started for home no later than 4:00 p.m.

Each state had a state NFA convention. Students would spend several days at a state land grant college to participate in NFA activities. In addition to competitive student events, the NFA members would hear from state and national leaders in agriculture and in agri-business. The NFA members would handle the business of the State NFA Association. They would also elect state officers for the next year.

The national NFA convention was rotated among cities in the South. In 1949, Atlanta, Georgia, became the home for national NFA conventions. During the life of the NFA, Atlanta, like the rest of the South, was segregated. Delegates and participants in the national convention would stay at the YMCA. Bunk beds would be brought to the Y and spread out on the gym floor. Delegates would eat in local restaurants, which served Negroes. The national NFA convention was held in the Atlanta Municipal Auditorium.

Delegates to the national convention were chosen at the state level along with the state contest winners who competed at the national level.

Most of the states had a state camp for NFA. The NFA camp in South Carolina was named Camp PeWilBurWhitCade, which was located approximately five miles out of Orangeburg, South Carolina. This camp was developed on sixty-two acres and was donated by a Negro man named Thomas Cade.

The South Carolina NFA camp was constructed with free labor, with assessments, and with donations. This amounted to $3,370.50. The South Carolina State Department of Education provided $2,773.40. The camp operated from June 1 to September 15 each summer. Approximately two hundred NFA members a week attended the South Carolina NFA Camp.

Campers came in on Monday mornings and left on Friday afternoons. During the week, campers maintained their barracks (living quarters) where they lived during the week. The barracks could sleep up to forty boys with upper and lower bunk beds. Each barrack also had an assigned detail to maintain the grounds, the dining hall, and leadership meeting building. Three meals were served each day. Meals were posted for the week in each barrack. At each meal, the NFA members sang the grace: "God is grace and God is good—and we thank Him for this food. By His hands we are fed. Give us, Lord, our daily bread. Give us, Lord, our daily bread. Amen."

After breakfast, devotion and leadership activities were held in Hickson Hall (leadership meeting building). Hickson Hall was named for Mr. W. F. Hickson, associate professor of agriculture at South Carolina State College and state NFA advisor for over twenty years. Hickson Hall was the only building at the camp, which was constructed with concrete blocks.

After lunch, organized recreational activities were held: baseball, horseshoe pitching, volleyball, billiards, table tennis, checkers, and badminton. Up until the middle 1960s, NFA members who could swim swam in the lake, which was located approximately five hundred feet from the main camp. Fishing in the lake was also permitted.

The barracks, meeting/recreational building, dining hall, and a cabin to house NFA advisors were constructed by teachers of agriculture from around the State of South Carolina. The camp was named to honor several prominent leaders in agriculture, the President of South Carolina State College, and the donor of the land for the camp. The meeting room was later named to honor Mr. W. F. Hickson, itinerant teacher-trainer and professor of agriculture at South Carolina State College. The camp housed two hundred boys a week, June to September, from across the State of South Carolina.

To finance the camp, each local NFA chapter was assessed $25. Each teacher of agriculture was asked to contribute $10. For the upkeep of the camp, each NFA member was asked to contribute fifty cents of his local dues. Each NFA advisor was asked to contribute $1 per year.

By contrast, the FFA in South Carolina had its camp located on the ocean at Cherry Grove Beach. The buildings were made of concrete blocks and brick. This was quite different from the wood frame buildings at the NFA camp, which was located in the woods near Orangeburg.

I worked for two summers as the youth advisor at Camp PeWilBurWhitCade. I was a student at South Carolina State College. My duties included cutting the lawn, leading the youth in devotionals, organizing the meals, ordering food items for the dining hall, getting the youth up in the mornings, leading the youth in morning drills, organizing recreational activities for the youth, and leading the youth in custodial and other maintenance activities for the camp. This was during the summers of 1963 and 1964.

My agriculture teacher was Mr. James C. Mattison. Mr. Mattison was from Honea Path, South Carolina. He was a very bright and dedicated teacher. You could immediately tell that he loved his profession and the students whom he served. He also found time to coach varsity basketball.

As a matter of fact, the agriculture teacher had a number of different roles in addition to teaching. He sponsored the NFA chapter and served as the club's advisor. As has been mentioned, he was expected to visit the homes and farms of his students.

Each student had to have a supervised farming program. Each student's program ranged from having a pig or swine project to managing acres of agriculture crops. To manage their project, each student had a recordkeeping booklet to maintain his records. These projects and records were reviewed and monitored by the agriculture teacher; therefore, home visits were required.

During the summer, the agriculture teacher had to operate a community cannery. The community cannery was the site where farmers and other local citizens brought their fruits and vegetables to be canned. Usually, these canned goods were used during the year, especially during the winter months when these foods were usually not available, except by cans bought from the grocery stores. These canned goods were often shared with family members and with neighbors.

Mr. Mattison was also responsible for building leadership skills of his students. This was done through NFA activities and contests.

My Agriculture Teacher and New Farmers of America Advisor
Mims High School in McCormick, South Carolina
Mr. James Claude Mattison

In 1968, I taught at a desegregated school (McColl High School). The school had less than ten black students. This picture shows a portion of my FFA chapter. The NFA was in the process of being assimilated by the FFA.

Location of NFA Chapters in South Carolina

Approximately 98 percent of the black high schools in South Carolina had NFA chapters because of the leadership and development skills which the NFA provided for its members. From schools that were considered rural to town or city schools, NFA chapters were located within those schools. Some of those schools were as follows: Granard in Gaffney, Long in Cheraw, Petersburg in Pageland, Pine Forest in McBee, Scott's Branch in Summerton, Manning County Training in Manning, Colleton in Walterboro, Butler in Hartsville, Mayo in Darlington, Rosenwald in Society Hill, Spaulding in Lamar, McCrory-Liston in Blair, Fairfield County Training in Winnsboro, Carver in Lake City, Gibbs in Pamplico, Rosemary in Andrews, Bryson in Fountain Inn, Sterling in Greenville, Edgewood in Ninety-Six, Emma Maddox in Ware Shoals, Wittemore in Conway, Barr Street in Lancaster, Bell Street in Clinton, Sanders in Laurens, Dennis in Bishopville, Mt. Pleasant in Elliott, Johnakin in Marion, Palmetto in Mullins, Terrell's Bay in Centenary, East Side in Bennettsville, Adamsville in McColl, Gallman in Newberry, Blue Ridge in Seneca, Carver in Cordova, Roberts in Holly Hill, Wilkinson in Orangeburg, Clearview in Easley, Booker T. Washington in Columbia, Eastern in Sumter, Manchester in Pinewood, Battery Park in Nesmith, C. E. Murray in Greeleyville, St. Mark in Kingstree, Tomlinson in Kingstree, Emmett Scott in Rock Hill, A. L. Corbett in Wagener, New Deal in Starr, Westside in Anderson, Michael C. Riley in Bluffton, Robert Smalls in Beaufort, Baptist Hill in Charleston, Burke in Charleston, Bonds-Wilson in Charleston, Latimer in Latta, Columbus in Lake View, Gordon in Dillon, Riverside in Pendleton, Wright in Abbeville, W. E. Parker in Edgefield, Riverside in Saluda, Wilson in Florence, Lincoln in Clio, Jackson in Camden, Chavis in Hemingway, Spearman in Williamston, Britton's Neck in Gresham, Mims in McCormick, Haut Gap on John's Island, Brewer in Greenwood, Geer Gant in Belton, and Schofield in Aiken.

Most of the names of these black high schools have faded into history. Whereas the names of most of the former white high schools still exist today. Oftentimes when you take away a name of a school or close that school without replacing it, you take away part of the culture and history of a people. This can have a long-term effect on a community.

The NFA: A Sophisticated Group of Young Black Men

The NFA Twenty-Sixth National Convention was held in Atlanta, Georgia. The dates were October 3–6, 1960. The site of the convention was the Municipal Auditorium.

I spoke at the convention in the National Public Speaking Contest, which I won. My prize was $200. My two major competitors were Earl Kagler of Lakeland, Florida, and Jimmy J. Altemus of Ville Platte, Louisiana, both of whom won $100 each. The public speaking contest was held on Thursday, October 6, 1960, at 9:00 a.m.

Again, these were the days of segregation. We could not stay at the white-owned motels or hotels in Atlanta. We had to stay at the YMCA building. Bunk metal beds were brought in for us to sleep, and there was always a line to use the restroom or to take a shower. Of course, we ate at segregated restaurants.

It was an amazing sight to see thousands of young black men with their advisors dressed in gold-and-black attire. Gold and black were the official NFA colors. Our jackets were gorgeous.

The NFA members were the focal point of the convention. There was a variety of student contests, the recognition of numerous student achievements, a variety of reports given, fair exhibits, and a number of challenging speeches given to the students.

The student contests included the public speaking contest, talent contest, quartet contest, livestock judging contest, and quiz contest. Student achievement awards included the Star Superior Farmer Degree, Farm Mechanics Award, Farm Electrification Award, Farm and Home Improvement Award, Soil and Water Management Award, Dairy Farming Award, and the H. O. Sargent Award.

The National NFA Chorus was entertaining and uplifting throughout the convention.

I have never observed student officers perform in such an outstanding fashion as did the NFA national officers at the 1960 National NFA Convention in Atlanta. They had been trained superbly. The introductory page to the program says it all. The NFA national officers met in Washington, DC, on August 10, 1960, to make final plans for the 1960 convention. It is well to note that Mr. William F. Hickson, professor and itinerant teacher-trainer, South Carolina State College, Orangeburg, South Carolina, was the Washington Section advisor. Mr. Hickson was also my major professor of agriculture. It is also well to note that the president of South Carolina State College, Dr. Benner C. Turner, spoke at the convention on Tuesday, October 4.

The convention started on Monday, October 3, and ended on Thursday, October 6, 1960. The opening and closing ceremonies were very impressive at this convention.

Pride was observed on the faces of all who attended the convention.

What an amazing event!

New Farmers of America Twenty-Sixth National Convention

An example of a first-class act convention was the Twenty-Sixth National Convention of the NFA, which was held at the Atlanta Municipal Auditorium, Atlanta, Georgia. The fact that this was the twenty-sixth was an indication that the NFA had enjoyed almost three decades, unlike any other organizations at that time.

Not only was the convention well organized, but some of the presenters, adult officers, and National Advisory Council represented the finest of educators in black America. Further, it also showed the acknowledgment of the NFA by corporate America.

Renowned black educators and black professionals in fifteen states had brought the NFA to be one of the most successful and organized groups for youth in America. It is unfortunate that such an organization no longer exists in the United States.

There was no merger of the NFA and the FFA. The NFA simply ended. The name of New Farmers of America, its youth officers, its adult officers, its black and gold colors, its creed, its creed song, its NFA Guide, its National Advisory Council, its national chorus, its activities, its constitution, its competitive events, and its success with black males in fifteen states faded away.

I have included a copy of the program for the Twenty-Sixth National Convention with this writing.

I attended this convention and participated in the National Public Speaking Contest. Although the convention was held in the Municipal Auditorium, we stayed at the YMCA Gym, where cots had been set up for us to sleep on because hotels had not been integrated to house us.

NEW FARMERS OF AMERICA

26th

National Convention

October 3 – 6, 1960
Municipal Auditorium
Atlanta, Georgia

DR. JAMES A. FRANKLIN SR.

National Officers
NEW FARMERS OF AMERICA—1959-60

Student Officers

President .... ROBERT MACK, Rt. 1, Box 84, Big Island, Virginia
First Vice-President .. ALFRED L. ROBERTS, Prairie View A. and M. College, Prairie View, Texas
Second Vice-President .... CLARENCE TURNER, Rt. 1, Box 239-M, Brandywine, Maryland
Third Vice-President .... ROBERT R. BEASLEY, 305 Brown Avenue, Eutaw, Alabama
Student Secretary .... JOHN MELVIN SMITH, Rt. 4, Box 186, Carthage, Mississippi
Student Treasurer .... JAMES M. GRIFFIN, Rt. 1, Box 440, Auburndale, Florida
Reporter .. HERMAN C. BURNETTE, Box 3017, Scott Hall, A. and T. College, Greensboro, N. C.

Adult Officers

Administrative Advisor, W. T. SPANTON, Office of Education, Washington 25, D.C.
Administrative Executive Secretary, R. E. NAUGHER, Office of Education, Washington, D.C.
National Advisor, G. W. CONOLY, Florida A. and M. University, Tallahassee, Florida
Executive Secretary, E. M. NORRIS, Prairie View A. and M. College, Prairie View, Texas
Executive Treasurer, W. T. JOHNSON, A. and T. College, Greensboro, North Carolina

National Advisory Council

W. T. SPANTON, *Chairman,* Office of Education, Washington 25, D.C.
R. E. NAUGHER, Office of Education, Washington 25, D.C.
G. W. CONOLY, Florida A. and M. University, Tallahassee, Florida
E. M. NORRIS, Prairie View A. and M. College, Prairie View, Texas
W. T. JOHNSON, A. and T. College, Greensboro, North Carolina
M. J. CLARK, Almot Sectional Advisor, Southern University, Baton Rouge, Louisiana
L. A. MARSHALL, Sargent Sectional Advisor, State Department of Education, Tallahassee, Florida
W. F. HICKSON, Washington Sectional Advisor, South Carolina State College, Orangeburg, S. C.

Director National NFA Chorus

I. S. GLOVER, Teacher Vocational Agriculture, Comer, Georgia

87

96

NFA 26TH ANNUAL CONVENTION
The New Farmers of America

THE NEW FARMERS OF AMERICA is the national organization of boys studying vocational agriculture in public secondary schools under the provisions of the National Vocational Education Acts. Launched at Tuskegee, Alabama, in August 1935, the organization has continued to develop rapidly. On June 30, 1960, the active membership totaled 52,209 in 1037 chapters in 15 states.

The primary aim of the New Farmers of America organization is the development of agricultural leadership, cooperation, citizenship and patriotism. Other purposes include: strengthening the confidence of farm boys and young men in themselves and their work; more intelligent choice of farming occupations; creating and nurturing a love of country life; improving the rural home and its surroundings; encouraging cooperative effort, encouraging thrift; improving scholarship; providing organized recreational activities for rural people; and supplementing, by means of boy-initiated and boy-directed activities, the systematic instruction offered to prospective young farmers regularly enrolled in day-school vocational agricultural courses. Its members learn through participating experiences how to conduct and take part in public meetings, to speak in public, and to assume civic responsibility. The NFA is an intracurricular part of vocational education in agriculture in the public school system of America. It constitutes one of the most effective devices for teaching through participating experiences.

The history of the NFA program in the United States has been, from the beginning, one of progress. The organization has not only grown in membership, but has each year improved its program of helping farm boys to prepare themselves better for citizenship and life on the farm.

DR. JAMES A. FRANKLIN SR.

NATIONAL OFFICERS AND SECTIONAL ADVISORS IN WASHINGTON, D. C., AUGUST 10, 1960

Seated, L. to R.—Herman Burnette, North Carolina, Reporter; Clarence Turner, Maryland, Second Vice-President; John Smith, Mississippi, Secretary; Robert Mack, Virginia, President; James Griffin, Florida, Treasurer; Alfred Roberts, Texas, First Vice-President; Robert Beasley, Alabama, Third Vice-President.

Standing, L. to R.—Martin Goodson, Alabama, Past President (1959); M. J. Clark, Louisiana, Almot Section Advisor; W. F. Hickson, South Carolina, Washington Section Advisor; G. W. Conoly, Florida, National Advisor; E. M. Norris, Texas, Executive Secretary; W. T. Johnson, North Carolina, Executive Treasurer; (not shown) L. A. Marshall, Florida, Sargent Section Advisor.

NFA 26TH ANNUAL CONVENTION

Program . . .

FOR THE TWENTY-SIXTH
NATIONAL N. F. A. CONVENTION

MONDAY, OCTOBER 3

8:00-11:00 A.M.   REGISTRATION—Lobby, Butler Street Y.M.C.A.

8:00-10:00 A.M.   MEETING OF NATIONAL BOARD OF TRUSTEES AND
REHEARSAL OF CEREMONIES —Room 4

9:00-11:00 A.M.   REHEARSAL OF NATIONAL CHORUS—Room 7

10:00-11:00 A.M.   MEETING OF COACHES OF LIVESTOCK JUDGING—Room 4

12:00   M.   NATIONAL N. F. A. CHORUS AND JUDGING TEAMS LEAVE
Y.M.C.A. FOR FAIR GROUNDS—Delegates and Advisers
12:15 P.M.

FAIR GROUNDS PROGRAM:
1) 1:00 P.M. NATIONAL N.F.A. CHORUS
2) 1:30 P.M. NATIONAL N. F. A. LIVESTOCK JUDGING
CONTEST
3) OBSERVING THE FAIR EXHIBITS

OPENING SESSION—Exhibition Hall, Municipal Auditorium

7:30 P.M.   OPENING CEREMONY—National N. F. A. Officers, Roll Call
of States and Seating of Delegates

NATIONAL N. F. A. CHORUS, Ira S. Glover, Teacher, Vocational Agriculture, Comer, Georgia, Conducting

INVOCATION—Clarence Turner, Second National
Vice-President

GREETINGS FROM ATLANTA—Dr. Albert E. Manley, President
Spellman College, Atlanta, Georgia

NATIONAL N.F.A. CHORUS

GREETINGS FROM F. F. A.—Jim Thomas, National President
Future Farmers of America, Patterson, Georgia

ILLUSTRATED LECTURE—Latin American Agriculture—
J. M. Carter, President, National Vocational Agricultural
Teachers Association, Wellsville, New York

SPECIAL ANNOUNCEMENTS FOR THE WEEK

CLOSING CEREMONY

9:30 P.M.   REHEARSAL—Star Superior Farmer Ceremony

NFA 26TH ANNUAL CONVENTION

Program . . . Continued

TUESDAY, OCTOBER 4

SECOND SESSION—Exhibition Hall, Municipal Auditorium

9:00 A.M.   OPENING CEREMONY

INVOCATION—Robert Beasley, Third National Vice-President

GROUP SINGING

AWARDING SUPERIOR FARMER DEGREES

HONORING PARENTS OF NATIONAL OFFICERS

AWARDING HONORARY SUPERIOR FARMER DEGREES

RESPONSE—Dr. B. C. Turner, President, South Carolina State College, Orangeburg, S. C.

• GROUP SINGING

APPOINTMENT OF CONSTITUTIONAL COMMITTEES
  a) Nominating
  b) Program of Work
  c) Auditing

CLOSING CEREMONY

1:30 P.M.   TOUR—(See Special Feature Leaflet)
McKinley Wilson, Conductor. (NOTE.—All who have no assigned duties, assemble in front of Y. M. C. A. for the tour).

THIRD SESSION—Exhibition Hall, Municipal Auditorium
F. F. A. FOUNDATION DONORS NIGHT

7:30 P.M.   OPENING CEREMONY

NATIONAL N. F. A. CHORUS

PRESENTATION OF ESTABLISHMENT IN FARMING AWARDS BY NATIONAL N.F.A. OFFICERS
  a) Farm Mechanics—Second Vice-President
  b) Farm Electrification—Reporter
  c) Farm and Home Improvement—Third Vice President
  d) Soil and Water Management—First Vice-President
  e) Dairy Farming—Treasurer

MASSING OF STATE FLAG

N F A 26TH ANNUAL CONVENTION

Program . . . Continued

PRESENTATION OF STAR SUPERIOR FARMER AWARDS

RECESSIONAL—Flag Bearers

MUSIC —National N.F.A. Chorus

SEATING ON THE STAGE, ALL F.F.A. FOUNDATION DONOR REPRESENTATIVES

MUSIC—National N.F.A. Chorus

INTRODUCTION OF PLATFORM GUEST BY— R. E. Naugher, Officer of Education, Washington, D. C.

REMARKS—Russell DeYoung, Goodyear Tire and Rubber Company, Akron, Ohio

WEDNESDAY, OCTOBER 5

FOURTH SESSION—Exhibition Hall, Municipal Auditorium

9:00 A.M. OPENING CEREMONY

INVOCATION—James Griffin, National Treasurer

NATIONAL N. F. A. CHORUS

ADDRESS—Howard McClarren, Director of Youth Education, American Institute of Cooperation, Washington, D. C.

QUARTET CONTEST — Conductor, James Griffin—National Treasurer

REPORT OF NATIONAL N. F. A. BOARD OF TRUSTEES

RESULTS OF NATIONAL N. F. A. QUARTET CONTEST

10:30 A.M. RECESS FOR COMMITTEE WORK

FIFTH SESSION—Exhibition Hall, Municipal Auditorium

1:30 P.M. OPENING CEREMONY

REPORTS OF NATIONAL OFFICERS
President
First Vice-President
Second Vice-President
Third Vice-President
Student Reporter

TALENT CONTEST—Conductor, Clarence Turner, Second National Vice-President

NFA 26TH ANNUAL CONVENTION

Program . . . Continued

REPORTS OF NATIONAL OFFICERS
National Student Secretary
Executive Secretary
National Student Treasurer
Executive Treasurer

RESULTS OF NATIONAL TALENT CONTEST

CLOSING CEREMONY

8:30 P.M.
to
10:30 P.M.
ATLANTA NIGHT—Amateur Program and N. F. A. Social—
Exhibition Hall, Conducted by
McKinley Wilson, Fort Valley, Georgia

THURSDAY, OCTOBER 6

SIXTH SESSION — Exhibition Hall, Municipal Auditorium

9:00 A.M.   OPENING CEREMONY

INVOCATION—James Griffin

NATIONAL N.F.A. CHORUS

NATIONAL PUBLIC SPEAKING CONTEST—Conductor,
Robert Beasley, Third Vice-President

MUSIC—Winning Quartet, Almot Section

REPORT OF CONSTITUTIONAL COMMITTEES
Auditing
Program of Work

ANNOUNCEMENTS OF WINNERS OF:
Public Speaking Contest
Quiz Contest

CLOSING CEREMONY

SEVENTH SESSION — Exhibition Hall, Municipal Auditorium

1:30 P.M.   OPENING CEREMONY

NATIONAL QUIZ CONTEST—Conductor, Herman Burnette,
National Reporter

RESULTS OF NATIONAL QUIZ CONTEST

NFA 26TH ANNUAL CONVENTION

Program ... Continued

2:30 p.m. (1) Election of National Officers—polls open 2:30-3:30 p.m.

3:30 p.m. Tabulation of Ballots and Announcement of Winning Candidates—Nominating Committee

EIGHTH SESSION—Exhibition Hall, Municipal Auditorium

7:30 p.m. Opening Ceremony

National Chorus

Presentation, H. O. Sargent Awards

Installation of New National N.F.A. Officers

Presentation of Awards by National N.F.A. Officers

1. F.F.A. Foundation Awards
   a. Quiz—*Treasurer*
   b. Quartet—*Second Vice-President*
   c. Public Speaking—*Third Vice-President*

2. N. F. A. Awards
   a. Talent—*First Vice-President*
   b. Livestock Judging and Showmanship for Holders of Livestock—*Reporter*
   c. Exhibits—*President*

Unfinished Business

Closing Ceremony and Final Adjournment

NFA Public Speaking Contest Participant

I was a member of the Mims High School NFA Chapter. As a freshman, I was encouraged to participate in the public speaking contest.

Mr. James C. Mattison, our agriculture teacher and NFA advisor, wrote the speech to be used by his NFA students in the public speaking contest. Miss E. V. Massey, our English Department chairperson, edited the speeches for Mr. Mattison. The speeches had to last between eight and ten minutes. If an NFA member spoke less than eight minutes or more than ten minutes, a severe deduction would be taken from his final score.

Students who were interested in competing learned by hard (rote memory) their speech. No notes were allowed. At the end of his speech, the judges had five minutes to ask questions about his speech.

The participants spoke in the school's auditorium before the student body. Three teachers served as judges. The first speech that we learned was "The Importance of a Supervised Farming Program." I was fortunate to win at the school level. The next level of competition was at the federation level. The federation level was composed of ten schools. I won at the federation level. The next level was at the district level. The district was composed of three federations. I lost at the district level. Later, I was told that the reason that I lost was for an incorrect answer I gave to one of the judges (Mr. Ward, a professor of agronomy at South Carolina State College). He asked, "Who is responsible for a supervised farming program?" My response was, "I believe that it was Dr. George Washington Carver." The correct answer was simply "Me." Each student was responsible for a supervised farming program.

I tried it again when I was in the tenth grade. This year's topic was "The Past, Present, and Future of Agriculture." I won at the school, federation, and district levels but lost at the state level. The state contest for South Carolina was always held at the NFA State Convention in Orangeburg, South Carolina, at South Carolina State College. Did I stop? No, I tried again in the eleventh grade. This year, the topic was "South Carolina's Farmers and Her Future in the

Forest." I used everything that I had learned the past two years and used my talents to win at the school, federation, district, and state levels, and I was named winner of the National NFA Public Speaking Contest at the National NFA Convention, which was held in Atlanta, Georgia. This was in 1960. I received a plaque and a check for $200. My plaque was given to the school to display in its trophy case. I had never seen that much money. I established a checking account at the Dorn Banking Company in McCormick. Thrift was important to all NFA members, and managing the $200 was important. I was able to use the money in my hog production project and for senior expenses.

Each vocational agriculture program had a cannery, which operated each summer. By its name, farmers and gardeners brought their fresh vegetables and fruits to the cannery to be canned and used primarily during the winter months or off-season. There was only one cannery in each community. White patrons came on certain days, and Negro patrons came on other days. The white agriculture teacher from the white school worked with the white patrons, and the Negro agriculture teacher from the Negro school worked with the Negro patrons.

Back in the day, a few white families had a type of refrigerator while all black families and some white families had an icebox. Obviously, you had to put ice in the icebox on a daily basis. We did not have a milkman to deliver milk every day, but we had an iceman to deliver ice every day. The icebox was constructed in such a way that the ice would be put in the top of the icebox, and you would spread your perishables around the ice and under the ice in aluminum containers. Although most of the iceboxes had some type of insulation, the ice usually did not last until the next day. This was especially true for houses with large families because you not only used the ice to keep perishables from spoiling, but you chipped off the ice to make iced tea, lemonade, Kool-Aid, and ice water. A side effect of poverty back in the day was those persons who did not have a refrigerator also did not have electricity or running water and bathrooms inside their homes.

At any rate, as refrigerators and freezers became more prominent, with electricity being installed in homes, the use/dependence of the cannery lessened. Another important component of the cannery was the sheller, which shelled beans and peas.

Some NFA chapters operated greenhouses. Greenhouses were used to grow plants under controlled conditions. Plants were propagated in the greenhouse. From floral plants to hardy yard shrubs, the greenhouse was used to nurture seedlings or to grow plants from seeds.

At the appropriate stage of growth, plants were sold by NFA students as a fundraiser. The funds were used to replenish the greenhouse and for other NFA sponsored events.

Most greenhouses were constructed using an oval metal frame. Heavy plastic was used to cover the greenhouse. There were openings, which could be opened or closed, depending upon outside conditions. Back in the day, a water hose was used for watering and spraying the plants. Later on, some greenhouses installed a more sophisticated irrigation system, which included vapor mists.

Work Experience for NFA Members

Each NFA member was required to have a supervised work experience program on his home farm or to contract with a local farmer, with a local cannery, with a local tobacco market, with a local forester, with a local grocer, with a local cotton gin, or with a local farm mechanics shop. Thrift was a component of his work experience program. The key thing about thrift was the emphasis that it placed on to student to have a savings account or funds invested in his farm enterprise.

The work experience program provided training in farming, livestock production, farm mechanics, record keeping, financial management, and human relations. The agriculture teacher taught in the classroom, taught in the agriculture shop, monitored all his students, visited the students' homes and places where the students performed the work experience, talked with the students' parents, and encouraged his students to work hard. He also encouraged his students to attend church, and he promoted academic success for all his students. The agriculture teacher was recognized as a community leader, and he promoted leadership for his students.

As a vocational agriculture teacher, it was the responsibility of each agriculture teacher to teach each one of his students a vocation, a trade, or a skill that the student could use for an individual life of work or to use to work for someone else. Today, the words "marketable skills" are used. They mean the same thing, and the goals are the same.

A Famous Motto for NFA Members

"He who plants the seed beneath the sod trusts in God" (author unknown).

A county agent in Columbia, South Carolina, used this motto each time his morning show on agriculture would end. This motto was remembered by numerous NFA members who had field crops as their work experience projects.

When I graduated from Mims High School in McCormick, I enrolled at South Carolina State College (S. C. State) in Orangeburg, South Carolina. I wanted to follow in the footsteps of my agriculture teacher, Mr. James C. Mattison.

While at S. C. State, I became caught up in the modern civil rights movement. I became a foot soldier in the army that was led by Dr. Martin Luther King Jr.

Foot Soldier from McCormick

As a foot soldier for Dr. Martin Luther King Jr., I marched in Orangeburg, South Carolina, in Columbia, South Carolina, and in Washington, DC. Like thousands of other students, I was jailed in Orangeburg until students filled up that jail (the Pink Palace), then we were moved to a state prison in Columbia. Like so many other students, I spent ten days in jail. Certainly, Dr. King had inspired all of us to be nonviolent as we were subjected to dogs, water hoses, racial epithets, and other forms of degradation.

The nonviolent marches and demonstrations were being followed as advocated by Dr. King and his followers. He was first introduced to the subject by Dr. Benjamin E. Mays, president of Morehouse College, when Dr. King attended as a student. Dr. Mays had been introduced to the concept by Mr. Mahatma Gandhi of India.

I never met Dr. King personally because he was surrounded by huge crowds wherever he led us in a march. I did meet Dr. Mays on several occasions. I introduced him when he spoke at South Carolina State University (South Carolina State College at the time) for his annual Easter sermon. Dr. Mays also happens to be a fraternity brother (Omega Psi Phi Fraternity Inc.).

This little boy, who grew up in Dorn's Alley of the Town of McCormick, had been touched by two great men whose teachings and practices changed the course of history.

At any rate, the civil rights activities which started in Orangeburg, South Carolina involved students at South Carolina State College, at Claflin University, and students from Wilkinson High School. These activities started in the late 1950s and continued for more than a decade, when in 1967, tragedy struck, resulting in the Orangeburg Massacre. While the activities of the students were nonviolent, the activities of the state police were not. Students were confronted by members of the South Carolina Highway Patrol on the front campus of South Carolina State College.

What provoked these armed state troopers to fire into this crowd of students is still uncertain, even today. We have heard rumors about someone throwing objects at the troopers. What happened that day cannot be justified by anyone. The barrage of bullets from the troopers killed three students—two South Carolina State students and one Wilkinson High School student. Twenty-seven other students were wounded. I have not heard of any state trooper being injured during the melee.

Although the matter was "investigated," no one was ever punished for what happened to those students. I had graduated for State two years earlier, but any person who had marched in Orangeburg was touched by this tragedy. I was no different.

But it did not end with South Carolina State because two years later, at Jackson State in Jackson, Mississippi, two more students were killed on a college campus by city and state police. The students had been demonstrating because of a rumor that Mayor Charles Evers, brother of slain civil rights worker Medgar Evers, and Mayor Evers's wife had been assassinated.

Seventy-five policemen and Mississippi Highway Patrol officers responded to a call about the demonstrators. It was reported that around 12:05 a.m. on May 15, 1970, the officers shot into the crowd of students, killing two students and wounding twelve others. As with the Orangeburg shootings, one of the slain students was a high school student. As with the Orangeburg shootings, no one was held accountable for the slain and injured students.

Do black lives really matter?

After graduation from South Carolina State College, I was employed as the teacher of agriculture at Latimer High School in Latta, South Carolina. I worked at Latimer High for three years, beginning in 1965. This was an all-black high school in Dillon County, South Carolina.

The agriculture teachers met on a monthly basis at the district level. There was a district supervisor who was employed by the South Carolina Department of Education. There were six districts for agricultural education, and all the supervisors were white. My supervisor was Mr. L. J. Carter. He had an assistant named Mr. J. Earl Frick Jr., also white.

We would meet in a short general session (white and black teachers together), and then we would separate with the white teachers remaining in the room, and the black teachers would be sent to another room in the building. Mr. Carter remained with the white teachers, and Mr. Frick led the meeting with the black teachers. If there was anything that any teachers had in common, it was the work of the agriculture teachers. This was the late 1960s. We saw each other at the tobacco markets and at other farming dealers and markets. We operated the agriculture canneries together in our communities. We ran into each other as we visited farms. Most of us had cordial relationships. Although segregation was still "legal," we found it somewhat strange to be separating at our district meetings. We basically covered the same things in our "separate" meetings.

At any rate, as with all agriculture teachers, I was the NFA advisor. This was a most enjoyable experience. In addition to instruction in the classroom, we started many school and community projects. We developed a fencing project for the school, thinned the school's pine forest, constructed trash receptacles in the school's shop, distributed food bags for the needy at Christmas, presented leadership workshops at neighborhood churches, and expanded the young farmer and adult farmer programs. The student's family became an integral part of the student's NFA Supervised Farming Program. Each student was required to have a supervised farming program.

NFA students connected NFA advisors to their families. An example of this occurred when NFA student Larone Jackson had a supervised farming program, which included cotton and tobacco. Through Larone's program, I met his father, Wally Jackson, who became a part of my adult farmer program.

Although there were some large Negro-owned farms, most were small farms. This provided for the opportunity, and also the challenge, for small farmers to form a cooperative. While teaching vocational agriculture at Latimer High School in Latta, South Carolina, we formed the Latimer Farmers' Cooperative. This cooperative was formed by three Negro farmers: Mr. Wally Jackson, Mr. Floyd Bethea, and Mr. Herbert Belin. The Farmers Home Administration of the United States Department of Agriculture provided a farm loan

to support the cooperative. The cooperative was able to purchase a cotton sprayer and other implements for their farms, items that they could not afford as individual farmers.

The major crops in the Latta area of Dillon County, South Carolina, in 1967 were tobacco and cotton. The cotton sprayer was used to spray the leaves of the cotton stalks, which caused the leaves to dry up and to fall off the stalk. This allowed the farmers to operate their cotton pickers to pick the cotton from the stalks without leaves being harvested into the cotton picker. Therefore, the cotton sprayer and the cotton picker became the two most important machines to be used in the harvesting of cotton.

Mr. Herbert Belin's son became the operator of the sprayer and moved the implement between the three farms.

The three farmers had children in high school who happened to be vocational agriculture students and NFA members. The efforts through the cooperative helped to improve their farming operations.

South Carolina State College Supporters of the NFA

Dr. Laler C. DeCosta, Dean, School of Agriculture and Home Economics and Professor of Agriculture

Dr. Gabe Buckman, Professor of Agricultural Engineering

Dr. Robert Hurst, Professor of Agricultural Economics

Mr. William Hickson, Associate Professor of Agriculture and State Advisor to the NFA, Itinerant Teacher-Trainer

Mr. Joe B. Epps, Associate Professor of Animal Husbandry

Mr. William Warren, Associate Professor of Horticulture

Mr. Louis Ward, Associate Professor of Agronomy

Mr. McNewton Sullivan, Assistant Professor of Agriculture and Assistant State Advisor to the NFA, Assistant Itinerant Teacher-Trainer

Mr. Leon Chavous, Instructor of Poultry

Mr. Benjamin Murvin, Instructor of Agriculture

Ms. Charlsea Daniels and Ms. Helen Moss, Administrative Assistants

FIRST ROW: William Hickson, Advisor; Willie Green, Jr., Vice President; Joe L. Wilson, Reporter; Fred Broughton, President; Ralph Council, Treasurer; James Franklin, Secretary; William Clinkscales, Assistant Secretary. SECOND ROW: Wayman Stover, Harold Hutto, Julius A. Stephens, Clarence Lester, George Ulmer, Jake Buckland. THIRD ROW: Vance Marshall, George Cummings, William Ray, James Oglesby, Everette Sanders, Jame S. Grant, Reginald Green.

S. C. State College, May, 1964.

NEW FARMERS OF AMERICA

The Collegiate Chapter of New Farmers of America is an organization of college students enrolled in Agricultural Education. It has for its purpose the training of prospective teachers of vocational agriculture to become local advisors under the provisions of state plans for vocational education approved by the United States Office of Education. The organization provides an excellent opportunity for its members to develop leadership ability as well as character. Each year the chapter participates in the many social and religious activities of the college. The Collegiate Chapter works in harmony with the national organization of New Farmers of America.

DR. JAMES A. FRANKLIN SR.

S. C. State College, May, 1965.

FRONT: B. F. Marvin, Jr., Assistant Advisor; Russell M. Washington, Assistant Secretary; Stephen Odom, Jr., James Grant, Chaplain; Laval Oxendine, Reporter; Ralph Council, Treasurer; Reginald Greene, Secretary; William C. Hickson, Advisor. BACK: Harold Hutto, Wayman Stover, Douglas M. Jones, Hardy Johnson, George Cummings, Alphonso Hannah, James Franklin, James Archie, Arnold Fields, Song-leader; Robert Wright, Clarence Lester.

NEW FARMERS OF AMERICA

The South Carolina State College Chapter of New Farmers of America provides leadership training for its members in preparing them to become competent teachers of vocational agriculture and local NFA advisors. This term the chapter sponsored a fellowship meeting with all of the College sponsored organizations, a joint promenade with the New Home-makers Club, a Collegiate Judging Team, a Collegiate Quartet and a Senior Smoker. It also entertained and assisted with the State NFA Convention and gave a scholarship to a student enrolled in vocational agriculture who showed scholastic ability and the need for financial assistance.

NEW FARMERS OF AMERICA
S. C. State College, May, 1965.

The South Carolina State College Chapter of New Farmers of America provides leadership training for its members in preparing them to become competent teachers of vocational agriculture and local NFA advisors. This term the chapter sponsored a fellowship meeting with all of the College sponsored organizations, a joint promenade with the New Homemakers Club, a Collegiate Judging Team, a Collegiate Quartet, and a Senior Smoker. It also entertained and assisted with the State NFA Convention and gave a scholarship to a student enrolled in vocational agriculture who showed scholastic ability and the need for financial assistance.

Mr. William Hickson, Advisor, and Dr. Laler DeCosta, Dean of the School of Agriculture, present an achievement award to Arnold Fields, who is also a national officer.

Former NFA Member Dies in Vietnam

Ronnie Chavis was an outstanding member of the Latimer High School NFA Chapter. He was dedicated and sat on the front row of his class. He was confident and always smiled as he presented himself in class and in NFA meetings. As the secretary to his chapter, he recorded his minutes accurately and kept good records.

We knew him to be the kind of guy who would serve his country well. We had expected great things from Ronnie in whatever career that he chose. So many black men and former NFA members would serve in Vietnam.

The debate about black men serving in Vietnam, only to return home to a country where they were considered second-class citizens, continues until this date. When I taught Ronnie at Latimer High School, he could not attend Latta High School (the white school), but he was expected to fight side by side with his fellow white soldier in a country thousands of miles from home.

PFC Ronnie Chavis died in the Phuoc Long Province, South Vietnam, on September 3, 1970. He was only nineteen years old. I felt a tremendous loss had taken place. Ronnie is listed on the Vietnam Veterans Memorial, Panel W7, Line 35.

Transition to Future Farmers of America (FFA)

After three years as an NFA advisor, I was offered a position as an agriculture teacher at McColl High School, McColl, South Carolina. This school is located in Marlboro County, South Carolina. This would not have been unusual, except for the fact that this was a predominantly white school. The all-black school in the area was Adamsville High School.

I learned later that I was the first black agriculture teacher at a predominantly white school in South Carolina. I started work at McColl High School one month before Mr. Harvey Williams, another black teacher, started teaching at the school. We were the only two black teachers at McColl in 1968.

Mr. Wayne Polyak, principal, was friendly and welcoming. I can't say the same for some of our white coworkers. As black professionals, we had to "sell ourselves" to the other teachers, to the students, and to the community. To that date, they had known blacks at the school as janitors, maids, teacher aides, and lunchroom workers.

During those early weeks, there were racial epithets, keying of vehicles, distributor cap removals, flat tires, and manners of disrespect.

Mr. Williams and I were exceptional teachers and did an outstanding job at McColl. Mr. Williams had a most successful science fair, but he left the teaching profession after his first year and moved out of state.

In my second year at McColl, I sponsored a Miss FFA contest. At that time, we had about ten black students at the school, including three black boys. One day, when we were rehearsing for the contest, I had eight boys to serve as escorts for the sixteen girls who entered the contest. Two of the boy escorts were black. There were two black girls in the contest. I simply had the eight boys to start escorting the girls from the back of the auditorium down to the stage. The two black boys escorted the two black girls to the stage and got back in line. This time they ended up escorting two white girls. Oh, what a mistake.

After rehearsal, I was called into the office of the principal, Mr. Polyak. He informed me that he did not have a problem with the escorts, but that a white teacher had learned of the situation and complained to him. A local service station owner had heard and had called him. He was reportedly associated with the Ku Klux Klan.

Obviously, I changed the rotation. When the black boys had escorted the two black girls, I had them to retire to their seats. This allowed the white girls to only be escorted by white boys. Other than this bump in the road, the contest was a successful event.

I had been teaching parliamentary procedure to the FFA boys each year, and during my second year at McColl, we entered the Parliamentary Procedure Federation Contest. We won and entered the district contest. We then entered the state contest. When we arrived on the campus of Clemson University in Clemson, South Carolina, we were being introduced to the state FFA president. He casually said to me, "You must be an alternate," to which my students said back to him, in unison, "No, that's our teacher." My team was an all-white team. My students won first place in the South Carolina FFA Parliamentary Procedure Contest. My race and the race of my students showed South Carolina in 1970 that we can be very effective in teaching and learning, without regard to race.

McColl High School Future Farmers of America (FFA)
Chapter Wins State Parliamentary Procedure Contest

This team from McColl High School Future Farmers of America
Chapter won the State FFA Parliamentary Procedure Contest
during the 43rd annual SCFFA convention at Clemson University.
Team members include, left to right, Billy Graham, Larry Meggs,
Richard Grooms, J. A. Franklin, agriculture teacher and team
coach, Charles Hatcher, and Wayne Lockey. The team received a
$100 check and plaque.

New Homemakers of South Carolina

The New Homemakers of South Carolina organization was chartered with the secretary of state of South Carolina on January 16, 1942. Those persons listed on the charter are Ms. Lillian C. Hoffman of Columbia (advisor), Ms. Mattie E. Pegues of Orangeburg (asst. advisor), Ms. Willie Mae White of Florence (officer), and Ms. Lizzie M. Finch of Jamison (officer).

The purposes of the charter were educational and recreational. The headquarters were in Orangeburg and Columbia. In the declaration and petition for incorporation, Ms. Hoffman is identified as state supervisor of home economics in Columbia and Ms. Pegues is identified as a teacher-trainer at State College in Orangeburg.

The Columbia headquarters was the South Carolina State Department of Education, and the Orangeburg headquarters was South Carolina State College.

In 1960, the New Homemakers of South Carolina became the Home Economics Club of South Carolina.

According to the Ninety-Eighth Annual Report of the State Superintendent of Education, 1965–1966, pp.76–78, the New Homemakers of South Carolina (NHA) *combined into* one organization—South Carolina Future Homemakers of America (FHA) in 1966.

Per state records, the New Homemakers of South Carolina was "dissolved by forfeiture" on March 17, 1975.

New Homemakers of America (NHA)

The NHA curriculum was for students enrolled in the Home Economics Classes in black high schools throughout the South and in some border states. Some of the curriculum items of the NHA classes included child care, food service, sewing, clothing maintenance, interior design, and nutrition.

Curricular and extracurricular activities of the NHA included helping needy families, helping families suffering from prolonged illness, supplying food, clothing, and appropriate medical help to needy families, and volunteering for the Red Cross, Salvation Army, and other community organizations.

The NHA was a partner group with the NFA. These two groups co-sponsored a number of school and community activities. They sponsored units in local parades; sponsored exhibits at the local, regional, and state fairs; sponsored a local and federation dance; sponsored summer camp activities; sponsored activities for the needy; and sponsored joint leadership sessions.

New Homemakers of America

The NHA worked in harmony with NFA members. They shared resources, facilities, and activities. The NFA advisor and the NHA advisor coordinated all the programs of the two organizations, held departmental meetings, held joint chapter meetings, and supported the contests of the two organizations.

The NHA had many of the characteristics of the NFA with leadership being the most common trait. I will not include as much detail in this writing about the NHA as I did about the NFA, because of the universality of the two groups.

The local leaders at my high school included Ms. M. Perrin, Ms. Flora P. Miller, Ms. D. M. Mobley, and Ms. Annie Moore.

One can sum up the work of the NHA with an article written by NHA member and reporter, Cynthia Freeman. As a student at Mims High School, Cynthia was well involved in her chapter. She was a most dedicated member of the NHA. On Monday, May 22, 1961, she wrote, "The Mims Chapter of the NHA is proud to announce that the chapter has sixty-five girls as active members. Fifty-eight of these girls were initiated in September 1960."

All members have paid state and district dues, contributed to the scholarship loan fund, and have made other contributions, and ten members have made reservations to attend the one-week summer camp in Orangeburg. Seventy-three NHA and NFA members attended the state fair in Columbia.

At Christmastime, the NHA and NFA members prepared and gave away numerous baskets of fruit and other items to the sick, shut-ins, and aged members of our community. Also, toys made in the home economics department were given to small children.

The Mims chapter participated in 100 percent of the State NHA Health Card Campaign, and all members and their advisors secured a health card from the local Department of Community Health.

The Mims chapter was an award-winning chapter during the 1960–1961 school year. The chapter won a blue ribbon with a superior rating after having been named an honor chapter for entering all NHA contests, both district and state. This recognition was made on

March 4, 1961, at Westside High School in Anderson, and on April 28, 1961, at South Carolina State College in Orangeburg.

A first-place rating was given to the Mims NHA Chapter in the home project contest, in the yearbook contest, in the cotton dress contest, and in the renovated garment contest. Second-place honors were given to the chapter in the essay speaking contest and in the chapter name tag contest. Also, at the district and state levels, the chapter won second place in the coupon contest.

Cynthia summed up her report by writing, "As a daily guide, Mims chapter lives by the wisdom of the NHA Creed, Pledge, and in order to develop quality in our lives we must hitch our wagon to stars, think deep, and with a purpose, and strive constantly and hard." Cynthia represents thousands of NHA members who were educated in the Old South, in the old Negro schools, which created brilliant young men and young women, which made the South a better place to live, while carving out their "place in the sun."

DR. JAMES A. FRANKLIN SR.

South Carolina State College Supporters of the NHA

Dr. Laler C. DeCosta, Dean, School of Agriculture and Home Economics
Dr. Annabelle Sherman, Associate Dean and Professor of Home Economics
Ms. Mattie Pegues, Associate Professor of Home Economics, Itinerant Teacher-Trainer
Ms. Wilhelenia Funchess, Professor of Foods and Nutrition
Ms. Amelia Adams, Assistant Professor of Clothing and Textiles
Ms. Ophelia Williams, Associate Professor of Home Economics
Ms. Geraldine Penn, Professor of Home Economics Education
Ms. Eloise Morris, Assistant Professor of Home Economics Education
Ms. Gracie McBane, Instructor of Home Economics
Ms. Earlene Jackson, Director of Pre School
Ms. Noveline Williams, Instructor of Nursery School
Ms. Dorothy Jarvis and Ms. Margaret Roberts, Administrative Assistants

South Carolina Department of Education Supporters
of the NFA and the NHA During My Associations with
the NFA and the FFA

State Superintendent of Education State Director of Vocational Education
Mr. Frank R. Stover, State Supervisor of Agricultural Education, Columbia, South Carolina
Mr. Louis J. Carter, District Supervisor of Agricultural Education, Florence, South Carolina
Mr. Earl Frick, Assistant Supervisor of Agricultural Education, Florence, South Carolina
Mr. William Mahoney, District Supervisor of Agricultural Education, Anderson, South Carolina

Clemson University Supporters of the NFA and the FFA
Clemson University Agricultural Education Staff

Career Change

*Establishing a Halfway House
for Substance Abusers*

Substance Abuse Worker

In 1973, I became director of the Chesterfield-Marlboro Alcohol Program. This was a $50,000 antipoverty program that served two rural counties in South Carolina. The program had a director, two counselors, a driver-counselor, and a secretary. Individual counseling and family counseling were the most important components of the program.

Ancillary and referral program services included inpatient services at the South Carolina Alcohol and Drug Abuse Treatment Center in Columbia, halfway houses, and Christian homes for alcoholics. Support and group efforts included Alcoholics Anonymous, Al-Anon, and Alateen groups.

With state funding, the alcohol program expanded to become the Chesterfield-Marlboro Alcohol and Drug Abuse Commission. While serving as executive director of the commission, I wrote a grant to establish the first rural halfway house for substance abusers in the State of South Carolina.

This halfway house was established with the cooperation of the late Mr. Jonas Kennedy of Bennettsville, South Carolina. Mr. Kennedy was a large turkey and field crop farmer. He and his wife, Mrs. Odette Kennedy, had been schoolteachers, but they decided to leave the teaching profession to start a farming operation. This bold new step in the late 1950s established the Kennedys as millionaire farming operators by the late 1960s when they were highlighted in *Ebony* magazine.

The old home house of the Kennedy family became available, and the commission rented this house to become the commission's halfway house. The facility had eight beds for men on the second floor and four beds for women on the first floor. Mr. Kennedy agreed to employ residents of the halfway house on his farm. The halfway house had a manager and an assistant manager with services being provided by other commission staff members, with the assistance of staff from other helping agencies. It was a wonderful partnership. The halfway house lasted for many years until it was destroyed by Hurricane Hugo.

Mr. Kennedy was a former NFA member, and Mrs. Kennedy was a former NHA member and NHA advisor. They successfully put into practice much of what they learned as members of these two organizations.

These former members of the NFA and the NHA serve today as models for putting thrift into practice. They were so successful until they were able to donate a large sum of money to Claflin University in Orangeburg, South Carolina, where a building on that campus bears their name.

Education and Religion

*Hope for a Former
Enslaved People in the Old South*

Dr. William Samuel Mims was one of the early leaders of public education for blacks in the Old South. Having started his career in a church school, he later started the Mims public schools for blacks in McCormick, South Carolina.

Dr. William Samuel Mims

1967 Tribute To Dr. W. S. Mims

(This tribute was written to Dr. Mims by a
Committee chaired by Mr. J. C. Mattison.)

Dr. Mims recognized many years ago that our rapidly changing world
requires men and women trained in sound reasoning, intelligent in
their evaluation, curious and capable of new discoveries, and thirsty
for knowledge. He was determined to do his share in helping people, particularly the youths under his jurisdiction, to develop their
potentialities to the maximum, and to master the aforementioned
requirements. He was acclaimed as a man with vision, and rightly
so because with his extra-ordinary ability and faith, he has strug-
gled against obstacles to demand noted recognition. It was under
his supervision as teacher and principal, with thirty pupils in the old
Odd Fellows' Hall that his vision broadened. Each day he gathered
strength for his task from one of his favorite scripture verses: "Where
there is no vision the people perish…"

He believed so firmly in this scripture and worked so unselfishly
in rendering of his time, service, knowledge, and ability that he has
been able to see the one-teacher school develop into an ultra-modern
building.

Upon consolidation of the public schools of this state, his efforts
were again rewarded—the honor of having three elementary schools
and a high school in McCormick County carry his name. One of the
main streets of the town is named for this educator. How does he
accept such fanfare? Humbly. As an answer to questions concerning
the Mims schools of the county, and especially Mims High, he simply answered, "Well, I have been here all of my life."

We can see much more. Sure, he has been here, but because
he is a man with vision, with a humble heart and grateful service
to mankind, these schools stand as monuments of his trust in our
youths and his untiring efforts to provide means of helping all mankind to quench his thirst for knowledge and to help insure America
and the world of a safer, sounder, more intellectual future.

THE MIMS SCHOOL FOUNDED IN 1939 BY DR. WILLIAM SAMUEL MIMS

(Later named Mims Elementary School Number One)

DR. JAMES A. FRANKLIN SR.

MIMS ELEMENTARY SCHOOL NUMBER TWO (WASHINGTON SCHOOL AT PARKSVILLE, SOUTH CAROLINA)

MIMS ELEMENTARY SCHOOL NUMBER THREE (WILLINGTON SCHOOL AT WILLINGTON, SOUTH CAROLINA)

The "new" Mims High School, constructed in 1954, later becoming McCormick High School in McCormick, South Carolina. This school was closed as a school when the new McCormick High School was constructed in 2010.

THE LEGACY OF DR. WILLIAM SAMUEL MIMS

The legacy of Dr. William Samuel Mims lives on in the hearts and minds of those who loved and were benefited by his care, his compassion, and his love of Negro youth and the extended Negro community. Mr. Mims was a teacher and eventually the principal of the Bethany School, which was located at the Bethany Missionary Baptist Church on South Main Street in McCormick. The Bethany School was a day school and a boarding school for students who had to travel long distances to the school and had no way of getting to the school on a daily basis.

There were a two-story building and a single-story building at the site. The two-story building housed Mr. Mims and his family on the second floor, along with some faculty members. Boarding students were located on the first floor. Classes were held in the single-story building, which was located next to the two-story building.

Prior to Mr. Mims coming to the Bethany School, the headmaster or principal was the founder of the Bethany School, the Reverend James Foster Marshall, the son of a slave, who was also pastor of the Bethany Missionary Baptist Church, a church which Reverend Marshall started in 1882. Prior to Mr. Mims's tenure at the Bethany School just after World War I, an early student at the Bethany School in 1909 was a boarding student from Epworth, near Greenwood, South Carolina. His name was Benjamin Elijah Mays.

Epworth was too far to travel, so Mays resided at the boarding house of the Bethany School. Further, the farm wagons and mules were needed on his dad's farm. Benjamin stayed at Bethany School for two years. Rev. Marshall saw the potential of the young student and offered him a job to assist at the school while he continued to matriculate there. Benjamin turned down the offer and left the Bethany School to enroll at South Carolina State College in Orangeburg. This account is in May's autobiography, *Born to Rebel.*

It is not known if Mr. Mims had heard of this gifted student when he arrived at Bethany School. History will eventually tell us that these two men had a lot in common.

According to accounts, Mims was born just north of the town of McCormick on August 14, 1893. His parents were Mr. Samuel and Mrs. Elizabeth Mims, who had six other children.

The seven children faced a tremendous challenge early in life because of the untimely death of their father. This caused William and his siblings to have to take on responsibilities in which they were not prepared. Little did he know at the time that there was a Divine Plan to toughen him up for a greater calling in life.

This McCormick County native learned early in life that hard work, diligence, determination, fortitude, perseverance, commitment, and faith were important ingredients to face difficult times. Not only did he need these traits to make ends meet for the family after World War I days, but he would need them, especially as he tried to start a comprehensive countywide public school system for Negro youth in McCormick County in 1924. The doctor of divinity degree, which he received from his beloved Allen University, further prepared him for his decades of school and religious work.

Prior to Dr. Mims's efforts to consolidate public education for Negro youth in McCormick County, it is reported that thirty-nine church and community schools provided for the education of the youth of former slaves. They were Bethany School (McCormick), Bailey Bethel School, Chestnut Ridge School, Holy Springs School, Bethany School (Clarks Hill), Martha's Chapel School, Mount Zion School, Rockford School, Saint Charlotte School, Whitetown School, Zion Chapel School, Glover's Chapel School, Rock Grove School, Laurel Grove School, Branch School, Gilbert Rosenwald School, Hopewell Rosenwald School, Mt. Moriah School, Mulberry School, Rock Hill School, Sand Hill School, Wideman School, Mt. Lebanon School, Kitchen Town School, Little Mill School, Blue Branch School, Cedar Springs School, Green Olive School, Pine Grove School, Mt. Pleasant School, Robinson School, St. Mary's School, Springfield School, Young's School, New Hope School, Getar Springs School, Hosannah School, the Branch School, and Lyon Chapel School.

He started his first school in a two-room building up by the "branch" on what is now Kelly Street. The building was formerly a fraternal lodge. The lodge was called the Knights of Pythias Lodge. The lodge and its four acres were deeded to the McCormick County School District for the education of Negro children. It is well to note that the fraternal lodge was established north of the Mason-Dixon Line in 1864. The lodge became the first fraternal order to receive its charter under an Act of Congress during the presidency of Abraham Lincoln. How did the order get into the Deep South? The lodge designed its efforts "to the cause of universal peace." It is named for Pythagoras, the father of Greek philosophy.

According to research, this noble organization was lauded by President Lincoln, who said, "The purposes of your organization are most wonderful. If we could but bring its spirit to all our citizenry, what a wonderful thing it would be. It breathes the spirit of friendship, charity, and benevolence. It is one of the best agencies conceived for the upholding of government, honoring the flag, for uniting our brethren of the North and of the South, for teaching the people to love one another, and portraying the sanctity of the home and loved ones." It is suspected that this northern group came south, as did many others during reconstruction.

According to their website, the Knights of Pythias theme is "We Help People." The United States flag is given a place of honor at every lodge meeting, and the Holy Bible is the supreme book of law, all of which were ideals of Dr. William Samuel Mims, and ultimately his four schools.

In the beginning, several classes were housed in these two rooms. It was not until Mims built his first large school in 1939, that classes were divided up until the tenth grade. The two-room school was used until the early 1950s. The eleventh and twelfth grades were not added until the late 1940s.

Although the branch doesn't exist anymore, as you stand on the hill at the site of the 1939 Mims School, you can imagine the branch flowing downstream behind the two-room schoolhouse. The branch not only provided water for the little garden which existed outside the two-room building, but it was a source of clay, which was used to make projects by the students.

I attended first grade and second grade in this two-room building. Back in the day, there were no age requirements, nor a compulsory attendance law. Most Negro youth worked on farms, so you had students starting school at different times. It would not be uncommon to have students in a class, and the age difference could be three or more years.

In a narration written by Mrs. Leola Grant Walker, she wrote about the "branch" near the two-room school. She worked as a teacher in the early Mims School. She was born on Church Street in the community known as the Bottoms, which is located on the southside of the town of McCormick. Her place of birth is just a block from the original Bethany School, where Dr. Mims first taught and served as principal.

Mrs. Walker was the first person of her race from the Bottoms who graduated from College (Miss Leola Grant at the time). This 1946 graduate of Paine College in Augusta, Georgia, learned very early some of the challenges of teaching in a Mims School where she started her career. She wrote that all the grades were located in one building and that Dr. Mims, although the principal of the school, also taught a class. She wrote that her biggest challenge was trying to teach sixty or more students in one room at a time.

Through the decades that followed, students came to know Dr. Mims as a strong disciplinarian and a strong promoter of the academics, and he brought organized high school sports to a level from which they would never return. Sports, like academics to Dr. Mims, had to be clean, organized, sophisticated, and played with the same determination as was displayed in the classroom. Many of us can remember when we did not have a gymnasium. We practiced and played against other schools outside. Basketball became the first organized sport at the Mims School, and these games were played competitively against other Negro schools in the region. Dr. Mims required that the outside basketball field be painted/lined off as if an artist had painted a picture for exhibition.

Mrs. Walker also wrote that great changes were made over the years, from adding a twelfth grade to the move into a new high school in 1954. She wrote that the new high school was built across the branch. This is the same branch where the first two room Negro public schoolhouse had been established decades earlier. She also saw the establishment of all four Mims Schools in 1954. The old "white building," the original Mims School built in 1939, became Mims Elementary School Number One, Mims Elementary School Number Two (the old Washington School in Parksville), and the new Mims Elementary School Number Three in Willington.

In addition to Mrs. Leola Grant Walker, there were many other great teachers in the Mims Schools. It is well to note that most of the teachers in the Mims Schools came from communities outside of McCormick County. This required a sense of dedication in light of the fact that they earned less than teachers in other schools. Further, the teachers and students in the Mims Schools received used books and used furniture from other schools. The students in the Mims Schools were studying materials that were way out of date.

To help offset this phenomenon, Dr. Mims asked teachers to fundraise and to charge students a registration fee. Much of these funds were used to buy supplemental materials and teacher supplies.

I remember when each class was assigned a fundraising project. We did not have a lunchroom or cafeteria. Some students brought their lunch in a brown paper bag. Selling lunch items became fund-raising projects. Examples of items sold were: peanut butter sandwiches, peanut butter crackers (saltines and Ritz), lunch meat sandwiches, bologna sandwiches, pimento cheese sandwiches, candy, cookies, chips, fruit, and different flavors of Kool-Aid. No, we did not sell hot dogs and hamburgers because stoves did not exist at the early Mims Schools. Five-cent sock dances were also held during the lunch break.

To help with custodial efforts, girls were assigned to wash the blackboards and to wash the windows. Boys were assigned to keep the fire burning in the pot-bellied stoves during the cold weather. The boys used "fat lyder" to start the fires. They also had to go outside to get coal in a "coal scuttle" to keep the fires burning. No, there was no central heat or air conditioning in the early Mims Schools. For air conditioning, you just let up the windows and hoped that the wind was blowing. The girls and boys shared with the cleaning of the room at the end of each school day. The boys emptied the trash.

In spite of all these responsibilities *and teaching*, some of our teachers kept coming back. It is well to note that many of our teachers never married, especially our female teachers. One such teacher was Miss E. V. Massey from Abbeville, who spent her career teaching in the Mims Schools. Miss Massey came with an education by the college of Dr. Mims (Allen University) and by the college that educated Booker T. Washington (Hampton Institute), and she drilled into us the King's English.

When we say that there were no discipline problems in the Mims Schools, Miss Massey was one reason why. In addition to her outstanding ability to teach us, she controlled discipline by walking around the classroom as she taught, and if you looked like you wanted to be mischievous, she would pinch you. Take my word; no one wanted to be pinched by Miss Massey.

On a serious note, in a speech given by Miss Massey at the Mims Elementary School Number Three in Willington, she said, "A community may count with pride its factories, good roads, fine public buildings; yet these are not to be compared with the intellectual, spiritual, physical, and social growth of its youth." She concluded her talk by asking, "What shall it profit a community if it gains the whole world of wealth and lose its future—the future that is embodied in its boys and girls?"

Like Walker and Massey, the names of Wilburn, Smith, Tompkins, Watts, Holloway, Donaldson, Spearman, Miller, Wilson, Mattison, Earl, Nelson, Hackett, Holmes, Patterson, Martin, Quiller, Edwards, Talbert, Pierce, Norman, Johnson, Threatt, Williams, Mobley, Frazier, Robinson, Moore, Chaplin, Gray, McCombs, Statum, Goudy, Dozier, Louden, Singletary, Childs, Boyd, Lee, Rearden, Rhodes, Carter, Thomas, Strickland, Ballard, Mattox, White, Dean, Watson, Adams, Lockett, Posey, and countless others embraced the opportunities and challenges which presented themselves each day in a Mims School.

To help him with his mission to effectively educate all Negro children entrusted to him, Dr. Mims picked his team of teachers, teacher aides, custodians, cafeteria workers, and other staff as if he was an artist who had to select the colors to use in a masterpiece painting of a still life. We also remember his teachers and other staff members to be sophisticated, well-educated, strong disciplinarians, effective educators who loved their craft, and loved the students whom they faced each day.

Dr. Mims also supported a strong Parent Teacher Association (PTA). The PTA was actively involved in the Mims Schools. Some outstanding PTA presidents during the Mims Schools years were Mr. Harvey Lee Murray (Mims High School PTA president), Mr. James Morgan (Mims Elementary School Number Two PTA president), and Mr. Roy Smith (Mims Elementary School Number Three PTA president). While there were many objectives and a creed, the objective which mostly represented a Mims School was "to bring into closer relation the home and the school, so that parents and teachers may cooperate intellectually in the training of the child."

Dr. Mims was a compassionate man. As a minister, he showed pain and empathy toward those whom life seems to deal a bad hand. Whether attending the funeral of a fallen student or sitting beside the bed of a hurt athlete, Dr. Mims showed the care and compassion of a dedicated Christian soldier. Beneath that suit of armor, which we saw each day, there exhibited a warmth toward others whose lives were touched by sadness or grief.

Dr. Mims knew that the first school where he had worked (Bethany School) was an industrial-type school. Most early Negro schools were industrial schools, training schools, or normal schools. These concepts grew out of the Booker T. Washington practice at Tuskegee Institute. It also goes back to his "great speech" at the Atlanta Exposition, where he was quoted as saying, "There is as much dignity in tilling the fields as there is in writing a poem." Washington's beliefs also contrasted with those of Dr. W. E. B. Dubois, who promoted intellectual pursuits for the children of former slaves. At any rate, Washington won out, and skills development became the norm for Negro youth. In 1954, Dr. Mims used the opportunity to expand skills development in his schools. He brought Mr. Frank Earl to teach industrial arts (carpentry, electricity, painting, mechanical drawing, welding, and other skills), Mr. James C. Mattison to teach vocational agriculture (animal husbandry, horticulture, cannery operations, agronomy, agriculture mechanics, agribusiness/ management, and NFA leadership training), Mrs. Nannie Watts to teach office occupations (typing, filing, shorthand, business math, office procedures, and office management), and Mrs. Perrin / Mrs. Miller to teach home economics (foods and nutrition, canning and freezing, sewing, family living, and NHA leadership training). These hands-on subjects significantly helped those students who did not plan to go to college.

We wrote earlier about discipline in the Mims Schools. In the Mims School, all the men teachers were called "Prof" or "Professor," out of the respect required by Dr. Mims. Back in those days, no special title was required for female teachers other than "Miss" or "Mrs." It was natural for Negro students to show respect for female teachers. You can credit Negro female parents for this expectation. The same respect that Negro youth showed "Mama" was expected at school. In the Mims Schools and in the homes of Negro children, the mother, grandmother, or in some cases, the aunt (Annie) were better disciplinarians than any father. On a personal note, my father never "beat" me, but my mother did so on many occasions.

As a matter of fact, when my mother felt that I needed a whipping, she would send me to the tree to get a switch for my whipping. If the switch was too small, she sent one of my siblings to get a larger switch. No, I did not want that because they would get a much larger switch. Back in the day, these Negro females made for the almost nonexistence of discipline problems in the Mims Schools. You see, these second and third whippings for the same infraction were not welcomed by any of the Negro youth. Dr. Mims and his son, Mr. William Mims, used a paddle, and no one wanted to face the paddle.

When you were approached by Dr. Mims, especially if you had done something wrong, his facial expression was enough to make you quiver, and the use of his gravel toned voice was the knock-out punch.

One embarrassing moment occurred when former principal and former school board member Eddie Lee Talbert and I were cited in an assembly by Dr. Mims. Eddie and I had met some girls at a federation ball. The federated balls were a semiformal dance where you wore your Sunday best. They were held each year by the nine Negro schools that were members of a federation. At any rate, Eddie and I wanted to see the girls again. As some precocious boys would do back in the day, we came up with a way to see the girls, and neither one of us had a car. We knew that the US postal mail truck went to Anderson each day. The girls attended Westside High School in Anderson. We asked the mailman if we could ride in the back of the mail truck to Anderson and to return that afternoon when he went back to McCormick. Though reluctantly, he did say yes. He "charged" us fifty cents for the round trip.

We walked several miles from the post office to Westside. We hadn't expected to get caught because our goal was to filter into the student population. Yes, we saw the girls, but a faculty member reported that he saw some strange students on campus and inquired if the school had enrolled some new students. Yes, we were caught red-handed. We told the principal (Mr. Wakefield) that we were on a goodwill tour. He laughed and called Dr. Mims to report that he had two of his students at his school on a goodwill tour and asked Dr. Mims if he knew of such a tour from Mims High School. Eddie and I couldn't determine if Dr. Mims was angry with us or if he smiled at the length that two of his boys would go to see some girls. The most serious infraction was that we cut school. Of course, we were trespassing on the Westside School property. No, he never severely punished us, but we were ostracized by other students, especially the girls. He probably felt that this was punishment enough.

In later years, Negro male teachers were in large numbers in the Mims Schools. This was especially true for Mims High School. At one point, there were just as many Negro male teachers as there were Negro female teachers. This was true for school year 1966–1967 when there were eight female and eight male (with Mr. W. J. Mims as principal) and there were nine male teachers. In today's public schools, black male teachers are almost extinct.

Some of us can remember when the new gymnasium was constructed in 1954, and Mr. Mims would not let you walk on the gym floor without your tennis shoes on. We can also remember Mr. Mims's schools as being immaculately clean. He must have known some-thing about Dr. Booker T. Washington and his efforts to impress his teachers at Hampton Institute by double cleaning a room to impress them to admit him to study at Hampton Institute.

Dr. Mims was a sophisticated man of high intellect and made the word "Esquire" popular long before there was an *Esquire* maga-zine. His principals followed this pattern. From his son W. J. Mims, to J. C. Threatt, to G. N. Williams, to Alexander Wilson, they mod-eled the W. S. Mims mode of dress. So did his male teachers. The Mims Schools' female teachers always wore their Sunday best to greet their students.

As a preacher and as a presiding elder in the African Methodist Episcopal (AME) Church, he used his sermons to motivate his parishioners. As a principal, he used his messages to motivate his stu-dents in Friday assemblies at Mims High School. Yes, he was a moti-vational speaker long before today's motivational speakers were born. During his career, he served as a pastor of several AME churches, among which were Pine Grove AME Church, Zion Chappel AME Church, and Bailey Bethel AME Church. Like, Dr. Benjamin E. Mays, whether from the pulpit, from the classroom, from the audito-rium or gymnasium, or from the side of the road, Dr. Mims demon-strated the best of mankind. Though not perfect, he lacked many of the imperfections that are pervasive in society today. Though not unblemished, his demeanor was one in which we could emulate.

His preaching and pastoral duties required Dr. Mims to visit the sick while preaching Sunday morning and Sunday night services here in McCormick County. Additionally, as a full-time principal who found it necessary to be at his school no later than 7:00 a.m. each day (6:00 a.m. in the winter because fires had to be made in the classroom stoves), Dr. Mims had to board with several families in the county rather than to travel to Abbeville each night. Mr. and Mrs. Fredrick Jenkins was one such family with whom he boarded.

Leisurely, Dr. Mims loved to hunt and to work in his garden. It was not until later in life that he had the time to enjoy these hobbies. His favorite color was blue, and his favorite foods were corn and country ham. From the pulpit, he loved to lead his congregations in the singing of "Amazing Grace" and "O For a Thousand Tongues to Sing."

In the 1967 Mims presentation of "Labor Conquers All," the James C. Mattison Committee wrote in a tribute to Dr. Mims, "As a Final Word." By the way, Mr. Mattison was a prolific writer and a role model for countless Mims students. This writer is one of those students.

The tribute continued, "As a final word for the directions for tomorrow, I should like to tell you of the story of a young man and his leader on the night of his graduation from an institution of learning. To me, these are the very same unchanging directions that I should like to impress upon you today. This story as I remember it was called 'The Rules for the Game of Life.' This game was illustrated as a game of football in a world crowded with people, good people, evil people, sad people, frightened people, and yes, self-sufficient people. These people were from the many faces of life, huddled against the many gadgets and forces of our time, and the story goes.

"You've made the team, son," he said. "I am giving you the ball, and naming you the quarterback for your team in the game of life, I am your coach, so I'll give it to you straight.

"There is only one schedule to play. It lasts all your life but consists of only one game. It is long with no time out and no substitutions. You play the whole game—all your life, and then it might not end. The printed pages might immortalize you. You'll have a great backfield. You are calling the signals, but the other three fellows in the backfield with you have great reputations. They are named faith, hope, and charity.

"You'll work behind a truly powerful line. End to end, it consists of honesty, loyalty, devotion to duty, self-respect, sturdy cleanliness, good behavior, and courage.

"The goalposts are the gates of heaven. God is the referee and sole official. He makes the rules, and there is no appeal from them.

"There are ten rules. You know them as the Ten Commandments, and you play them strictly in accordance with your own religion.

"There is also an important ground rule. It is, as you would that men should do to you, do ye also to them likewise."

"Here's the ball—it's your immortal soul! Hold on to it. Now, son, get in there and let's see what you can do with it. Time will tell for we know not, so prepare yourself, aim high, drive toward the goal and watch your end. The door of opportunity stands ajar. Good luck!" the Mattison Committee Report concluded.

The other members of the Mattison Committee were Mr. W. J. Mims (son of Dr. Mims), Mr. J. C. Threatt, Mr. G. N. Williams, Mr. Alexander Wilson, and Mr. Fletcher Pierce. The committee also used the phrase "Labor Omnia Vincit" to describe the legacy of Dr. Mims. This phrase means "Works Conquers All."

At a time when most former all-Negro schools have "faded away," the legacy of the Mims Schools continues to have a place in the minds and hearts of countless black students and their parents who were fortunate to have been touched by this giant of a man!

The Mims Foundation is named for Dr. William Samuel Mims. The foundation started in the year 2000 in the basement of the MACK Building in McCormick. The foundation is a 501 3 tax-exempt (federal ID number 61-1415080) organization by the Internal Revenue Service of the United States. It is also chartered (state ID number 10432) with the Secretary of State of South Carolina as a nonprofit organization. As such, we solicit donations to be used to give scholarships to needy and deserving students who graduate from McCormick High School each year.

The scholarship program started in 2004. Students from McCormick High School are invited to apply for two scholarships, each in the amount of $1,000, from the Mims Foundation. The criteria are submission of their high school transcript, evidence of acceptance at a four year accredited institution, SAT/ACT scores, evidence of a minimum GPA of 2.5 on a 4.0 scale, be ranked in the top fifteen of the graduating class, two letters of recommendation, and to submit an essay of two hundred words or more in his/her own handwriting, explaining why the applicant is deserving of the scholarship. The foundation feels that Dr. Mims would have wanted these type criteria. From 2004 to 2018, twenty-six students received

scholarships from the Mims Foundation. We are now receiving scholarship applications for 2019. The deadline is May 1 of each year. Award winners are recognized on the Annual Awards Day Program at McCormick High School.

Former recipients of Mims Scholarships are Jarvis Adams, Tonesia Cartledge, Natoya Cartledge, Verronda Kelly, Ashlej Cartledge, Ongela Hill, Marissa Timpson, Geneva Green, Tierra Robinson, Brandon New, Laneshia Kelly, Markeydes Nelson, Miles Sibert, Crystal Reid, Tyliah Yarbought, A'siuan Freeman, Alexis Browning, Ashley Hill, Chelsey Johnson, Corjnthin Martin, Jasmine Callaham, Kitlyn Foster, Leah Anthony, Robin Harris, Tyrhea Mason, and Tymira Booker.

The foundation wanted to establish a memorial site for the Mims legacy. The names of all the schools which he started were a thing of the past. When the foundation was started, the only remembrance of Dr. Mims was the street, Mims Drive.

The old Ebenezer AME Church property, owned by the McCormick County Board of Education, was vacant. This great church served the Negro community from August 23, 1894, until August 18, 1970. Over the years, the membership dwindled. The few remaining members (Mr. John Bell, Mrs. Laura Ann Bell, Mr. H. W. Walker, Mr. Moses Franklin [my father]) and a few others moved their membership to the Shiloh AME Church. As time passed, the building deteriorated and was torn down. The property was deeded to the McCormick County Board of Education. The Foundation requested that site for the Mims Memorial. Under the administration of Superintendent Dr. Lloyd Hunter and with the leadership of school board chairman, Mr. Oscar New, this request was granted.

The memorial site has Dr. Mims, many of his teachers, his students, and other staff acknowledged at the site. Mrs. Seleda Mims, wife of Mr. W. J. Mims and Dr. Mims children, are also acknowledged. The site has six flags: four American flags, which represent the four Mims Schools; one Christian flag that represents Dr. Mims as a preacher and a presiding elder in the African American Episcopal AME Church; and another Christian flag that represents the former Ebenezer AME Church. A marker also salutes this great church. This church is where Dr. Mims held his graduation exercises each year because the high school at that time did not have an auditorium.

The Mims graduation exercises were most impressive and held in the great traditions of class and sophistication. Baccalaureate sermons on the Sundays preceding graduations were profound and challenging. At the commencement exercises, when the pianist began to play "War March of the Priests," observers were overcome with joy, pride, and adulation. As the pianist played "Pomp and Circumstance" at the end of the exercises, some tears began to flow as graduates exited the church.

What happened to the Mims students/graduates? Northern migration, which started during Reconstruction, continued with the Mims graduates, until after school integration in the 1970s. Locally, Mims graduates found jobs as janitors, pulpwood and timber workers, sawmill workers, and farmers and in other low-paying jobs. Skilled labor positions were not available for Mims graduates. Mims female graduates found it much harder to find a job of any kind, other than domestic labor. Locally, there were no skilled jobs available for Mims graduates.

Most Mims graduates did not remain in McCormick County. They, as their ancestors, moved north to find good-paying jobs, or they entered the armed forces. Five of my brothers, who were Mims graduates before me, entered the United States Navy. Still, other Mims graduates entered and graduated from college. Mims students/graduates have excelled all over the United States in business, law, medicine, engineering, education, technology, social work, government, manufacturing, architecture, theology, chemistry, nursing, and in a variety of other areas.

When the new McCormick Schools Complex was constructed, and students moved into those new buildings, this created some vacant properties where the 1939 Mims School was built, and near the site of the original two-room schoolhouse, which was deeded to the McCormick County School Board by the Knights of Pythias Lodge for the education of Negro youth. The foundation requested one of these buildings. Under the administration of superintendent

Dr. Sandra Callaham, and with the support of school board members Mr. Oscar New and Mrs. Kathy DuLaney, the request was granted.

This successful effort to secure a facility was highlighted in one of Mrs. DuLaney's (another prolific writer) final commentaries to the *Messenger*. In her column entitled "Between Friends," Mrs. DuLaney included the following: "Another of the vacated buildings at the old high school will go to the Mims Foundation. No longer will we just drive by and see the monument and flags in memory of Dr. Mims. Now the Foundation will have a building and the possibilities have endless potential to keep the Mims message alive in McCormick. 'Good, Better, Best! Never let it rest until good is better and better is best!'…The message is a great one to keep in your head, but more importantly it should be a constant call to action for everyone," Mrs. DuLaney concluded. The foundation building has historical documents, artifacts, Negro history materials, local history, and the Mims story materials. It is also used for meetings by families, for meetings by former classes of the Mims Schools, for baby showers, and for civic meetings.

The foundation is now preparing for events, which it has every two years. These events are called the Mims Schools Reunion. These reunions started in the first year of the foundation's existence, 2000. The 2019 reunion of the classes of the Mims Schools was held on June 28–30. Registration and reception were held on the night of June 28. The Mims Memorial Parade was held on June 29, beginning at 10:00 a.m. The parade started at the site of the old Bethany School, where Dr. Mims first worked (now the Bethany Missionary Baptist Church on South Main Street), travel through town, and disband at the old ginhouse. The Mims Memorial Program was held at the rear of the MACK near the hour of 1:00 p.m. A special part of this program was the platting of the Maypole, a favorite of Dr. Mims. Anyone could participate in the parade; however, registration was required. The units were judged, and the winners were announced at the MACK program. As in the past, the judges' table was across the street in front of the Messenger News Office. Vendors were invited to register to sell food at the time of these events. Registration was required. The reunion banquet was held Saturday night in the

Talmadge Center. This year's Mims scholarship winners spoke at the banquet. The reunion church services was on Sunday morning.

Dr. William Samuel Mims and his wife, Mrs. Alma P. Mims, had three sons. Their oldest, William J. Mims, followed in his father's footsteps. He was a teacher and principal in the McCormick Public School System. I was quite familiar with his paddle. He paddled me when I was in the seventh grade while he was principal of Mims Elementary School Number One. Unfortunately, he passed away while serving as a high school principal. He was married to Mrs. Seleda Mims. The 1984 *Chieftain* (McCormick High School Yearbook) was dedicated in memory of Mr. William J. Mims. Another son, Talmadge Tennyson Mims, was a veteran of the United States Air Force and a career diplomat where he spent a number of years with the United States Embassy in Athens, Greece. He is now deceased. He was married to Mrs. Brenda Gregitis Mims of London, England. His third son, Thales Mims, taught Spanish in Cuba and in several high schools and colleges in the State of South Carolina. This Fulbright Fellow was also a musician extraordinaire and served as a church musician for more than thirty-five years. Thales, now ninety-two years "young," lives in Abbeville, South Carolina. He also serves as parade marshal in the Mims parades in McCormick, South Carolina.

While the memorial site, foundation building, and reunion events will serve to remember the legacy of Dr. William Samuel Mims; the Mims scholarships will foster the continued production of scholarly students who are expected to demonstrate the grand motto of Dr. Mims: "Good! Better! Best! Never let is rest until Good is Better and Better is Best!" Remembering the Legacy of Dr. Mims will ensure a brighter future for all who love and respect our great nation and its people.

The little boy from Epworth became Dr. Benjamin E. Mays, a recipient of over fifty honorary degrees and a PhD degree from the University of Chicago, a preacher and orator known the world over, a mentor and teacher of Dr. Martin Luther King Jr., the eulogist for Dr. King's funeral, an educator and president of Morehouse College, president of the Atlanta Board of Education, a community activist, an advocate for Mahatma Gandhi's nonviolence efforts, and an advisor to presidents. The common thread between Dr. Mims and Dr. Mays was the Bethany School. Maybe it was "something in the water."

Dr. William Samuel Mims, what a legacy! He worked for the citizens of McCormick County for over sixty years. He was an educator, a parent, a husband, a patriot, a theologian, and a servant for the people.

Mims High School Students (circa 1940s; Dr. Mims is pictured on the second row from the top on the left)

Mims Elementary School Students (circa 1940s)

146

Tributes To Mims Educators

TRIBUTE TO MIMS PRINCIPALS

They roamed the schools throughout the day
Trying to keep things straight
Beneficiaries to laughter and tears
Such great memories to relate.

Their jobs were filled with stress
For they really cared
So many concerns to address
Futures to get prepared.

Yes, they were Mims and Mims
Wilson, Threat, Williams,
Rhodes, Talbert, Merritt, and Robinson.
Great principals all.

Their students were their tomorrow
They knew this well
They were role models from which to follow
In time their work will tell.

Principals hated to say goodbye
Memories of students come and gone
They had to look back and not question why
As they prepared so many for a world unknown.

TRIBUTE TO MIMS SCHOOLTEACHERS

We had teachers with special gifts for learning
And with hearts that deeply cared
They added a lot of love
To everything that you shared.

And even though they shared
And even though
They meant a lot
They will never know just how much.

They helped to change the world
Through every one of us whom they taught
They sparked the creativity
In all the students they touched.

You were Massey, Watts, Dean, Earl, Mattison, Wilburn,
Holmes, Smith, Tompkins, Donaldson, Wilson, Walker,
Patterson, Miller, Perrin, Martin, Booker, Spearman, Johnson,
Freeman, Pressley, Reynolds, Burton, Brown, Nelson,
Harley, Hodges, Jones, Goodwin, Chaplin, Moore, Norman,
Wideman, Lockett, Merritt, Bell, Frazier, Palmer, Holmes,
Adams, Carter, Banks, Gilchrist, Yeargin, Rhodes, Hines,
Thomas, Chenault, Jenkins, Talbert, Franklin, Callaham,
Posey, and so many others.

They helped students to strive for goals
That could not be bought
They were such special people
That no words can truly tell
However much they are valued
For the work that they did with us so well.

A MEMORIAL TRIBUTE TO A 1946 MIMS HIGH SCHOOL GRADUATE

Dorothy Wilma Searles was a graduate in the class of 1946 of Mims High School. She graduated on May 14, 1946.

In 1946, the graduating class of Mims High School held its graduation ceremonies at the Ebenezer African Methodist Episcopal Church, which was located on what is now the Mims Memorial Site. This site was adjacent to the Mims High School building, thereby making it convenient for the graduating class to practice and to hold its graduation ceremony at that site. Ebenezer was a somewhat large wood-frame building and could hold a large audience. Mims High School did not have an auditorium at this time. Graduations were held here until Dr. Mims had constructed an addition to the large white school building. The addition included an auditorium and four additional classrooms.

For decades, Dr. W. S. Mims, principal, held a baccalaureate sermon. The sermon for Dorothy's graduating class was delivered by Rev. C. T. Screen. The sermon was preached on May 5, 1946, at Ebenezer. Ten days later, Dorothy and her fellow seniors graduated at that same site. Rev. Butler delivered the commencement address.

In 1946, there were certain superlatives which may not be used for today's graduating classes, for example, most beautiful, most handsome, class poet, and class prophet. For the Mims High School class of 1946, Ruby Lee Searles was the Most Beautiful, Marion Parks was the Most Handsome, and Zelma Lue Settles was the Class Prophet. Other superlatives included Marion Parks as the Most Popular Boy, Helen Saxton as the Most Popular Girl, and Doris Louise Searles as the Class Historian. The class sponsor was Ms. Mary Alice Booker.

The valedictorian of the Mims High School class of 1946 was Lillie M. Turner. The salutatorian was Dorothy Wilma Searles. The class officers of the class of 1946 were Dorothy Wilma Searles, president; Marion Parks, vice president; Minnie B. Harris, secretary; and Milwee A. Parks, treasurer.

Dorothy Wilma Searles was selected by her classmates to give the farewell message for the class of 1946.

This has been a memorial tribute to one of the founders of the Mims Foundation, who also served as the foundation's first treasurer, Mrs. Dorothy Wilma Searles Freeman.

"STONE OF HOPE"

"Out of the Mountain of Despair, a Stone of Hope"

These immortal words are inscribed on the Dr. Martin Luther King Jr. Memorial in Washington, DC. Dr. King represents the stone of hope. And so it is with the Mims family, who, under very trying times, attempted to educate the sons and daughters of former slaves at the turn of the twentieth century and beyond. As we look back over the decades of strife and struggle faced by Dr. Mims and his family, we can say with marked assurance that Dr. Mims, like Dr. King, was also a stone of hope.

There were other players in the Mims legacy. We have acknowledged that Dr. Mims had coworkers who worked under very dire conditions, and with little pay, each day to present a brighter day to children starving for a good education.

The other players included the Mims family.

Mrs. Alma Patterson Mims, wife of Dr. W. S. Mims, was a key player in the life of Dr. Mims. She knew that part of her job was to stand by her man and to support him as a strong, dedicated spouse. Then there was William, who traveled in his father's footsteps. He was an outstanding educator who became a principal, following his father. His wife, Saleda, was also an educator who helped to mold the minds of countless youth while being an outstanding volunteer in community life. His son, Thales, a brilliant personality, who shared his knowledge and skills with young people whom he taught, was recognized very early as a literary student of the arts and foreign languages. Thales used his intellect to guide students into more intellectual endeavors. Dr. Mims's son, Talmadge, chose a different route to excel as an embassy official and an Amtrak employee.

The Mims stone of hope is located at the Mims Memorial Site on Mims Drive in McCormick, South Carolina.

The School Song of Mims High School

Dear Old Mims High

Dear Old Mims High, we love and cherish thee. In all our strife, we'll always strive to be loyal and true, faithful and ever honored. Dear Old Mims High, you are our all and all. Loyal and true, faithful and ever honored, dear old Mims High, you are our all and all.

The way seems dark. We never, ever depart. Your guiding light will always shine before us. We'll always keep fond memories of you, Dear Old Mims High. You are our all and all. We'll always keep fond memories of you, Dear Old Mims High. You are our all and all.

The schools that educated black people in McCormick County before the Mims Schools are church and local community schools.

DR. JAMES A. FRANKLIN SR.

A TRIBUTE TO THE EDUCATORS
AND SUPPORTERS WHO WORKED
IN THE OLD NEGRO SCHOOLS

THEY "BROUGHT US A MIGHTY LONG WAY.

SCHOOLS THAT EDUCATED THE NEGRO YOUTH
IN MCCORMICK COUNTY BEFORE THE MIMS SCHOOLS

Bailey Bethel School	Bethany School (Clarks Hill)	Blue Branch School
Boyds Chapel School	Branch School	Cedar Springs School
Chestnut Ridge School	Gilbert Rosenwald School	Green Olive School
Holy Springs School	Hopewell Rosenwald School	Pine Grove School
Martha's Chapel School	Mount Moriah School	Mount Pleasant School
Mount Zion School	Mulberry School	Robinson School
Rockford School	Rock Hill School	Saint Mary's School
Saint Charlotte School	Sand Hill School	Springfield School
Whitetown School	Wideman School	Youngs School
Zion Chapel School	Mount Lebanon School	New Hope School
Glover's Chapel School	Kitchen Town School	Getar Springs School
Rock Grove School	Bethany School (McCormick)	Hosannah School
Laurel Grove School	Little Mill School	Lyon Chapel School

A Talk about Dr. Benjamin Elijah Mays and Dr. William Samuel Mims and the Challenge to Today's Youth

Dr. Benjamin E. Mays

MAYS, MIMS, AND THE IMPORTANCE OF EDUCATION

Almost one hundred years ago, a man came to McCormick to be the principal of a school, which was named Bethany School. This school was located on South Main Street in McCormick and next to the Bethany Missionary Baptist Church. This man's name was William Samuel Mims.

A few years before Mr. Mims came to this school, a student from Epworth, which is located up the road near Greenwood and Ninety-Six, by the name of Benjamin E. Mays, had spent two years at the Bethany School.

The Bethany School was not a public-sponsored school. It was sponsored by a church, the Bethany Missionary Baptist Church.

Ever since the end of slavery, the church saw that its role was to meet the spiritual needs of its people in preparing them to go to heaven. It also saw its need to get its people ready to survive and thrive here on earth. The way to do that was to educate its people. Therefore, churches all over the South started schools for the children of former slaves.

Some of these churches also had a boarding house which was located next to the church. This was needed because it was too far for many of its students to travel each day. Back in those days, students traveled by walking to school, by mule, by wagon, or by horse and buggy. For many of them, it would have taken all day just to get to school.

Benjamin E. Mays was one of those students. Since he lived about thirty miles from the Bethany School, he stayed in the Bethany Boarding House and went home only on major holidays.

Not only did the church see the importance of getting an education for its members, but these two men, Mr. Mims and Mr. Mays, knew that it was important for children and adults to get a good education. They got a good education for themselves, and they made way for countless others to get a good education.

Mr. Mims went back and got additional college degrees and became Dr. William Samuel Mims. With his training, Dr. Mims started four public schools in McCormick County for black children who had no other public schools to attend. Dr. Mims knew the importance of education. Dr. Mims also served as a principal and a central office administrator. He was also a preacher and an elder in the African Methodist Episcopal Church.

There is a street in McCormick named after Dr. Mims, a county events center named after Dr. Mims, a scholarship named after Dr. Mims, a community center named after Dr. Mims, a foundation named after Dr. Mims, and a memorial named in his honor.

Benjamin E. Mays went on to finish high school and got several college degrees and became Dr. Benjamin E. Mays. After teaching at several colleges and universities and serving as a university administrator, he became president of Morehouse College, president of the Atlanta Board of Education, and advisor to presidents of the United States. He was also a world-renowned preacher and orator.

Dr. Mays taught Dr. Martin Luther King Jr. when Dr. King was a student at Morehouse College and influenced Dr. King to get more education by going to Boston University to get his doctorate degree. Sadly, Dr. Mays preached Dr. King's funeral after he was assassinated in Memphis, Tennessee. Dr. Mays was honored with more than fifty honorary doctorate degrees. There arc streets and schools named for him all over America. Mays Crossroads in his home area is named for him. There is a Mays Center in Greenwood, and Dr. Mays is memorialized on the campus of Morehouse College in Atlanta.

These two farm boys, who were touched by McCormick County, became known and made their mark in the world because they saw the importance of education.

McCormick and a Distinguished American

Dr. Benjamin E. Mays was a world-renowned educator, theologian, philosopher, scholar, orator, college president, and author of several books and numerous manuscripts. He is most famous for being an influence on one of his students when he was president of Morehouse College in Atlanta, Georgia. This student was Martin Luther King Jr. Dr. Mays was also the one who preached the funeral of this student several decades later when this former student was then a world-renowned theologian and civil rights leader.

Dr. Mays was an advisor to Presidents John F. Kennedy and Lyndon B. Johnson. He hosted world leaders, famed author Robert Frost, and other celebrities at Morehouse College. He earned three university degrees (bachelor's from Bates College and master of arts and doctor of philosophy from the University of Chicago). He was also awarded forty-nine honorary doctorate degrees from some of the world's most renowned universities, to include one by Lander College of Greenwood in 1974. At the hooding ceremony by Lander College, it was Representative William Jennings Bryan Dorn, in a tribute to Dr. Mays, who said, "Greenwood County has produced no more illustrious son than Dr. Mays, who was, I am proud to say, born only a short distance from where I now live." Dr. Mays received numerous other honors during his lifetime. Several schools bear his name, and his portrait was hung in the South Carolina State House in July 1980. He was also inducted into the South Carolina Hall of Fame, and in 1981, in a ceremony which included Mrs. Coretta Scott King (wife of the slain civil rights leader Dr. Martin Luther King Jr.) and a major tribute from Dr. Larry Jackson, president of Lander College, Mays Crossroads was dedicated in Greenwood County. (Note: A historical site honoring Dr. Mays has been established in Greenwood. The site was dedicated on Tuesday, April 26, 2011.

In addition to his other contributions, Dr. Mays was most proud of his service as chairman of the Atlanta Board of Education for twelve years.

Little do many of us realize that the great Dr. Mays had a McCormick connection in a variety of ways. Benjamin was born up the road in Greenwood County in a small community called Epworth. As a young boy, he received part of his early education here in McCormick.

In his autobiography, *Born to Rebel*, he writes, "When I was fifteen, Pastor Marshall persuaded by Father to let me go to a small Baptist Association school in McCormick, South Carolina. I was spending four months a year in school, and after two years in McCormick, I had to go back to the farm. I was seventeen." This Baptist Association School consisted of a boarding facility and the Bethany Colored School. They were located at the Bethany Missionary Baptist Church which is located on South Main Street here in McCormick.

The boarding facility was a two-story building. The principal and his family, along with some faculty members, lived on the second floor with boarding students living on the first floor of the two-story building. The second building was the schoolhouse, a one-story building (the Bethany Colored School). The Baptist Association (Simmon Ridge Samaritan Baptist Association) consisted of a group of colored churches, which held numerous events together and operated the school at Bethany and its boarding facility. The Bethany Missionary Baptist Church was also a member church of the Baptist Association.

Mays also wrote, "McCormick is twenty-four miles from Greenwood; and it was a wonderful day for me when I got on the Charleston and Western Carolina Railroad and rode those twenty-four miles. It was a new experience. It was at McCormick that I decided that if I could continue my education I would be a mail clerk on the railway." Mays continued, "The idea of being a railway mail clerk came to me because there was a Negro mail clerk on one of those trains that ran through McCormick, and just seeing him at work made a tremendous impression on me."

Pastor Marshall was Pastor James Marshall, pastor of Mount Zion Baptist Church, Mays's home church which was/is located in Epworth. The Baptist Association wanted Benjamin to return to the Bethany Colored School the next year to teach, but he chose to go to South Carolina State College to continue his education. Dr. Mays didn't mention in his autobiography, but it is well known that graduations from the Bethany Colored School were held in the Bethany Missionary Baptist Church since the Bethany Colored School did not have an auditorium; therefore, Benjamin may have also marched in the graduation exercises at the Bethany Missionary Baptist Church.

Dr. Mays's education, career, and travels would take him all over the world. He traveled to India, where he met with Mahatma Gandhi on December 31, 1936. During this ninety-minute conference with the great Indian activist, Mays talked with Gandhi about nonviolence and the Indian caste system.

Upon his return to Morehouse, Dr. Mays began teaching his students about the use of nonviolence and its impact upon change. Martin Luther King Jr. would become aware of this concept in Dr. Mays's 1948 chapel address when this address focused on Gandhi's philosophy and use of nonviolence. As most of us know, this practice became the basis of all of Dr. King's work as a leader in the modern civil rights movement in the United States.

During the 1950s and early 1960s, Dr. Mays had a standing invitation as the preacher of the annual Easter sermon at South Carolina State College (his alma mater), in Orangeburg, South Carolina. In 1964, while a student at South Carolina State College, I had the privilege of introducing Dr. Mays to the students, staff, and community in the auditorium of White Hall. I represented the Student Christian Association. Also, on program was another student, Dewey Jeffries, who also represented the Student Christian Association. Dr. Benner C. Turner was president of the college. Dr. Mays's sermon was oratorical and filled with dramatic gestures, which had made him famous the world over. His deep baritone voice kept the packed audience spell-bound as he talked of the "momentous sunrise" and its relevance to humankind.

Dr. Mays was well dressed, polished in every manner, and walked with dignity, grace, and pride. He was a proud and distinguished gentleman. I feel that this demeanor had an impact on our own Dr. W. S. Mims because one could say the same things about him.

Although we will never know how much, we do know that Dr. Mays's two years in McCormick at the Bethany Colored School on the campus of the Bethany Missionary Baptist Church from 1909 to 1911 did make an impression on him, if only from his own writing, "just seeing him at work made a tremendous impression on me," when talking about the "Negro mail clerk."

Upon his death in 1984, it was Senator John Drummond (senator for Greenwood and McCormick Counties), in a memorial service to Dr. Mays at Mt. Zion Baptist Church who said, "We are glad that history will always link his name to this church, to my hometown of Ninety-Six, and to the little community of Epworth where he entered this world. We will say with pride that we were his home folks. And we will be the beneficiaries of the works of a man who found this world a troubled place, and made it better." Other tributes were given to Dr. Mays from all around the world, but Dr. Mays would probably have appreciated most one by writer, Orville Vernon Burton, who simply wrote, "This story of Benjamin E. Mays is important to all people because it proclaims a truly heroic example of striving for a better world."

As McCormick citizens, we can take "part ownership" to this distinguished American.

A few parting notes: At the time that Benjamin E. Mays was attending school here in McCormick, my mother joined the Bethany Missionary Baptist Church as an eight-year-old girl. If she were alive today, I would ask her if she may have known the young Benjamin. Also, one who would become one of McCormick's greatest educators, Dr. William Samuel Mims, began his career as a teacher and director (principal) of the Baptist Association facilities in the 1920s. What might this tell us about the Bethany Colored School?

There are also numerous persons living today who studied at the Bethany Colored School. The school's last official year of operation was the 1938–1939 school year. Dr. Mims opened the new Mims School in 1939. By the way, the new Mims School did not have an auditorium; therefore, graduations were held in the Ebenezer AME Church, which was located next door to the school. Both facilities no longer exist.

The former Baptist Association buildings operated as rental property until the facilities closed in the 1950s.

Dr. Mays died on March 28, 1984, and is buried on the campus of his beloved Morehouse College, in Atlanta, Georgia. He was eighty-nine years old.

The life of Dr. Benjamin Elijah Mays, an outstanding American, who received his early education from the Brickhouse School in Epworth and from the Bethany School in McCormick, really makes us proud of the efforts of rural educators in the South who worked very hard to educate Negro boys and girls over one hundred years ago.

McCormick schools (church, community, Mims, and McCormick public schools) have produced some outstanding citizens who have excelled in their chosen professions. Dr. Benjamin E. Mays was one of them.

Dr. Benjamin E. Mays Delivers the Annual Easter Sunday
Sermon at
South Carolina State College in Orangeburg, South Carolina
Easter Sunday, 1964

(From left to right: Dr. Benner C. Turner, president of South
Carolina State College; Mrs. Julia Turner, wife of the President; Dr.
Benjamin E. Mays; Mrs. Sadie Gray Mays, wife of Dr. Mays; and
student representatives James A. Franklin Sr. and Dewey Jeffries.)

Characteristics of a Black Community in the Old South

THIS IS THE story of a black community in the Old South. This section was compiled and written from oral and written histories by persons who lived in the Bottoms, a community in McCormick, South Carolina, during the early to the mid-twentieth century. This is where my family moved as Dorn's Alley was being transformed to the site of the new Main Post Office, the site of the new county library, and to the site of homes for the Aged.

We will start with the Bethany Missionary Baptist Church, my home church. I was baptized there and still attends Bethany to this day.

THE BETHANY MISSIONARY BAPTIST CHURCH

The Bethany Missionary Baptist Church was organized by Rev. James Foster Marshall in 1882. He was pastor here for fifty-four years.

Rev. Marshall was a great visionary leader. He ministered to the whole person. Former slaves and the children of slaves needed to be educated while being ministered unto for their spiritual needs, so Rev. Marshall founded schools for children and adults. Rev. Marshall established the Bethany School at this church. Under the leadership of Rev. Marshall, the Bethany Missionary Baptist Church also constructed a boarding facility at this church. At the time, the Bethany School and the Bethany Boarding School were the centers of education for black people in McCormick County. Other churches had church schools but did not have boarding facilities.

Under Rev. Marshall's leadership, Bethany grew in numbers and in activities. He even recruited the famous Dr. Benjamin E. Mays to come to the Bethany School for two years as a young boy from Epworth, in Greenwood County. Benjamin boarded at the Bethany School.

Bethany has seen a number of pastors during its 133 years. They include Rev. C. C. Garrett, Rev. W. E. Laws, Rev. M. L. Mines, Rev. J. S. Harrison, Rev. S. L. McCain, Rev. Mark Adams, Rev. Robert Haskell, and now Rev. Keith Gordon. There have been a number of deacons who have served this church. They include Deacon Willie Marshall, Deacon Charlie Grant, Deacon J. W. Callahan, Deacon Alexander Wilson, Deacon J. C. Mattison, Deacon Joseph Franklin, Deacon Robert Lee Franklin Sr., Deacon George C. Franklin, Deacon Robert Lee Sibert Jr., Deacon Roosevelt Haskell, Deacon Philmore Dean, and Deacon Bobby Gilchrist.

A number of members have become ministers while attending Bethany. They include Rev. Robert Haskell, Rev. Billy Gene Jones, Rev. David Tompkins, and Rev. Eric Butler.

The Bethany Missionary Baptist Church continues to be a beacon of hope for those persons who need a spiritual home and for those seeking more purpose in life. Back in the day, Bethany and the Bethany Masonic Lodge worked together on a variety of projects in the Bottoms, to include meetings, turnouts, and other celebrations.

THE BETHANY MASONIC LODGE

The Bethany Masonic Lodge started under the leadership of Rev. James Foster Marshall and others. Rev. Marshall knew that black men needed an organization, which could be used to feed the self-esteem needs of black men who were embarrassed, humiliated, and denigrated by the dominant society. For this need and others, the Bethany Masonic Lodge was born. In addition to Rev. Marshall, some of the other leaders over the years have included Mr. James Sibert, Mr. James Thomas Wideman, Mr. Amos Hardy, and Mr. Tom Wideman.

Businesses in the Bottoms: Garrett's Lumberyard, Garrett's Barbershop, Garrett's Consulting Services, Naomi Weaver's Beauty Shop, Eula Mattison's Sandwich Shop, Jasper Tolbert's Barbershop, Lillie Rogers' Store, Walker & Letman Funeral Home (Now Walker's Funeral Home), Francis Callaham's Beauty Shop, Lucille Brown's Store (white owned), Joe "Moncks" Hamilton's Store (white owned), Washerette (white owned), Troy & Louise West Icehouse (white owned), Walker's Soda Shop and Pool Hall, and Albert Tolbert's Barbershop.

Businesses owners from the Bottoms: Willie Perrin's Service Station, Charlie Grant's Blacksmith Shop, Charlie & Candice Berry Shoe Shop (this was the first black owned business on Main Street), and Bernard and Etrulia Walker (restaurant and other businesses).

Church and civic buildings: Bethany Baptist Church and Bethany Masonic Lodge.

Talent from the Bottoms: Banks Family, Banks sisters, Johnnie Callaham (guitarist and singer), Billy Gene Jones (singer), Willie Joe Perrin Jr. (singer), John Cade (singer), and James Parker (songwriter).

Outstanding people from the Bottoms: Dr. John Cade (college dean), George Franklin (teacher, school administrator, and probation officer), Maria Walker (physician), Angela Walker (college president), Willie Tompkins's Funeral Home and Real Estate, Greta Franklin (teacher and speech therapist), George Perrin (businessman), Emma Grant (teacher), Leola Gran (teacher), Alvene Banks (teacher), Hervey Walker Funeral Home and Real Estate, Eric Butler (pastor), Billy Gene Jones (pastor), Thales Mims (teacher), William Mims (teacher and principal), Thelma Grant (teacher), Wilena Grant (nurse), and Eddie Lee Talbert (teacher, principal, and school board member).

The only two people who were born in the Bottoms back in the day and never left are Mrs. Catherine Cade Wilkerson and Mrs. Leola Grant Walker.

A SHORT HISTORY OF THE BOTTOMS

The Bottoms started over one hundred years ago, just after slavery ended in the South. We could not find out the name of the first family which settled in the Bottoms. The Bottoms probably got its name from its geographical location in the town of McCormick. It was composed of the bottom section of Church Street, the bottom section of Carolina Street, and an adjourning section between Carolina Street and Hammond Street. If you went up the hill from Carolina Street, you were in the white section. The other streets/roads in the Bottoms were Collier Street and Marshall Street. South Main Street was the "front street" for the Bottoms. The Bottoms section was composed mainly of black people who lived in the southeastern part of the town of McCormick.

The houses were mainly of wood frame construction. Back in the day, Mr. John Garrett had the largest house in the Bottoms. The size was only exceeded by the Bethany Church, Bethany Boarding House (formerly Bethany School), Bethany Church, and Bethany Masonic Lodge. The first brick structures in the Bottoms came from the construction of the McCormick Housing Project. The first cement block structures came from the construction of the Bethany Masonic Lodge and the Dewey Harmon Home. Walker and Letman Funeral Home was started in the Bottoms by Mr. Hervey Walker Sr. and Mr. Herbert Letman. Mr. Hevey Walker had a career as a minister and as a presiding elder in the AME Church. Mr. Herbert Letman was a wealthy landowner, logger, and businessman who lived north of the town of McCormick at the intersection of Highway 28 and Highway 10. They combined their resources and started the Walker and Letman Funeral Home in the Bottoms. Before this time, black people were buried by two white funeral homes: McCain Funeral Home and Strom Funeral Home. Mr. Walker and Mr. Letman bought the McCain Funeral Home.

In the beginning, the people in the Bottoms had no running water or electricity in their homes. They used kerosene lamps for light and outhouses for restrooms. They had a faucet (spigot) or wells from which to draw water. Their homes were heated with wood-burning stoves, coal-burning stoves, or fireplaces. Most of the cooking was done on a kitchen wood-burning stove or in the fireplace.

BOYS WILL BE BOYS

Boys in the Bottoms swan/played in Deason's Pond. Deason's Pond was located on the southside of Bethany Church and behind Deason's Florist. The boys would swim until Mr. Deason came out of his house. He would shoot his shotgun in the air, thereby running the boys out of the pond.

THE WASHPOT

How did the families in the Bottoms use the washpot? The washpot was a large black pot made of heavy cast iron, which would hold about twenty gallons and made like a large bowl. You would build a fire around the washpot, which sat on three to four bricks in order to prop the pot off the ground so that the wood or coal could get under and around the pot to heat the water in the washpot. The washpot had metal protrusions (legs) from the bottom used to place the pot on the bricks. In addition to heating water, the washpot was used to make crackling from the skin of the hog, used to make grease to cook with, used to wash white clothes by boiling them in water, used to make lye soap used to wash clothes in the number 3 washtub and used to take a bath, among other things. The washpot was used to heat the water during hog-killing time. The water was boiled in the washpot and used to scrape the hair from the hog before the hog was cut up into different parts.

THE NUMBER 3 TUB

Oh yeah, the number 3 tub, everybody had two or more tubs. We washed clothes in one with the use of the rubboard, and remember the lie soap, now it was used to rub on the clothes as they were being washed on the rubboard in the number 3 tub. The tub was made of heavy tin. The rubboard was made of wood and metal. The frame was wood, and the ridges on the board were made of metal. The rubbing of the clothes on the rubboard created friction, thereby causing the dirt to be released from the clothes. The second number 3 tub was used for rinsing the clothes. Back in the day, the clothes were wrung out by hand before being placed on the clothesline. The clothesline was usually made of metal or twine and strung between two posts or trees. Each clothesline had a prop, usually made from a limb or from a long piece of wood. The prop was used to prop the clothes up high enough so that the clothes would not touch the ground as the clothes dried in the sun/wind. The clothes were kept on the line with the use of clothespins.

The number 3 tub was used to bathe the children in the Bottoms, usually on a Saturday night. The smaller children were washed first, and the same water was usually used to wash a larger child before the water was changed for other children or for the parents to take their baths. During the week, there was a foot tub to wash up with between the Saturday night baths. The foot tub was a metal tub about a third of the size of a number 3 tub. And then there was the wash pan, which was used to wash our faces or hands, as needed, during the day. The wash pan was usually made of metal with a white enamel coating.

SUPPLEMENTING OUR MEALS

Many of the parents in the Bottoms used to supplement their meals with wild game. This included squirrels, coons, possums, quail, rabbits, deer, and others. The rabbits and squirrels were usually skinned in such a way to protect the skin. The skins of rabbits and squirrels were cleaned, stuffed with cotton, and mounted. They were then sold to persons who wanted them for their homes.

The catching of fish from our ponds and streams was also used to supplement meals for the families in the Bottoms.

Childhood Memories in the Bottoms
by Malinda Franklin

Back in the day when I was a young girl, I used to go up to Mrs. Mozelle Tompkins's house with my godmother (Cai), Mrs. Carrie Bussey. At the house were Mrs. Mozelle (Mrs. Dewey), Ethel Harmon, David Tompkins, Michael Tompkins, Curtis Tompkins (King Bee), Willie Tompkins (Sugar Babe). Mrs. Dorothy Franklin would be next door on her porch. Ms. Clifford Williams would be sitting on their porch with her shades on. Mrs. Mozelle would have some old rags, burning them, so that the smoke would try to kill the mosquitoes or to keep them away from us. She would have two old pans, full of old rags or old clothes. We would laugh, talk, and have fun. Mrs. Dewey would break out in some hymns. We would sit out there until 11:00 p.m. or 12:00 a.m. We had no televisions to watch. Those were the good old days.

My momma, Mrs. Carrie Bell Roman Franklin (nicknamed Little Baby), was a jack-of-all-trades. She was the head of the Bethany Baptist Church Usher Board. She would lead the twelve tribes of Israel. It was always a success. I was always right there at my momma's dress tail. I was told that my sister, Sandra, and I became ushers. It was a big usher board back then.

We used to ride on the back of Mr. William Gunter's pickup truck. He always had chairs on the back of his pickup truck, and the chairs were covered so we wouldn't mess up our pretty white dresses. Some of the time the truck was so full, we used to ride in my cousin George Franklin's car. George was also called Car-Car. He had a blue Chevrolet that we used to ride in. I remember, at one time, when we were going to this particular church. His car was full of members. I told Car-Car that he had it, but he ignored me. I was just trying to help. He ignored me and said, "I do my own driving," and backed straight into the ditch. I kept my head down. I was just giggling, but Car-Car was disappointed. But he was nice enough to carry us to different churches to sing. We always had fun riding with Car-Car.

You would think that my family was some kin to the Beverly Hillbillies. My momma made lye soap, at least three times a week.

We used lye soap to wash our clothes. We had a partial farm, with chickens, a big garden, dogs, and some cats. My momma would hang the chickens on the clothesline by their feet (when she was ready to kill them for food). When she was getting ready to kill them, she would twist their necks and cut them off. She would clean them and cook them, even the chicken feet. We never bought eggs. We had a hen house, where the chickens laid their eggs. Momma would have pieces of cloth, which she used to make quilts. She sewed them together by hand and made some pretty quilts. The quilts were used to keep us warm in the wintertime. She also canned vegetables from our garden. She also canned fruit. My momma could really sing. She loved to laugh, and she could cook anything.

My brother, Tyrone, built a spinning jenny for us and the kids from the Bottoms to ride on. It was made of wood. He also made a see-saw. Angela and Maria Walker were our neighbors back then, and they used to come over to ride. Tyrone made the biggest and baddest basketball court in the Bottoms. We had guys from McCormick, Greenwood, Abbeville, and Edgefield, coming to our backyard to play ball.

We had a Little League Bottoms team. I used to play on the team with Paul Cade (Wilkerson) all the time because Paul's team used to win all the time. Leon "Pig" Franklin and Tyrone had a Big League in the Bottoms. We also had a bad softball team. Of course, I was on the Team with Paul Cade.

John Cade, Sadie Gunter, Louise Sibert, and Glossie Rogers were my sister Sandra's (Babe's) best friends. John used to come over to our house every night and stayed until 11:00 p.m. or 12:00 a.m. When he got ready to go home, he was so scared of the dark. He used to sing really loud, or sound like a siren, so that he could wake up everybody, in case someone tried to mess with him. My best buddies and friends were: Ann Rogers, Jack Rogers, Cynthia ("Cent"), and Yvette Banks.

My sister, Sandra, Glossie Rogers, John Cade, Louise Sibert, and Sadie Gunter used to go and take pictures in the white neighborhoods, in front of the nice houses and cars. They would tell people that there was where they lived and that those were their cars. You see, all of us lived in old wooden broken-down shacks.

Easter Egg Hunts in the Bottoms by Amy Wilkerson

I have many fond memories growing up in the Bottoms. One of my favorite things was our yearly Easter egg hunt. Mrs. Dorothy Franklin would announce after the Easter program on Easter Sunday that there would be an egg hunt for all the children the following Monday.

We were told to meet at her house at a certain time and bring a cup and one boiled egg. All the children would then go to Bethany Church for activities. While we were at the church, some of the parents would take the eggs across the railroad tracks to a big field in front of the church and hide the eggs. The children would be escorted across the road to hunt eggs.

After the hunt, we would all gather back at Mrs. Dot's house for snacks that the neighborhood parents had brought. Remember that cup? Well, that was for the punch, and we had cookies and goodies to go with the punch. We could also eat an egg.

It was truly a fun time for all. Mrs. Dot did this for many, many years.

Voting Efforts in the Bottoms by Barbara Sibert

In the early 1960s, after moving to the Bottoms, I met a lady by the name of Mrs. Dorothy Franklin. We became friends. She encouraged me to become a registered voter, and I voted in 1961. After voting, I became involved with the Democratic Party, along with Mrs. Franklin. We went out talking to people trying to get them up and out to vote so they could become full-fledged citizens and be able to voice their opinions to help to make decisions for the Bottoms. We picked up people and took them to the polls to vote on election day.

There were times when Mrs. Franklin, Mrs. Amy Wilkerson, and I were not allowed on the courthouse steps, but we got the message to our people, explaining to them how to go in and vote, telling them if they needed help, we would have people there to help them. The early 1960s was just the beginning that black people were going out to get people to vote. Others involved in these efforts from the Bottoms were Mrs. Essie T. Banks and Mr. H. W. Walker. They were also part of the Democratic Party. I thank God for having the opportunity to participate in these voting efforts.

Brick Wall at the Bethany Church

The brick wall at the side of the church was done by the late Woodrow "Toot" Wilson. Because of his untimely death, the wall was never completed. He donated his time and efforts to construct the wall.

CANNING

Canning was a summertime activity for the families in the Bottoms. Wild plums, blackberries, peaches, apples, muscadines, and scuppernongs were some of the fruits used to make jelly or preserves. Canning was also used to can vegetables.

Canning was very popular because back in the day, no one had a refrigerator in the Bottoms. Canning was a way to preserve food items to be used during the winter when a lot of fruits and vegetables were not available. Everybody in the Bottoms remembers using Mason jars. The process for canning was to boil the Mason jars and lids in hot water and to place them on a sterile towel to dry. The items to be canned were well prepared properly before being placed in the jars. The home canning process was an art form.

CHILDREN AT PLAY

Kids in the Bottoms rode bicycles, played with the Western Flyer red wagon, played tag, rode tricycles, made bows and arrows, played cowboys, played hopscotch, made pop guns, played football, played baseball, shot/played marbles, played with dolls, played beauty shop, played Old Maid cards, played checkers, climbed trees, played house, rolled tires, rolled other children inside tires, swung on vines at the branch, played with whistles, etc.

HOG-KILLING TIME IN THE BOTTOMS

Hog-killing time in the Bottoms was a community/neighbor activity. Neighbors helped neighbors. Hogs were killed during the coldest months of the year. Everyone knew when hog killing was going on in the Bottoms. All you had to do was to follow the smoke coming from the big fire or to hear the hog squealing as they were being taken to be slaughtered. Everyone came to help, especially to keep the fire going.

Only one or two persons cut up the hog. Other persons sorted the meats, which were being cut from the hog. Just about everything from the hog was to be used in some way. The head was used to make hog's head cheese for souse meat, the skin was used for a variety of purposes, the intestines were used as chitterlings, and the hooves were used to make "tea" or some form of "medicine." The blood was sometimes given to persons who wanted to make blood pudding. Blood pudding was made similar to liver pudding. Poor people knew how to make it for their families in the Bottoms. Most people in the Bottoms were poor financially, but they didn't know that they were poor because everyone lived basically with the same standards. When the tasks were finished, everyone who helped received a share of the hog.

CRAFTS IN THE BOTTOMS

Crafts included carving, making brooms, making whistles, making rabbit boxes, making ladders, stuffing animal skins, making pop guns, making bows and arrows, etc.

Rev. James Foster Marshall and Dr. Benjamin E. Mays

In 1851, a child was born during slavery, who would grow up to be an outstanding clergyman. James Foster Marshall was born. He was born in the Bordeaux Section of McCormick County. His father was Mr. Lalson Marshall. The name of his mother is unknown.

Rev. Marshall spent most of his life in the town of McCormick and in the Bordeaux section of McCormick County. He was married twice. His first wife was Mrs. Frances E. Marshall. To this union, eight children were born. The names of their children were James A. Marshall, Luther J. Marshall, Author D. Marshall, Carrie L. Marshall, Athel A. Marshall, Ruth E. Marshall, Fannie Lee Marshall, and Addie May Marshall. Upon the passing of his first wife, he met and married Mrs. Fanny Marshall. They had no children.

Early in James Foster Marshall's life, this former slave accepted the call to become a preacher, not just an average preacher, but a preacher whose guidance and direction were divinely inspired to establish churches for former slaves and their children. He preached in the brush arbors, which were often just fields. Other brush arbors were established in the brush and made of beams from trees as the frame with limbs and the brush used to cover the frame. Still, other brush arbors were cut from within a group of trees with the larger trees remaining to support the frame of the church. Some brush arbors had benches on which to sit, and some did not. The tops were designed with as much brush as possible to keep out the sun and the rain while they worshipped. The brush arbors could easily be expanded to hold more worshippers.

From the brush arbors to more permanent structures, Rev. Marshall traveled around McCormick County and touched the lives of former slaves to establish Holy Spring Baptist Church, New Hope Baptist Church, and Bethany Baptist Church. In Greenwood County, he preached at Old Mount Zion Baptist Church for fifty years and at Young Mount Zion Baptist Church for eighteen years.

According to records, the Holy Spring Baptist Church "was an outgrowth of slave worshippers of Buffalo Baptist Church, off Highway 28." It could not be determined if Rev. Marshall continued to preach at the Holy Spring Baptist Church when he was hired to organize the New Hope Baptist Church in 1879. According to records, Rev. Marshall was a member of Mount Moriah Baptist Church when he helped to organize Holy Spring and to eventually serve as Holy Spring's pastor. According to public records, a Holy Spring colored school was built for the Buffalo Section of McCormick County.

Rev. Marshall led New Hope Baptist Church from the brush arbor in 1879 to the construction of a more permanent structure in 1880. The first New Hope School was built at the turn of the century. The school closed in 1949. Rev. Marshall served as pastor of New Hope for fifty-seven years.

Rev. Marshall traveled by the Bottoms each time he went to the New Hope Baptist Church. He noticed some brush arbor efforts going on in the Bottoms. Rev. Marshall organized the Bethany Baptist Church in the Bottoms in 1882. He was pastor there for fifty-four years.

In almost every county in South Carolina, black and some white groups established an academy, industrial, or graded school for the children of former slaves. The Simmon Ridge Samaritan Baptist Association wanted to start a school in McCormick County. Through the capable leadership of Rev. Marshall, the Bethany School was established. Soon thereafter, a boarding facility was added. The boarding school was established by Rev. Marshall so that students could attend from other counties.

In 1908, there were two teachers and thirty students at the Bethany School. In 1909, one of the students at the school was Benjamin E. Mays from Epworth (Greenwood County). He attended the school for two years.

In his autobiography, *Born to Rebel*, Dr. Mays writes, "When I was fifteen, Pastor Marshall persuaded my father to let me go to a small Baptist Association School in McCormick. I was spending four months a year in school; and after two years in McCormick, I had to go back to the farm. I was seventeen. This Baptist Association school was the Bethany School."

It turns out that Pastor Marshall, pastor of Old Mount Zion Baptist Church, Dr. Mays's pastor when he was a youth, was also pastor of Bethany Missionary Baptist Church in McCormick.

This great visionary leader accepted the challenge to minister to the whole man. Former slaves and the children of former slaves needed to be educated so he founded schools for children and adults. It was reported that he had only five years of schooling, but that he was a self-taught man. Rev. Marshall established the Bethany School, the New Hope School, and it was reported that he established the Holy Spring School.

Under the leadership of Rev. Marshall, the Bethany Missionary Baptist Church, the Bethany School, and the Bethany Boarding Facility were the most significant locations in McCormick County for the education and training of the children of former slaves. Numerous other Negro churches in McCormick County had schools, but they were day schools. During my research, I could not find another Negro church in McCormick County with a boarding facility.

Rev. Marshall knew that adult black men needed an organization that could be used to feed the self-esteem needs of black men who were embarrassed, humiliated, and denigrated by the dominant society. For this need, Rev. Marshall helped to establish the Bethany Masonic Lodge.

Rev. Marshall also started the Liberty Spring Baptist Church School. During his lifetime, he also served as moderator of the Union Third Division of Baptist churches. While serving as moderator, he helped the union to purchase one hundred acres of land.

It is obvious that the Rev. Marshall had the vision of a Booker T. Washington and the intelligence of a W. E. B. DuBois.

About Rev. Marshall, Dr. Mays also wrote, "The Reverend James F. Marshall was hardly more than a fifth-grade scholar, but he knew the Scriptures, at least so far as knowing where certain passages were to be found. He could quote almost any passage of Scripture from memory. He accepted the Bible as it was printed and held it was "wicked" to doubt any part of it.

"We thought he was the best preacher in the world (our world was Greenwood County). He was eloquent. He could moan and did. Almost invariably he made some of the people shout. If he did not moan a bit and make the people shout, his congregation felt he had not preached well. The intellectual content of his sermons was not nearly as important as the emotional appeal," said to Dr. Mays.

Dr. Mays continued to write: "The Reverend Marshall set a good example for the people, f believe no one ever accused him of any dishonesty or immorality. Wives and daughters were safe in his presence. He did not touch liquor. The same could not be said of all the ministers who pastured in Greenwood County. The Reverend Marshall, who lived twenty-four miles away from the church, usually held Conference on the second Saturday afternoon and stayed overnight with a family of the church. It was a rare privilege to have the pastor spend the night in one's home. The house was spic.

"By the way, during the time of Rev. Marshall's death, there were no black-owned funeral homes in McCormick. Two white owned funeral homes handled Negroes: G. P. McCain, and J. S. Strom. J. S. Strom handled Rev. Marshall. Rev. Marshall's funeral was held at the New Hope Missionary Baptist Church with interment in the New Hope Cemetery.

"This giant of a man had lived during the most turbulent times in United States history: slavery, the Civil War, reconstruction, Jim Crow laws and practices, the Spanish-American War, and the Great Depression, while poverty and ever-present racism loomed over his head. Through it all, this clergyman kept the Faith and was a beacon of Hope for countless others.

"Indeed, Rev. Marshall was a 'preacher's preacher.' Preachers from other churches, including members of the white clergy, would often come to hear him preach. Dr. Mays called his preaching 'an opiate.' Not only was he a good preacher, but Rev. Marshall was also a good pastor and a good manager.

"When the first New Hope School was destroyed, he built a new one. Two sanctuaries were also built at New Hope, under his leadership. While serving as pastor of Young Mount Zion Baptist Church in 1919, the church was enlarged and new pews were purchased. At Bethany, the first school he built was destroyed and a new school and a boarding facility were constructed to replace the first Bethany School.

"Rev. Marshall held church conferences on Saturdays and usually stayed in the communities overnight for services on Sundays. He spent time in the communities served by his churches, because as Dr. Mays put it: He needed to know his members.

"Rev. Marshall left a trail and a legacy for clergymen to follow and to emulate. Indeed, it is a privilege to honor this man and to say to clergymen, in general, thanks!

"To help to honor the memory of Rev. Marshall, the Union Third Division of Baptist churches established the Marshall-Peterson-Gordon Scholarships. These scholarships are given annually to deserving students. Rev. Peterson was pastor of Springfield Baptist Church for a number of years and Rev. Gordon served as a pastor of Cedar Spring Baptist Church.

"With the dedication of the Marshall Memorial, this Man of God will be remembered for decades to come. He had almost been lost and may have been 'Gone With the Wind.' Some research on Dr. Benjamin E, Mays, an outstanding clergyman in his own right, led me to my discovery of the late Rev. James Foster Marshall. As he sacrificed and worked so hard to help so many others, beginning this day, with the Marshall Memorial, we will remember this Man of God for a long time.

"It is fitting that we are celebrating the life of this clergyman on this, the 150th anniversary of the effect of the Emancipation Proclamation which was signed in 1962 by President Abraham Lincoln and to become law on January 1, 1863. This law, which freed the Negro slaves, freed James Foster Marshall, who had been a slave for twelve years. To put this in perspective, Booker T. Washington, the famous black educator, was born as a slave in 1856, in Franklin County, Virginia; five years after Marshall was born.

"Although their paths may have never crossed, both men had similar feelings about the future progress of their people. Both men were public speakers, both men built schools and other institutions, both men felt that the freed slaves needed some kind of trade to earn a decent wage, or to set up their own business. Booker T.'s work ended with his death in 1915. Marshall's work continued for twenty-one more years. Rev. James Foster Marshall will be forever connected to 'the Bottoms.' and span when the preacher came, and the best food was served. He was the only hero we had around Zion to worship. So impeccable (or discreet) was the Reverend Marshall's conduct that the only story circulated about him was that once he got up in the middle of the night and left a certain woman's house because she had approached him in an immoral way."

Dr. Mays further wrote, "The Reverend Marshall's preaching was highly otherworldly, emphasizing the joys of heaven and the damnation of hell. He preached funerals according to the life the deceased had lived. He didn't hesitate to preach the dead 'smack into heaven' or into hell, according to the life he or she had lived. The church was usually full at funerals, especially if the deceased had been well known; and when a man of bad reputation died, the church was jammed. The people wanted to hear what kind of funeral sermon Marshall would preach. I am sure that a burning hell and a golden-street heaven were as real as their farms to a majority of the people in Mount Zion and in the community at large. They believed the trials and tribulations of the world would all be over when one got to heaven. Beaten down at every turn by the white man, as they were, Negroes could perhaps not have survived without this kind of religion. There was no doubt in the minds of some that Marshall had special Power with God."

Additionally, Dr. Mays wrote, "Although Marshall taught the people to be honest and upright, the Gospel he preached was primarily an opiate to enable them to endure and survive the oppressive conditions under which they lived at the hands of the white people in the community. Fighting and heavy drinking on church property were common practices in many churches, but not much of this went on at Mount Zion, thanks largely to Rev. Marshall. The Reverend Marshall baptized every member in my family, including Mother and Father. Father did not join the church until after the earthquake in 1886. My parents told me that, after the quake, the Reverend

Marshall baptized a hundred men at one session. 'God moves in mysterious ways!'"

Finally, Dr. Mays wrote, "Now and then, Rev. Marshall would invite white ministers to preach at Mt. Zion…and the few Negroes who attended the Rev. Pierce Kinard's (white preacher) tent meetings were thoroughly segregated." It could not be determined if this was by a plan or by choice. At any rate, it appears as though Rev. Marshall was working to promote inter-racial church activities over a hundred years ago. Here, in 2020, we still have made very little progress in this area.

The churches and the community lost their pastor in 1936. Rev. Marshall contracted the flu sometime around February 1. He contracted pneumonia on February 3 and passed away on February 8. He passed away at his home. His second wife, Mrs. Fanny Marshall, was at his bedside. He was eighty-four years old. Rev. Marshall was living in the town of McCormick at the time of his passing.

During my research, I learned that Rev. Marshall purchased four lots in the town of McCormick, two on Walnut Street and two on Oak Street, on May 6, 1916, from Mr. Elijah Williams of Greenwood. These properties were considered to be in the white section of town. He paid $250 for the four lots. By the time of his death in 1936, Rev. Marshall owned sixteen lots and one house in McCormick.

Rev. Marshall had served churches in the McCormick-Greenwood area for over sixty years. He preached two to four times, somewhere, on most Sundays.

At the time of his passing, Rev. Marshall was pastor of Bethany Missionary Baptist Church in McCormick, New Hope Missionary Baptist Church in Plum Branch, Old Mount Zion Baptist Church in Epworth, and Young Mount Zion Baptist Church in Chappells.

Memories by Catherine Wilkerson

In the early 1960s, I began traveling around with a friend and neighbor, Dorothy Franklin. We would travel to Frog More, South Carolina, for about a week or two, for training as a community activist. We also traveled to Columbia, South Carolina, for meetings with James Clyburn and others. When voting time came, we would work at the polls (courthouse). Others from the Bottoms who worked were Dorothy Franklin and Barbara Sibert. A lot of times, we would be treated unfairly and had to leave the premises. Eventually, when a call was made to Columbia by Dot, Mr. John Freeman, Mrs. Essie T. Banks, and others, we got back on the job (we worked from 7:00 a.m. to 7:00 p.m.). Often, we would meet from house to house and from church to church. Others involved with us were Bob Gilchrist, Georgette Wiggleton, Harvey Lee Murray, Nellie Lee, Elizabeth Gilchrist, Harvey Tucker, and others. Although times were tough, we enjoyed socializing, eating, and communicating with each other. Voting was very important to us.

Poverty

Poverty was widespread in the Bottoms. Most of the houses were in need of constant repair. There were roof leaks, holes in the floor, and holes in the walls. It was not uncommon to see buckets on the floor when it rained. To keep the cold winds out of the house in the wintertime, a paste was made using starch which had been mixed with water or some other form of paste. The starch was applied to the paper (usually newspaper), and the paper was pasted over the holes in the walls. This helped to keep the cold winds out while keeping the heat inside the house. Pieces of wood or cardboard was tacked into the flood covering the holes. The walls were of a single-frame construction with no insulation. There was no government help or government subsidies back in the day.

The Iceman

The iceman came around about the same time daily. Back in the day, most homes in the Bottoms had no electricity and no running water. Water was usually gotten from a well or from a faucet (spigot). Faucet water came from the town's water system. Water from wells was gotten by dropping a bucket into the well and raising the water up using a pulley. Water from a well could also be gotten from a hand pump over a well. Water was used to prime the pump so that a steady flow would be able to be pumped from the well. At any rate, since most homes did not have electricity, they did have an icebox. The icebox was of several different designs, but a white upright unit, made of a metallic outside with some insulation in the walls of the structure. Ice was placed in the top portion of the unit to keep milk, meats, and some other food items cool in order to keep the foods from spoiling. The ice would melt overnight, and you would have to buy ice each day. The iceman would come by each day, usually in a pickup truck. He would have blocks of ice on the back of the truck, which would be covered by a canvas. The color of the canvas was usually green and designed to keep the ice from melting so quickly. He would also have an ice pick and some ice hooks. The ice hooks were used to lift and to measure the amount of ice purchased from the iceman. He would also have some ice string. When you purchased your piece of ice, he would tie a piece of string around your piece of ice so that you could carry the ice into your house. Every house in the Bottoms also had an ice pick so that they could chip the ice into smaller pieces. Back in the early 1950s, ice was usually sold for one cent a pound.

The Apron

Back in the day, most mothers and grandmothers wore an apron. The main use of the apron was to protect the dress underneath since she had only a few dresses. The mother's apron served to dry the tears of children, to be used as a pot holder, and on occasion may have been used to clean out dirty ears. The apron was used to collect vegetables from the garden or to collect eggs from the chicken house. It was always amusing to see a bashful child hide behind his mother's apron. Sometimes Momma used her apron to wipe her brow. She brought in wood chips and kindling wood in her apron. After she shelled the peas, her apron was used to carry out the hulls. In the fall, the apron was used to bring in apples and pears from the fruit trees. Each family in the Bottoms tried to have at least one fruit tree. Yeah, Momma also used the apron for minor dusting. Were there ever any germs on Momma's apron? Are you kidding?

Cotton and Peach Picking by Workers
from the Bottom by Barbara Sibert

As a child, the young people would always pick peaches during the summer to have money to buy school clothes, to attend the McCormick County Fair, or to go to the McCormick Theater, and to free our parents from having to give us spending change in the summer. Mrs. Corrie Martin, Mrs. Jessie Bell Sibert, and Mrs. Pauline Heath were some of the drivers of the peach trucks. They would pick up the young people from the Bottoms and take them to the peach fields and peach-packing houses in Johnson and Trenton, South Carolina. The hours varied from picking peaches all day until working in the packing houses until two or three in the morning. It depended upon how ripe the peaches were and the need to refrigerate them for long trips up north. We worked each day, regardless of how long you worked the day before. As young boys and girls, we seemed to have endless energy. Of course, the most exciting part was getting paid each week. A lot of us wore long sleeves because of the peach fur that got on us while picking the peaches from the trees. Boy, did we itch! We ate very fancy back in those days: bologna, saltines, Vienna sausage, cinnamon rolls, souse meat, cookies, pork and beans, and candy and cookies for dessert. Some of us got a chance to eat an overripe peach. Yes, the peach picking summers were long and hot, but the Bottoms children learned how to do hard work. Cotton picking was worse. Picking was a sunup to sundown job. You only had a lunch break. The water that you drink was hot. The sun was hot. There were no shade trees, just long, long rows of cotton. To pick cotton while standing straight was tough, but when you got to the short stalks, bending became a task. It was not uncommon to have backaches from bending over picking cotton. Boy, you talk about a suntan. All you had to do was to go to pick some cotton. Music was always a comforter. It was not uncommon to hear singing or humming in the cotton field. Yeah, as kids, we had some fun too! That did help us to cope with the long hours and the long days. By the way, we got paid two cents a pound, for a hundred pounds of cotton, we got paid $2. Most kids picked less than one hundred pounds a day; however, some serious adults from the Bottoms picked as much as 250 pounds a day. I picked cotton for Mr. Author Thompkins.

The Insurance Man

The insurance man was a white man who came door to door in the Bottoms to collect money for life insurance. They would come every week to collect as low as five cents for each policy. For example, if you had five children with a life insurance policy, the insurance man would collect twenty-five cents. The amount of the policy ranged from $100 to $500 worth of life insurance. For families who could not afford to pay each week, the insurance man came every two weeks. Yes, there was such a thing as a nickel policy.

Gathering at the Holy Tree

There was a tree in the Bottoms, which was located in the yard of Mr. and Mrs. Robert Lee Sibert. This is where the children had chairs, stools, and buckets to sit on. Children would gather here to talk, play, and laugh. There were never any disagreements, fights, or arguments, just friendly relationships. One Saturday, a motorcycle came down Pine Street, failed to stop, and hit a car on Carolina Street. The motorcycle landed in the yard near the tree where children often assembled. No one was hit or hurt. Because nothing "bad" never happened in or around this tree, Mrs. Ethel Harmon called the tree the Holy Tree.

Bell Ringing at the Bethany Church
by Shirley Callahan

The Bethany Church had a bell tower. The bell in the tower weighed over one hundred pounds. The bell was used to let everyone know that it was time for Sunday school and for any time that a church event was being held, such as evening church and for revivals. Back in the day, Bethany had two services on Sunday, a Sunday morning service and a Sunday evening service. The bell was also used to announce funerals. The person with the longest tenure as a bell ringer was Deacon Marion Thompkins.

The Blue Bird Beauty Shop by Barbara Sibert

Mrs. Naomi Weaver was the owner/operator of the Blue Bird Beauty Shop. The shop was located at the corner of Carolina Street and Pine Street. This black-owned business in the Bottoms had three "chairs" with as many as three beauticians working at the same time. The waiting area consisted of several chairs around the wall as persons waited for their appointment. Workers in this shop included Naomi, Ruth Leverette, and Alfredia S. Norman. The shop closed when Naomi moved to Greenwood.

Walker Funeral Home by H. W. Walker Jr.

I am the owner of the Walker Funeral Home. A lot of persons probably think that my father operated the funeral home; however, he never was the official operator. He and the late Mr. Herbert Letman purchased the old McCain Funeral Home Service from the late Mrs. McCain after which they hired me to run the new business because I was the only one licensed to operate a funeral home by South Carolina law. Therefore, I have been the operator since its beginning. My father, who operated a funeral home in Clinton, South Carolina, in the late 1930s, was able to operate the Walker Funeral while I was in the armed services from 1951 until 1953 at which time I returned and resumed the operation of the service. Most services have not made a drastic change from the early ages of funeral service until this present day. Families sometimes would ask that their deceased relative be brought back to the home to spend the last night (setting up) before the service at the church, but this was not a common practice because only a few homes were large enough to accommodate the family and friends who would visit that day or night. Homes now are large enough to have a last night visitation, but most families use the funeral home facilities rather than have the remains brought back to the homes. Having a visitation or what is commonly called a *wake* is now accepted in most situations. However, the practice of a wake is not as popular as one would think because some persons look on it as a nighttime funeral and a continuation into the next day for final services. All of these services are possible and can be provided whenever a family desires to ask for this service. I hope that these few words and statements will help someone to understand the few changes that have occurred over the past fifty or more years.

Living in the Bottoms by Jeanette Reid

We lived in the Bottoms, my mother (Mutt) and stepfather (Big) Leverette and my sisters and brothers. We lived in an apartment next to Junior Sibert and his family. On the other side was Mrs. Catherine Cade. Across from us was Mrs. Mozelle Tompkins and Mrs. Dorothy Franklin. My mother, Mutt, used to beat my brothers with a switch. I never got into trouble, so she did not beat me. One day, my brothers went to the store up the street, Mrs. Lucille Brown. They got some candy and some oranges and walked back to the house. My mother asked them where they got the stuff. They told her that they got it from Mrs. Brown's Store. She asked them where they got the money. They said that they didn't have any money. My mother got them by the hand and the unfinished candy and oranges and took them to Mrs. Brown's Store and told Mrs. Brown that they picked it up. My mother beat them in the store with a switch, and when she got them back home, she beat them again. She would not let them go back to the store for a long time. The current Mr. Walker's Funeral Home is where Mrs. Brown's Store used to be. The Lay's man (potato chip man) used to come by Mrs. Brown's Store on Friday, and he would park on the side of the road by Mrs. Mozelle Thompkins's house, and he would go to the back of the truck, and he would throw bags of chips (probably out of date) out on the ground just to see children run to pick them up. We used to run by a neighbor's house in the Bottoms because a rumor was going around that she had a gun and that she would shoot you. Mrs. Lizzie Calhoun lived across the street from our house, and she would make tea cakes, and she would always give us some. We didn't have a car and had to walk everywhere we wanted to go, to church, to school, uptown, etc. We always had food to eat, clothes to wear, and shoes on our feet. At Christmas, we got a white doll, one orange, and one candy cane. We were happy. We never had to lock our doors in the Bottoms. When we left the house, my mother kept the switches with her. Thank God, we made it!

Memories of My Early Childhood in the Bottoms by Thales Mims

My earliest childhood memories go back to the home of my grand-parents. It was a two-story house in a farm setting. My uncle ran the farm, and my grandfather worked on the railroad near the town. There was a pecan tree in the front yard and a very large wisteria vine on the right side of the house, which reached above the top of the porch. I was very interested in that vine for a very specific reason. I was fond of grapes, which grew in bunches like the blossoms of the wisteria vine. I waited in great anticipation for those blossoms to develop into grapes so that I could have as many grapes as I wanted and whenever I wanted them. Summer passed and I began to wait on the first day of school. My first-grade teacher was Ms. Georgia Dean. I later learned that she was from Ninety-Six. She was an excellent teacher—firm but fair and caring. Who can't remember the first lesson in that book that was prefaced by a full-page picture of Baby Ray? I loved to hear Ms. Dean read. With her voice inflections, it was as though Baby Ray was actually in the room. I credit Ms. Dean for giving me a strong foundation in my early education. I wish that I could express my appreciation to her because I feel that it was from her efforts that I later became a Fulbright student in Europe and a Buenos Aires Convention Fellow in Latin America. I remember that on a fall afternoon, Mr. Jeff Tolbert, who lived down the road toward Plum Branch, gave my brother William a brindled bulldog puppy. We named the puppy Benny. Why Benny? I don't remember. The thrill of having Benny was momentarily turned into tears because we could not find him the next morning. Later in the morning, we found him curled up and basking in the sunshine next to the chimney behind Aunt Liddie's house. I suppose that her name was Lydia, but she was known as Aunt Liddie by the neighbors.

I remember as though it were yesterday seeing my brother, Talmadge, in his nightgown walking across the grass and accompanied by Benny, a large dog at this time. Talmadge would occasionally trip on his gown. Faithfully, Benny would stand next to him and wait for him to get up as they continued their trek across the grass to Mr. Herbert Walker's house to have breakfast with him and his wife, Mrs. Lorena. Mr. Walker always referred to Talmadge as "My Man." Next to Mr. Walker's house and across the street from Mrs. Catherine "Cat" Cade's and Mrs. Atrene's house was my father's garden. It was always productive. I can still visualize the long rows of beans as resembling rows of teepees. My favorite food from my father's garden was corn.

I can still remember how fascinating it was to watch the water cascade down the tall structure of the icehouse, which was across the street. But of course, things always seemed larger than life to small children. Near the icehouse was the filling station (as service stations were called back then). Mr. Brown owned the filling station. For some strange reason, I thought that the image on the penny was that of Mr. Brown. Whenever I came across a penny, I always gave it to Mr. Brown in exchange for candy. The sucker was a popular piece of candy during my childhood. It was sweet and lasted a long time. My favorite type of sucker was one, which had candy on each end of a stick, and my favorite flavor was strawberry.

Who can forget Mrs. Dena's chickens—all separated into a little individual pen! As a boy, I didn't understand why they were separated in that manner. Leaving Mrs. Dena's and coming toward the street that led to the Bottoms lived Mrs. Dewey and Dorothy. On the other corner, on the same side, lived Cat and Mrs. Atrene. I don't remember anyone else on that side as the street descended, but for some reason, the name Aunt Niecy comes to mind. Coming back up the street on the left side lived the Marshalls—Mrs. Candice, Margie, and another sister whose name I don't remember. Also coming to mind is the name Ethel Roman; on the same street at the corner lived Mr. and Mrs. Charlie Grant and the grandchildren.

Close by Mr. Grant lived a man called Uncle Jim, who shared the house with his sister. Uncle Jim lived on one side, and his sister lived on the other. I can remember no one entering the abode of Uncle Jim. He was handicapped but rode a bicycle quite expertly. We didn't have a community clock, but everyone knew when it was one o'clock in the afternoon because Uncle Jim would yell loudly and accurately at one o'clock each day.

Further up the street lived Mr. Willie Marshall and his wife, Mrs. Ann. Mrs. Ann was from Georgia, and I understand that she was a great cook. I don't remember much about their children as they were not of my age group. There was a house below Aunt Liddie's house, but I don't remember who lived there. Coming full circle on the corner of the highway lived Mr. Harmond and niece (or daughter), Inez. I remember Inez returning from a trip (Ohio, maybe) and telling me about a ride that she had taken, which was higher that a two-story building. Today, I think that she was referring to a Ferris wheel. Inez was very talented and drew very well.

I have talked about my neighborhood and many of the personalities who lived there. Now let me talk about what I remember as the school which my father started. The school was located on the southside of Bethany Church.

The school consisted of two large buildings. We lived on the second floor along with part of the faculty. Were it not for my mother, that building would have burned to the ground, and I would not be alive to tell you this story. In the comic strip, Mutt (the short one) and Jeff (the tall one), I perceived that the character Little Chester was about to be harmed in some way, so I decided to punish the aggressor by burning him with a match. When I lit the paper, I dropped it, and I got under the bed covers. After I fell on the bed covers, the burning paper caused the bed covers to ignite. My mother smelled the bed covers burning, and she came into the room and rescued me while putting out the fire. It is still vivid in my mind how I popped the paint blisters on the wall, which had been caused by the fire.

Except for the airplane swing that Joseph Norman and my brother made there was not much play equipment available. Oh, there were the swings made of automobile tires and what was more fun than curling up inside of a car tire and being rolled around on the grass. In those days, we had to be creative and to make our own equipment and games. For the older people, there was the Mott Brown Band.

Bethany Church was the place where graduations were held. I can remember Uncle Cliff giving a graduation speech at the church.

His topic was "Climb though the Road Be Rugged." Of course, I and other children in the community said our Easter speeches at Bethany.

The time came for us to leave our beloved McCormick and the Bottoms. We moved to Abbeville. For some reason, we had to leave Benny behind. I believe that it was Mr. Willie Marshall, who took care of Benny. Whenever we returned to McCormick to visit, the first thing that was on my brothers, and my agenda was to find Benny. Whenever we found him, he would swish his tail "a mile a minute" with joy on seeing us. On one occasion, when we came to visit Benny, our little world seemed to crumble when we were told that there was no more Benny and obviously no more tail swishing. Benny had been involved in a fight with a dog that was rabid. Benny and the rabid dog had to be destroyed.

Going back to the Bottoms was often a fun thing to do, but it was never the same without our Benny.

The Negro Leagues

Negro League players and teams existed throughout most of the country. We had several teams in South Carolina. Mr. John Wesley "Agg" Zimmerman was the coach of a Negro League team in McCormick. One player from the Bottoms who played on this Negro League team was Joseph "Joe" Franklin. Joe played several positions to include a pitcher and a catcher. The Negro League teams wore the same type of uniforms and used the same type of gear as Big League teams.

Garrett's Barbershop and Wood Yard

Mr. John Garrett opened a barbershop in the 1950s on his property in the Bottoms. At the time, it was the most modern barbershop in South Carolina. Everything was new—the building, all the chairs, and all the equipment. Nothing was secondhand. One of the early barbers in the new shop was John T. Moore of Parksville. He had just finished barbering school. Mr. Garrett also operated a wood yard. His business had a very large saw run by electricity, which was operated by a belt on a pulley. His men would cut wood (logs, saw pulp, and some boards) all day to be sold as firewood. He also had a large delivery truck. Persons could go to his wood yard to buy some wood, or he would have the wood delivered to your home.

THE NEGRO LEAGUES (Continued) MR. AGG ZIMMERMAN'S NEGRO BASEBALL TEAM BY JACKIE RODGERS

McCormick once boasted of its Negro League baseball team. It was often referred to as Agg Zimmerman's Baseball Team. The team consisted of the following players from the 1940s to the 1950s: Robert "Bob" Bell (centerfield), Nero Talbert (pitcher), Ulysses Murray (pitcher), Gordon Moore (catcher), Foster Rodgers (third baseman), Rufus Mattison (second baseman), Leonard Jenkins (first baseman), Coleman Rodgers (shortstop), Arch Covington (umpire), Arthur Smith (catcher), Goober Timpson (catcher), and Mr. Agg Zimmerman (manager). The team played surrounding areas: Promised Land, Troy, Willington, Bradley, Mt. Carmel, and Ninety-Six. (Note: We understand that Mr. Agg's name was Mr. John Wesley Zimmerman. Also note: Joseph "Joe" Franklin was also on this team and played as a pitcher and sometimes as a catcher.) Several of these team members lived in the Bottoms.

It was rumored that two of the team members were scouted for tryouts with the big Negro League teams. Some of the family members had reservations about how they would be treated and how they were to be paid; therefore, they forbid them from trying out. After the family members found out about the team and saw them play, they regretted not allowing them to try out for the Big League.

MRS. LOUISE JOHNSON SEARLES

Mrs. Searles lived next door to Mrs. Janie Bell Walker on Carolina Street. She rented two rooms in the back of a house. The front of the house was used as a barbershop by Mr. Jasper Talbert, who was Mrs. Walker's uncle. Mrs. Eddie Mae Haskell, aunt to Rev. Robert Haskell, also had a store in the same building, at one time.

MRS. LILLIE C. RODGERS BY JACKIE RODGERS

Mrs. Lillie Calhoun Rodgers was born on January 3, 1897. She was the wife of Coleman Rodgers. She was the mother of sixteen children. In 1947, Mrs. Rodgers's son, Elijah, had a house built for her on Carolina Street.

Mrs. Rodgers was a no-nonsense kind of a woman with one arm. She could outcook anyone. She never let her disability disable her. Mrs. Rodgers raised her children and many of her grandchildren and great-grandchildren. If you ever received a "whooping" from her, you never wanted to misbehave again! She believed in not sparing the rod, switch, or belt! She was always helping others, feeding the town winos, giving shelter to others, even when her house was already full. She was truly a *phenomenal woman*, who lived to be ninety-eight years old.

THE OUTHOUSE, PRIVY, OR TOILET

Back in the day, everybody in the Bottoms had one.

The outhouse, privy, or toilet was a mainstay at homes, schools, and churches during the first half of the twentieth century and before that time. Most of the outhouses were built of wood, although the very rich had brick outhouses. This wood constructed facility was constructed over a hole in the ground. Most of the floors of these toilets were made of concrete to keep them from deteriorating since these floors were in contact with the ground.

As these toilets filled with waste, they were moved to another location at the home, school, or church. Over the years, it was not unusual for the location of the outhouse to be repeated in the location scheme used by men who dug holes for toilets. Like those men who dug graves, it took some experience to dig holes and to properly locate the outdoor toilet.

Usually, the men would dig the hole for the new location, move that soil to the side, and on rollers, move the outhouse to its new location. The soil taken from the new hole was used to fill in the old toilet site. Some type of outhouse or open ditches are still used in some parts of the world, especially in very poor communities.

I know there are some things that you want to forget. Then I won't talk about the slop jar. Who wanted to go outside to use a privy when it was ten degrees outside.

"We have come a long way, baby!" Don't forget where you came from. Our history helps to keep us focused.

Some Highlights and Challenges of Blacks in the Old South

Suffering as a Black Southerner

SLAVERY HURT VERY deeply for black people. To bring human beings here in 1619 to work as slaves was the most dehumanizing practice of modem history. History had taught the world from biblical times to the Anglo-Saxon colonization of Africa that slavery was wrong, violated the laws of God, and violated the Constitution of the new republic—the United States of America. Note: All slavery in the United States should have ended at least by 1776. After all, it was Crispus Attucks, a black man, who was the first to die for the American Revolution. As we all know, slavery in the United States did not end in 1776.

When you dehumanize a race of people, officially as property and not as human beings from 1619 until 1863, this does irreparable damage on said race for centuries to come.

To think that the stroke of a pen in 1862 could bring a race from hell's doorsteps to full-fledged psychological, sociological, economic, and physiological health in a prejudiced and hateful society was a joke. Most of the South couldn't care less about what happened to the Southern Negro.

The *Dred Scott* decision further enflamed a segment of the United States to continue to see the black race as less than human. To be seen as three-fifths of a man would be disconcerting to any black person.

When the Northern contingent left the South too early during reconstruction, an uneducated, poor, and unskilled populace fell back into semi-slavery roles of sharecropping and tenant farming and continued second-class citizenship, which was supported by Jim Crow laws and practices and the rise of hate groups. The US Supreme Court got it wrong in *Dred Scott*, and it got it wrong in *Plessy v. Ferguson*. As the United States was dealing with the "Indian Problem," it sought to deal with the "black problem." This was a country that wanted to be controlled by whites and for white interests. The reservation was chosen for the American Indian, although this was "his country" and not a country "discovered" by Christopher

Columbus in 1492. As the story goes, the Indian was already here. It was Columbus who was lost.

There was no reservation for blacks, so the practice was to make America "separate but equal." What evolved were white neighborhoods and black neighborhoods, usually divided by a railroad track, a major highway, or "your side of the town." And so, it was with schools when the US Supreme Court ruled in *Plessey v. Ferguson* to have "separate, but equal" schools. History has taught us that this did not work.

Things stagnated until the late 1940s and early 1950s when the NAACP (National Association for the Advancement of Colored People) started challenging *Plessey v. Ferguson*. Therefore, after fifty years, the South started to implement *Plessey v. Ferguson* in public schools. New, modern schools were being built all across the South. In the rush to set up these schools, these new schools for blacks had no new student desks, no new textbooks, and no new other learning materials. These items were sent over from the white schools. I remember sitting in Mims High School, a new modern facility, with old items from the white high school in town. Little did people acknowledge, but most black boys played with white boys until sixth grade, so we were able to recognize the names of our former playmates whose names were carved in the old desks which we received. We also recognized their names in the old textbooks which we received. Therefore, much of what we were taught was old knowledge from old textbooks. This simply put black students further behind our white counterparts.

Sharecropping

The practice of sharecropping existed in my home county. This practice started after the Civil War when former black slaves had no land (no, they did not get the forty acres and mule) or jobs to support themselves and their families. A number of former slaveholders had land but very little money because most of their financial resources had been used to support the War for Southern Independence, the name given to the Civil War by most Southern whites.

Many blacks and some poor whites "agreed" to stay on farms and to share in its harvest. The original idea may have been good but turned sour because of the records kept by the landowner. Old slave cabins were used to house some sharecroppers and their families. Additional tenant houses or cabins were also constructed. All of this housing was located on the white landowner's property. Since these were farmworkers, they could just come out of their doors and go to work.

The landowner would provide the seed, fertilizer, other chemicals, house the workers, and approve the workers "buying from the local store," usually owned by the landowner. Since the former black slaves could neither read or write, he was at the mercy of the landowner. Other than from memory, he did not know what he had "purchased or did not purchase" from the store. He did not know what had been the costs of the seeds and other items used by him to work the farm. He did not know what the landowner had made from the harvest and from the work of the sharecropper and his family. Usually, the sharecropper and his family went in the hole each year and, therefore, could never leave the farm. Additionally, his children had to work the farm so they could not go to any of the church schools started by numerous black churches after the Civil War.

Most black sharecroppers had no money and got further into debt each year. In my community, this practice continued until the 1950s.

Lively Debate on Segregation Hits
My Hometown in 1954

McCormick residents were informed of the debate between the supporters of two candidates for governor of South Carolina on June 3, 1954. On this date, two ads appeared in the *McCormick Messenger* newspaper. One ad was called "The Big Lie Exposed!" In this ad, the supporters of candidate George Bell Timmerman Jr. wanted to distance Mr. Timmerman from "a political debt to Mojeska Simkins, the Lighthouse and Informer, James M. Hinton or the NAACP?" The ad further reads, "Mr. Timmerman has publicly said he does not want the support of any of them. He has repeatedly denounced and repudiated them. This Bates has not done." Lester L. Bates was Mr. Timmerman's opponent in the governor's race. The ad, which was paid for by a Mr. Roy R. Whitney and other friends of George Bell Timmerman Jr., was designed to distance Mr. Timmerman away from the NAACP, which supported the integration of schools in the State of South Carolina. The "Big Lie" evolved from "an editorial post-dated May 1, the Lighthouse and Informer, with Communistic cunning, pretended that Timmerman favored mixed schools. Speaking in Charleston that night, Timmerman denounced this editorial as the "big lie" of the campaign."

The second ad is entitled "NAACP Denounces Bates" for his position "after a speech in Charleston, October 16, 1953." It reports that candidate for Governor Lester L. Bates said, "We must guarantee separate schools to both white children and Negro children in South Carolina for the peace, happiness and contentment of both." Finally, the ad reports Bates as saying, "I shall never recommend or approve mixed schools." According to the *Messenger*, this ad was "paid for by Friends of Lester L. Bates."

It appears as though each campaign was trying to stress their positions on keeping schools segregated while distancing each campaign as far away as possible from the NAACP. This was the year of the 1954 decision of the United States Supreme Court that outlawed the segregation of schools in the United States. Most of the governors and obviously some candidates for governorships in the South were taking a stand against this decision. We all remember the words of Governor George Wallace of Alabama: "Segregation now, segregation tomorrow, segregation forever."

Mob Violence against Blacks

Mob violence against blacks was not always limited to Mississippi, Alabama, and other Deep South states. A classic example happened in the spring of 1930, when seventeen white men in Oconee County, South Carolina, dragged a Negro man from jail and riddled his body with multiple gunshots, killing him instantly. Among the mob was the mayor of Walhalla, R. L. Ballentine. The Negro man was Allen Green, fifty years old, who had been arrested for something common in the Old South, assaulting a white woman, similar to the Emmett Till Story, twenty years later.

The Mysterious Fire

Just twenty-three miles north of my hometown of McCormick is the town of Abbeville. In 1885, an agricultural college was established for the training of Negro youth by Rev. Emory Williams of Washington, DC. After experiencing financial difficulties, the school was relocated and named Harbison College in 1901. In 1910, three students living in a dormitory lost their lives when arsonists burned Harbison Hall. Several other students were injured. No record could be found where the arsonists were caught and brought to justice. The school then relocated away from Abbeville.

Loss of Black Identity in Schools

White resistance to the integration of schools continued for many years after *Brown*, the 1954 decision of the Supreme Court. The first practice was the construction of new and "equal" school facilities, even though these new schools were filled with used desks and used textbooks from the white schools. "With all deliberate speed" was not happening. There was massive Southern resistance to integration with many examples to cite: from the Little Rock Nine in Arkansas to Governor George Wallace's proclamation of "Segregation now! Segregation tomorrow! Segregation forever!" in Alabama, and according to a paper written by Christopher P. Lehman, Governor Paul Johnson in Mississippi was renaming the NAACP from the National Association for the Advancement of Colored People to "Niggers, Alligators, Apes, Coons, and Possums."

It was not until after the 1964 Civil Rights Act that we saw any major strides in the integration of schools. Formerly segregated school districts were required to submit desegregation plans. Most desegregation plans continued to delay full integration. A variety of plans were submitted to the US Department of Education in Washington, DC: voluntary, involuntary, student and staff assignments, quotas, and plans, which included busing. Full integration to the extent possible did not occur until the 1970s. Delay practices also gave time to start private schools or academies for white students only. In essence, the integration of black and white students in schools gave rise to segregated white schools.

Then there were other issues. Most public schools were governed by white policy makers. They did not want white kids to attend school originally named for reputable black citizens or black leaders. Many of these schools were renamed, thereby starting a black identity problem, which continues until this day. Most black principals became assistant principals or classroom teachers. Many black teachers became teacher assistants or teacher aides. The use of the National Teacher Examinations also contributed to this happening. Instead of integration, it became "black absorption into white schools." With the closing of many former black schools, came the loss of black student organizations (New Farmers of America, New Homemakers of America, and other vocational clubs). Extracurricular activities changed such as the prom, beauty pageants, daily and weekly devotionals, daily Bible verses by each student, the Pledge of Allegiance being recited each day, the singing of patriotic songs, and baccalaureate sermons.

Then came higher standards for teachers, such as the National Teachers Examination. Blacks were not resistant to higher standards but did voice that the general teacher examinations were not culturally fair. These exams were prepared by white developers for white participants. As was predicted, blacks did not perform as well as whites, and many did not meet the score requirements established by white governing bodies, resulting in the loss of countless numbers of black teachers across the South, many becoming teacher assistants and making approximately 50 percent or less in salary than they had earned as teachers. Of course, many black teachers left the profession. This shortage of black teachers continues until this day. Critical to this shortage is the black male teacher. In the "integrated school," it is not uncommon for a black student to come into contact with a black male teacher only by the time the black child gets into middle school or even high school.

An Example of Segregated Classes
within an Integrated School

The Cades-Hebron Elementary School in Cades, South Carolina, was cited for having segregated classes in its school. School boards and school administrators around the South used "ability grouping," parents being able to request their child's teachers, and predominantly black classes being taught by black teachers and predominantly white classes being taught by white teachers. "Low-level" classes were being taught by black teachers, and "academic" classes were being taught by white teachers. These practices became known as segregation within an integrated school.

According the *State* newspaper, "as more white students started attending Cades-Hebron Elementary School over the past three years, some classes taught by white teachers got whiter, while most black teachers' classes kept black majorities." The *State* went on to report that "one eighth-grade class is all black, and several other classes are mostly black. But several classes are mostly white." The State also reported that the school had "a form letter allowing parents to request certain teachers."

The knowledge of these practices by the white community caused white parents to use vans to pick up white students to attend Cades-Hebron Elementary School. Also, according to the *State* newspaper, "whites have come to the school from the private Williamsburg Academy or from other school zones. Some black parents have speculated that the white students were coming to Cades because of the imbalanced classes."

Whites Oppose Being in Black County

During the summer of 1983, Hemingway, South Carolina, residents opposed the consolidation of all black Battery Park High School with predominantly white Hemingway High School. This was a plan by the Williamsburg County School Board Trustees. The division was so great until the white school board members from the Hemingway area did not sit with the black school board members at the community meeting in Hemingway. Instead, those white school board members sat in the gymnasium bleachers. The consolidation effort seemed to bring attention to deep-seated problems regarding race in the Hemingway area.

According to published reports, local Hemingway attorney and Williamsburg County School Board member, William Chandler, filed a suit to prevent the consolidation of Battery Park High School with Hemingway High School. Chandler, a white male, claimed that his white child would be adversely affected by the consolidation.

Ultimately, the Williamsburg County School Board trustees implemented the plan to consolidate the two schools. This led to a discussion of annexation by citizens from the Hemingway area. To prepare for a referendum on annexation, there was an effort to annex certain areas around the town of Hemingway to be included in the area to be annexed. These "certain areas" were predominantly white populated areas.

The issues in Williamsburg County involved more than its schools. According to the *Wall Street Journal* newspaper, an article entitled "Carolina Town Seeks a Brighter—Some Say Whiter—Future" in its December 10, 1993 edition, "the official line in Hemingway is that the secession movement is motivated by economics, not race."

Others contend that race has always been the problem. Before the Voting Rights Act, whites controlled everything in Williamsburg County. In a predominantly black county, blacks held no responsible positions in the county government. Whites were in power, and the black population feared their participation because the jobs and economics were controlled by the minority white population.

According to an article in the *Los Angeles Times* newspaper entitled "S. C. County Mirrors Gulf Between Races in the South" in its
November 28, 1993, edition, "blacks in the majority begin to wield
political clout; whites react angrily." For decades, the county had
held an Old-Fashioned Days Festival. According to the article, "they
[blacks] drew no pleasure from the spectacle of Confederate flags
lofted above the streets of their town. They gritted their teeth when
black sanitation workers trailed behind horses in the parade, cleaning
up the droppings. They cringed when black women paraded in 'Aunt
Jemima' attire and black men posed lazily in overalls in the backs of
hay wagons for the amusement of the assembled throngs."

Things changed when the local school superintendent challenged the event by withholding the participation of public school
groups at the festival. Whites were extremely critical of the superintendent's decision and began to demand his resignation. Whites
hadn't gotten over the superintendent's efforts to place two monuments on the Williamsburg County Courthouse grounds. He had
provided the leadership to place a monument of Dr. Martin Luther
King Jr. and a monument of Supreme Court Justice Thurgood
Marshall, with a fountain separating the structures. He had also provided the leadership to name two major highways for these two men
through the county, all of which stand today.

The local school superintendent had also stopped salary assignments. For a school district employee to get a loan from a local lending institution, the employee's monthly check had to be made out to
the employee and to the lending institution. They had to go to the
lending institution to cash their check. He found this to be belittling
and demeaning.

At any rate, it was not until ten years after the discussion of
secession began that the Hemingway area planned for a referendum
on whether the predominantly white Hemingway area would secede
from predominantly black Williamsburg County to predominantly
white Florence County. The referendum was planned for January 18,
1994.

The Williamsburg County School Board trustees and the
NAACP filed a lawsuit in federal court against the referendum being

held. Allegations were that the proposed annexation would violate the 1971 School Desegregation Plan and a violation of the federal Voting Rights Act. Another lawsuit was filed against Governor Carroll Campbell, the Hemingway Town Council and mayor, and the Election Commission of the Hemingway area. The lawsuit also addressed the annexations by the town of Hemingway to bring more whites into the proposed annexation area, while leaving blacks out of the proposed area.

A three-judge federal panel was requested to hear the lawsuits in federal court in Florence, South Carolina. The case was heard in federal court in Florence. The final decision of the court was that the referendum would violate the allegations made by the plaintiffs. The referendum request was denied.

The superintendent during these times was the writer of this transcript.

Man Shot by Tax Collector

At the time that I was working as a shoeshine boy at Lowe's Shoe Shop in McCormick, a Negro man by the name of Mr. Sammy Lee Wakefield was shot by McCormick County tax collector, Mr. E. L. Hollingsworth, on Main Street in McCormick, just approximately thirty feet from where I was working. We heard the shot and focused our attention on the scene of the shooting.

According to reports, the tax collector claims that the victim advanced on him with his right hand in his pocket and that the victim struck him on the head. He also claims that he only questioned Mr. Wakefield about his delinquent taxes. Now, this happened on a Saturday in June 1958. During this time, the Main Street in McCormick is full of people. Of the many people who observed the incident, none agreed with the version of the tax collector. Also, according to reports, the tax collector was placed under "technical arrest," but the citizens never learned of any "punishment" for the shooting by the tax collector or of the reasons why he had a loaded gun on his person.

Black Combat Veterans for US
"Fight" to Join VFW Post

In 1999, fifty years after President Harry Truman integrated the United States Armed Forces, and after fighting side by side as American combat soldiers in the Korean War, in the Vietnam War, in Desert Storm, and in other conflicts, black veterans in Durham, North Carolina, reported that the American Legion Post No. 7 had problems admitting them. According to news reports, "eight black veterans said that the Post didn't want their memberships." The post commander was also quoted as saying, "There are three other posts in Durham, and they keep coming to Post 7." However, he also reportedly said, "Everyone is treated the same. Race makes no difference." The black veterans seemed to be frustrated with the "cold reception" they received when they tried to join the post.

McNair Takes Blame

In an article in the *State* newspaper (Columbia, South Carolina), on Friday, July 14, 2006, former governor Robert E. McNair is reported to accept blame for the Orangeburg Massacre.

The massacre occurred in February 1968 when South Carolina State Troopers fired into a group of black students on the campus of South Carolina State University in Orangeburg, South Carolina. Three black students were killed and twenty-seven others were wounded. The troopers had been sent to the campus after several days of protests by students against a segregated bowling alley. In the article, Mr. McNair was quoted as saying, "The fact that I was governor at the time placed the mantle of responsibility squarely on my shoulders, and I have borne that responsibility with all the heaviness it entails for all those years."

Surprise by Civil Rights Icon

One of the most surprising things was to learn that James Meredith, who broke the color barrier as a student at the University of Mississippi in 1962, and who was shot during the civil rights movement, would become an adviser to conservative Senator Jesse Helms of North Carolina. According to reports, while Mr. Meredith was fighting for civil rights in the 1960s, Mr. Helms was growing in stature and recognition as a conservative television personality who was critical of the civil rights movement.

(Washington, Associated Press, about 1989–1990)

Silent March

On Saturday, August 26, 1989, I participated in the NAACP Silent March on Washington. I traveled on an NAACP designated bus from South Carolina. The bus picked up NAACP members from across the state of South Carolina.

We had received an announcement earlier in the week to wear all black, including footwear. We traveled all night Friday night, stopped at a truck stop in Virginia, took a sponge wipe off, got a snack, and reboarded the bus to enter DC.

The march was entirely silent: no talking, no eating, no singing, no inappropriate gestures, and no whispering. The march was a response to recent US Supreme Court decisions. The court had voted four times in 5–4 decisions, which seemed to reverse civil rights gains. It was felt that the US Supreme Court was not a friend to civil rights gains, which had helped black people. The march ended at the United States Capitol. The only stop along the way was a stop at the US Supreme Court building where the multitude was led in prayer. A number of speakers spoke at the Capitol: Rev. Benjamin Hooks (NAACP executive director), Dr. William Gibson (chairman of the NAACP board of directors), Mayor Marion Berry (mayor of Washington, DC), Dr. Dorothy Height (president of Black Leadership Forum), Mr. Walter Fauntry (congressman of District of Columbia), Dr. Joseph Lowery (president of the Southern Christian Leadership Conference), and Rev. Jesse Jackson (president of Rainbow Coalition).

A highlight of the assembly was a fifteen-minute litany, which was led by Dr. Hooks. The litany was a "why we march" litany, which reviewed the civil rights movement and provided challenges for the future. The final unity response said it all: "We march because we have heard the admonitions of the prophets of old; we march and will continue to march until the hungry are fed, the homeless in this nation are sheltered, those who are sick and do not have health insurance coverage can see a doctor, until sexism and racism are removed from our nation's landscape, and in the words of Amos, until 'Justice will run down as waters and righteousness as a mighty stream.'" Over two hundred agencies and organizations endorsed the silent march of 1989.

Two Remarkable Figures Who Impacted The Old South

**Dr. Martin Luther King Jr. and
Supreme Court Justice
Thurgood Marshall**

THIS TOPIC IS about two men of color who worked so that color would no longer be a barrier to anyone. These two men waged a war against racism, discrimination, and the unfair treatment of their fellowmen.

The war that they waged had very unusual weapons. Although all warriors need cunning, intelligence, strength, and strategy, warriors usually must also possess other weapons from a knife to a nuclear bomb. Attorney Thurgood Marshall and the Reverend Martin Luther King Jr. were cunning, possessed intelligence, possessed strength, and could strategize. Beyond those traits, they had nothing.

Neither man possessed or used destructive weapons. No, each man went off to war, one with the Constitution and the other with the Bible. They knew that they needed unusual weapons for an unusual war.

Thurgood Marshall was born in 1908 in Baltimore, Maryland. His mother, Norma, was a schoolteacher, and his father, William, was a Pullman porter.

The Constitution became a companion of Marshall early in his life. When he was a high school student, Thurgood did not respond well to corporal punishment for misbehaving, so his principal would often send him to a small room at the school and require that he memorize certain sections of the United States Constitution. Little did Marshall know that this document would become his constant companion throughout his years.

Unable to enter the University of Maryland because of his race, Marshall chose to go to Lincoln University in Pennsylvania, a small private black college. He graduated with honors in 1930 with a bachelor's degree in one hand and an arm around the waist of his wife, Vivian Burey, whom he had married during his senior year.

It was Vivian who encouraged her husband to go to law school. For some reason, Marshall thought that the University of Maryland had changed during the past three years. He applied. He was rejected.

Being unable to attend law school at home and without adequate funds to go off to school, Marshall thought that law school would only be a dream. Upon learning of this, Thurgood's mother vowed that law school would not be a dream for her son. This schoolteacher saw to it that her son would enter law school through sacrifice and devotion. Marshall entered and was graduated from Howard University Law School, Washington, DC.

Martin Luther King Jr. was born in 1929 in Atlanta, Georgia. Thurgood Marshall was studying at Lincoln University in Pennsylvania when King was born. Their ages were twenty-one years apart. His mother, Alberta, was a musician, and his father, Martin Sr., was a Baptist minister.

A son of the soil of the Deep South, Martin just naturally attended an all-black college. He graduated from Morehouse College at the young age of nineteen with a bachelor's degree.

King did not experience the problems which Marshall had experience regarding college entrance. Although he may have thought about going to a Southern all-white college, he chose to follow in his father's footsteps to become a trained minister. He received a bachelor of divinity degree from Crozer Theological Seminary, graduating first in his class, and a doctor of philosophy degree from Boston University. Like Marshall, King married while in college. While at Boston University, he met an accomplished singer named Coretta Scott, who was studying music at the New England Conservatory of Music.

By the time King graduated from Morehouse in 1948, Marshall had worked as an attorney for fifteen years, the last eleven of which had been as legal counsel for the NAACP.

While at Morehouse, King became influenced by another minister, Dr. Benjamin E. Mays. Dr. Mays was a Baptist minister as well as the college's president.

It is significant to note that Dr. Mays was born and spent his early life in Epworth, a small community in Greenwood County, South Carolina. A marker along Highway 78 between Greenwood and Saluda presently marks the birthplace of Dr. Mays. Mays, a distinguished orator, minister, and educator, in his own right when King was at Morehouse came to be the final force in King's decision to become a minister. King had earlier contemplated law and medicine.

While King was matriculating in high school and college, several significant things were happening, which caused many to say that the 1954 decision was just a matter of time.

1. As the United States was about to enter World War II, President Franklin Roosevelt issued Executive Order 8802, which outlawed discrimination against blacks who worked in defense plants. Roosevelt also established the Fair Employment Practices Commission.
2. On July 26, 1948, President Harry S. Truman issued Executive Order 9981, which ordered the end of racial discrimination in the armed services.
3. In 1948, former first lady Eleanor Roosevelt helped to draft a resolution that was passed by the United Nations. This resolution is called the Universal Declaration of Human Rights.
4. Also, in 1948, Strom Thurmond and Hubert H. Humphrey were thrust to the forefront of American politics but with different agendas about the race question. Thurmond is quoted as saying there are "not enough troops in the army to force the Southern people to break down segregation and admit the Negro race into our theaters, into our swimming pools, into our homes and into our churches."
5. Humphrey countered, "To those who say that this civil rights program is an infringement on states' rights, I say this, that the time has arrived in America for the Democratic Party to get out of the shadows of states' rights and to walk forthrightly into the bright sunshine of human rights."

Although some walls were falling down, Marshall knew that he and his colleagues had an uphill battle in this war for civil rights. Although he had an intelligent and sophisticated group of soldiers in his command, the "enemy" had *Plessy v. Ferguson*, Jim Crow, and the 1927 case called *Gong Lum v. Rice*, where a unanimous United States Supreme Court known as the William Howard Taft Court had ruled that Chinese students did not have to be allowed to go to school with whites.

Marshall attacked the *Plessy* angle by showing that Clarendon County, South Carolina, was spending $1,432.35 to educate white students and $350.20 to educate colored students. The pupil-teacher ratio for white students was 1 to 23 and 1 to 67 for colored students. This, Marshall insisted, was not "separate but equal."

Kenneth Clark, a noted psychologist from New York, performed tests on colored students and demonstrated with the use of dolls and other techniques that colored students had been adversely affected by segregation.

Marshall left South Carolina in 1951, feeling good about the *Briggs* case. He was devastated on June 21, 1951, when the South Carolina lead attorney with the *Briggs* case, Attorney Harold Boulware, called to inform him that the federal panel had voted against Briggs.

Although disappointed, Marshall knew that he would appeal to the US Supreme Court.

THE LEADING ATTORNEYS IN THE *BROWN* CASE BEFORE THE UNITED STATES SUPREME COURT

The attorney for South Carolina was John W. Davis of New York. He was eighty years old and had been the Democratic Party's presidential candidate in 1924. He was assisted by Robert McFigg of Charleston, South Carolina. Davis was considered an expert on constitutional law and well respected in the legal profession.

Thurgood Marshall presented the case for the plaintiffs. Marshall argued that "any segregation, which is for the purpose of setting up class or caste distinction, is of itself in violation of the 14th Amendment."

In an article appearing in the Atlanta Constitution, Friday, April 23, 1954, Aurelius S. Scott wrote, "I would like to support the idea that the Negro operating his own schools will solve most of south's educational problems."

The Negro has successfully operated his churches and secret orders. Booker T. Washington's Tuskegee Institute proves irrefutably that he can run educational institutions. The late Mr. Washington was the founder of the first and only Negro curriculum.

"The core of the miseducation of the Negro school child is in the curriculum. Better school plants will not solve the problem. At present, there are no curricula, no teachers, white or colored, for mixed schools," the writer concluded.

The message in this communication seems to support segregated schools. This appeared less than a month before the *Brown* decision.

Martin left Boston University the year of the *Brown* decision (although he completed his dissertation and was graduated in 1955) with intentions to return to the South and to pastor a church. It was almost to the day that King preached his first sermon at the Dexter Avenue Baptist Church in Birmingham, and the *Brown* decision was ordered.

Everything was falling in place for the young minister for roles which he and the world never dreamed of before. Neither, at this time, did Martin know of his destiny.

King knew that Thurgood had been fighting, using the Constitution, for over a decade. He was inspired by Thurgood and the *Brown* decision.

Although neither man was patient with the slow pace of equal rights, King was less patient than Marshall. Marshall knew that laws had to be changed for equal rights to be available and perpetual for all people. He had learned from his law professor and mentor at Howard Law School, Dean Charles Houston, that however slow the process may seem, the law was the route to take. This philosophy helped Marshall to win twenty-nine of thirty-two cases that he argued before the United States Supreme Court.

However, the impact of the *Brown* decision appeared to be moving too slow for King. Finally, on May 17, 1957, this new type of "rebel" from the South was one of the leaders of the Prayer Pilgrimage to Washington. Along with Roy Wilkins, A. Phillip Randolph, and Adam Clayton Powell, King blasted the country on segregation from the steps of the Lincoln Memorial. King was never more eloquent than he was on that spring day. From that day until his death, other civil rights leaders marched in his shadow.

The civil rights movement was abruptly interrupted in 1960, with the assassination of President John F. Kennedy.

"This is sick. You just can't do right and survive in this nation. This is going to happen to me, also. You know, I don't think I will live to reach forty because this country is too sick to allow me to live."

STATEMENT OF DR. MARTIN LUTHER
KING JR. UPON LEARNING OF
THE ASSASSINATION OF PRESIDENT JOHN F. KENNEDY

IT IS SO
ORDERED.

THE WORDS "IT IS SO ORDERED"

The words "It is so ordered" were never more welcomed by significant numbers of Americans than they were when the highest court used them in the *Brown* decision.

Included in this section are excerpts and statements regarding the cases, attorneys, and actions of the courts that led to the decision of the United States Supreme Court on school integration.

The significant cases which ultimately led to the *Brown* case came from several parts of the country, Topeka, Kansas, Prince Edward County, Virginia, Newcastle County, Delaware, and Summerton, South Carolina.

Although other attorneys were assigned by the NAACP to work on different cases—i.e., Robert Carter and Jack Greenberg were assigned the *Topeka* case; Louis Redding, George Hayes, and Jim Nabrit, the *Delaware* case; and Spottswood Robinson, the *Virginia* case—and although Thurgood Marshall managed all the cases, he was the lead man for the *Clarendon County, South Carolina* case.

The *South Carolina* case, as taken from *United States Reports*, was known as *Harry Briggs et al. v. Elliot et al.* This case was heard during the October 1951 term of the United States Supreme Court by Chief Justice Fred M. Vinson, Associate Justice Hugo L. Black, Associate Justice Stanley Reed, Associate Justice Felix Frankfurter, Associate Justice William O. Douglas, Associate Justice Robert H. Jackson, Associate Justice Harold H. Burton, Associate Justice Tom C. Clark, and Associate Justice Sherman Minton.

OPINION OF THE COURT

APPEAL FROM THE UNITED STATES DISTRICT COURT FOR THE EASTERN DISTRICT OF SOUTH CAROLINA.

No. 273. Decided January 28, 1952.

The District Court in this case decided that constitutional and statutory provisions of South Carolina requiring separate schools for the white and colored races did not of themselves violate the Fourteenth Amendment, but ordered the school officials to proceed at once to furnish equal educational facilities and to report to the court within six months what action had been taken. After an appeal to this Court had been docketed, the required report was filed in the District Court. Held: In order that this Court may have the benefit of the views of the District Court upon the additional facts brought out in the report, and that the District Court may have the opportunity to take whatever action it may deem appropriate in light of that report, the judgment is vacated and the case is remanded for further proceedings. Pp. 350-352. 98 F. Supp. 529, judgment vacated and case remanded.

Spottswood W. Robinson, III, Robert L. Carter, Thurgood Marshall and Arthur D. Shores for appellants. Robert McC. Figg, Jr. for appellees.

Appellant Negro school children brought this action in the Federal District Court to enjoin appellee school officials from making any distinctions based upon race or color in providing educational facilities for School District No. 22,

Clarendon County, South Carolina. As the basis for their complaint, appellants alleged that equal facilities are not provided for Negro pupils and that those constitutional statutory provisions of South Carolina requiring separate schools "for children of the white and colored races" are invalid under the Fourteenth Amendment. At the trial before a court of three judges, appellees conceded that the school facilities provided for Negro students "are not substantially equal to those afforded in the District for white pupils."

The District Court held, one judge dissenting, that the challenged constitutional and statutory provisions were not of themselves violative of the Fourteenth Amendment. The court below also found that the educational facilities afforded by appellees for Negro pupils are not equal to those provided for white children. The District Court did not issue an injunction abolishing racial distinctions as prayed by appellants, but did order appellees to proceed at once to furnish educational facilities for Negroes equal to those furnished white pupils. In its decree, entered June 21, 1951, the District Court ordered that appellees report to that court within six months as to action taken by them to carry out the court's order. 98 F. Supp. 529.

Dissatisfied with the relief granted by the District Court, appellants brought a timely appeal directly to this Court under 28, U. S. C, (Supp. IV) 1253. After the appeal was docketed but before its consideration by this Court, appellees filed in the court below their report as ordered.

The Court has not given its views on this report, having entered an order stating that it will withhold further action thereon while the cause is pending in this Court on appeal. Prior to our consideration of the questions raised on this appeal, we should have the benefit of the views of the District Court upon the additional facts brought to the attention of that court in the report which it ordered. The District Court should also be afforded the opportunity to take whatever action it may deem appropriate in light of that report. In order that this may be done, we vacate the judgment of the District Court and remand the case to that court for further proceedings. Another judgment, entered at the conclusion of those proceedings, may provide the basis for any further appeals to this Court. **It is so ordered**.

MR. JUSTICE BLACK and MR. JUSTICE DOUGLAS dissent to vacation of the judgment of the District Court on the grounds stated. They believe that the additional facts contained in the report to the District Court are wholly irrelevant to the constitutional questions presented by the appeal to this Court, and that we should note jurisdiction and set the case down for argument.

NOTE: Judge Earl Warren was not a member of this court.

The NAACP petitioned the Court for three cases to be presented before the court during the October 1952, term. The NAACP asked that the Briggs (South Carolina) and Davis (Virginia) cases be joined with the Brown case into Brown et al. versus Board of Education of Topeka, et al. The composition of the court had not changed from the October 1951, term.

APPEAL FROM THE UNITED STATES
DISTRICT COURT FOR THE TOPEKA,
KANSAS DISTRICT, OCTOBER 8, 1952.

In two cases set for argument in October,
the Laws of Kansas and South Carolina providing for racial segregation in public schools
were challenged as violative of the Fourteenth
Amendment. In another case raising the same
question with respect to the laws of Virginia,
appellants had filed a statement of jurisdiction
and a motion requesting that all three cases
be argued together. There was pending in the
United States Court of Appeals for the District
of Columbia Circuit a case in which segregation
in public schools of the District of Columbia was
challenged as violative of the Fifth Amendment.

Held:

1. The Kansas and South Carolina cases are
    continued on the docket; probable jurisdic-
    tion is noted in the Virginia case; and argu-
    ments in all three will be heard in December.
2. Judicial notice is taken of the pendency of
    the District of Columbia case. The Court
    will entertain a petition for certiorari in that
    case, which, if presented and granted, will
    afford opportunity for argument of that case
    immediately following arguments in the
    other three cases.

Robert L. Carter, Thurgood Marshall,
Spottswood W. Robinson, III, George E. C.
Hayes, George M. Johnson, William R. Ming,
Jr., James M. Nabrit, Jr. and Frank D. Reeves for

appellants. Oliver W. Hill was also with them on the brief, in the Virginia case.

T. C. Callison, Attorney General of South Carolina, John W. Davis, Robert McC. Figg, Jr. and William R. Meagher for appellees in The Clarendon case.

J. Lindsay Almond, Jr., Attorney General, and Henry T. Wickham, Assistant Attorney General, for the State of Virginia, and T. Justin Moore, Archibald F. Robertson and John W. Riely for the Prince Edward County School Board et al., appellees in The Virginia case.

In two appeals now pending, Brown et al. v Board of Education of Topeka et.al., and Briggs et al. v Elliott et al., the appellants challenge, respectively, the constitutionality of a statute of Kansas, and a statute and the Constitution of South Carolina, which provide for segregation in the schools of these states. Appellants allege that segregation is, per se, a violation of the Fourteenth Amendment. Argument in these cases has heretofore been set for the week of October 13, 1952.

In Davis et al. v. County School Board of Prince Edward County et al., the appellants have filed a statement of jurisdiction raising the same issue in respect to a statute and the Constitution of Virginia. Appellees in the Davis case have called attention to the similarity between it and the Briggs and Brown cases; by motion they have asked the Court to take necessary action to have all three cases argued together.

The Court takes judicial notice of a fourth case, which is pending in the United States Court of Appeals for the District of Columbia Circuit, Bolling et al. v. Sharpe et al., on that court's docket. In that case, the appellants challenge that appellees' refusal to admit certain Negro appellants to a segregated white school in the District of Columbia; they allege that appellees have taken such action pursuant to certain Acts of Congress; they allege that such action is a violation of the Fifth Amendment of the Constitution.

The court is of the opinion that the nature of the issue posed in those appeals now before the Court involving the Fourteenth Amendment, and also the effect of any decision which it may render in those cases, are such that it would be well to consider, simultaneously, the constitutional issue posed in the case of Bolling et al. v. Sharpe et al.

To the end that arguments may be heard together in all four of these cases, the Court will continue the Brown and Briggs cases on its docket. Probable jurisdiction is noted in Davis et al. v. County School board of Prince Edward County et al. Arguments will be heard in these three cases at the first argument session in December.

The Court will entertain a petition for certiorari in the case of Bolling et al. v. Sharpe et al., which if presented and granted will afford opportunity for argument of the case immediately following the arguments in three appeals now pending.

IT IS SO ORDERED.

The NAACP petitioned to put the four cases together to include a Delaware case and to argue them versus Board of Education of Topeka et al. There was a new Chief Justice, Earl Warren. The other eight members of the court remained the same.

APPEAL FROM THE UNITED STATES DISTRICT COURT FOR THE DISTRICT OF KANSAS. Argued December 9, 1952.—Reargued December 8, 1953.—

Decided May 17, 1954

Segregation of white and Negro children in the public schools of a State solely on the basis of race, pursuant to state Laws permitting or requiring such segregation, denies to Negro children the equal protection of the Laws guaranteed by the Fourteenth Amendment—even though the physical facilities and other "tangible" factors of white and Negro schools may be equal.

(a) The history of the Fourteenth Amendment is inconclusive as to its intended effect on public education.

(b) The question presented in these cases must be determined, not on the basis of conditions existing when the Fourteenth Amendment was adopted, but in the light of the full development of public education and its present place in American life throughout the Nation.

(c) Where a State has undertaken to provide an opportunity for an education in its public schools, such an opportunity is a right which must be made available to all on equal terms.

(d) Segregation of children in public schools solely on the basis of race deprives children of the minority group equal educational opportunities, even though the physical facilities and other "tangible" factors may be equal.

(e) The "separate but equal" doctrine adopted in Plessy v. Ferguson, 163 U.S. 537, has no place in the field of public education.

(f) The cases are restored to the docket for further argument on specified questions relating to the forms of the decrees.

MR. CHIEF JUSTICE WARREN delivered the opinion of the Court.

In each of the cases, minors of the Negro race, through their legal representatives, seek the aid of the courts in obtaining admission to the public schools of their community on a nonsegregated basis. In each instance, they had been denied admission to schools attended by white children under laws requiring or permitting segregation according to race. This segregation was alleged to deprive the plaintiffs of the equal protection of the laws under the Fourteenth Amendment. In each of the cases other than the Delaware case, a three-judge federal district court denied relied to the plaintiffs on the so-called "separate but equal" doctrine announced by this Court in Plessy v. Ferguson, 163 U.S. 537. Under that doctrine, equality of treatment is accorded when the races are provided substantially equal facilities, even though these facilities be separate. In the Delaware case, the Supreme Court of Delaware adhered to that doctrine, but ordered that the plaintiffs be admitted to the white schools because of their superiority to the Negro schools.

The plaintiffs contend that segregated public schools are not "equal," and that hence they are deprived of the equal protection of the laws. Because of the obvious importance of the question presented, the Court took jurisdiction. Argument was heard in the 1952 Term, and reargument was heard this Term on certain questions propounded by the Court.

Reargument was largely devoted to the circumstances surrounding the adoption of the Fourteenth Amendment in 1868. It covered exhaustively consideration of the Amendment in Congress, ratification by the states, then existing practices in racial segregation, and the views of proponents and opponents of the Amendment. This discussion and our own investigation convince us that, although these sources case some light, it is not enough to resolve the problem with which we are faced. At best, they are inconclusive. The most avid proponents of the post-War Amendments undoubtedly intended them to remove all legal distinctions among "all persons born or naturalized in the United States." Their opponents, just as certainly, were antagonistic to both the letter and the spirit of the Amendments and wished then to have the most limited effect. What others in Congress and the state Legislatures had in mind cannot be determined with any degree of certainty.

An additional reason for the inconclusive nature of the Amendment's history, with respect to segregated schools, is the status of public education at the time. In the South, the movement toward free common schools, supported by general taxation, had not yet taken hold. Education of white children was largely in the hands of private groups. Education of Negroes was almost non-existent, and practically all of the race were illiterate. In fact, any education of Negroes was forbidden by law in some states. Today, in contrast, many Negroes have achieved outstanding success in the arts and sciences as well as in the business and professional world. It is true that public school education at the time of the Amendment had advanced further in the North, but the effect of the Amendment on Northern States was generally ignored in the congressional debates. Even in the North, the conditions of public education did not approximate those existing today. The curriculum was usually rudimentary; ungraded schools were common in rural areas; the school term was but three months a year in many states; and compulsory school attendance was virtually unknown. As a consequence, it is not surprising that there should be so little in the history of the Fourteenth Amendment relating to its intended effect on public education.

In the first cases in this Court construing the Fourteenth Amendment, decided shortly after its adoption, the court interpreted it as proscribing all state-imposed discriminations against the Negro race. The doctrine of "separate but equal" did not make its appearance in this Court until 1896 in the case of Plessy v. Ferguson, supra, involving not education but transportation. American courts have since labored with the doctrine for over half a century. In this Court, there have been six cases involving the "separate but equal" doctrine in the field of public education. In Cumming v. County Board of Education, 175 U.S. 528, and Gong Lum v. Rice, 275 U.S. 78, the validity of the doctrine itself was not challenged. (In more recent cases, all on the graduate school level, inequality was found in that specific benefits enjoyed by white students were denied to Negro students of the same educational qualifications.) Missouri ex rel. Gaines v. Canada, 305 U.S. 337; Sipuel v. Oklahoma, 332 U.S. 631; Sweatt v. Painter, 339 U.S. 629; McLaurin v. Oklahoma State Regents, 339 U.S. 637. In none of these cases was it necessary to re-examine the doctrine to grant relief to the Negro plaintiff. And in Sweatt v. Painter, supra, the Court expressly reserved decision on the question whether Plessy v. Ferguson should be held inapplicable to public education.

In the in state cases, that question is directly presented. Here, unlike Sweatt v. Painter, there are findings below that the Negro and white schools involved have been equalized, or are being equalized, with respect to building, curricula, qualifications and salaries of teachers, and other "tangible" factors. Our decision, therefore, cannot turn on merely a comparison of these tangible factors in the Negro and white schools involved in each of the cases. We must look instead to the effect of segregation itself on public education.

In approaching this problem, we cannot turn the clock back to 1868 when the Amendment was adopted, or even to 1896 when Plessy v Ferguson was written. We must consider public education in the light of its full development and its present place in American life throughout the Nation. Only in this way can it be determined if segregation in public schools deprives these plaintiffs of the equal protection of the laws.

Today, education is perhaps the most important function of state and local governments. Compulsory school attendance laws and the great expenditures for education both demonstrate our recognition of the importance of education to our democratic society. It is required in the performance of our most basic public responsibilities, even service in the armed forces. It is the very foundation of good citizenship. Today it is a principal instrument in awakening the child to cultural values, in preparing him for later professional training, and in helping him to adjust normally to his environment. In these days, it is doubtful that any child may reasonably be expected to succeed in life if he is denied the opportunity of an education. Such an opportunity, where the state has undertaken to provide it, is a right which must be made available to all on equal terms.

We come then to the question presented: Does segregation of children in public schools solely on the basis of race, even though the physical facilities and other "tangible" factors may be equal, deprive the children of the minority group of equal educational opportunities? We believe that it does.

In Sweatt v Painter, supra, in finding that a segregated law school for Negroes could not provide them equal educational opportunities, this Court relied in large part on "those qualities which are incapable of objective measurement but which make for greatness in a law school." In McLaurin v Oklahoma State Regents supra, the Court, in requiring that a Negro admitted to a

white graduate school be treated like all other students, again resorted in intangible consideration;
"...his ability to study, to engage in discussions
and exchange views with other students, and, in
general, to learn his profession." Such considerations apply with added force to children in grade
and high schools. To separate them from others
of similar age and qualifications solely because of
their race generates a feeling of inferiority as to
their status in a way unlikely ever to be undone.
The effect of this separation on their educational
opportunities was well stated by a finding in the
Kansas case by a court which nevertheless felt
compelled to rule against the Negro plaintiffs:

"Segregation of white and colored children in public schools has a detrimental effect
upon the colored children. The impact is greater
when it has the sanction of the law; for the policy of separating the races is usually interpreted
as denoting the inferiority of the Negro group.
A sense of inferiority affects the motivation of a
child to learn. Segregation with the sanction of
law, therefore, has a tendency to (retard) the educational and mental development of Negro children and to deprive them of some of the benefits
they would receive in a racially integrated school
system."

Whatever may have been the extent of
psychological knowledge at the time of Plessy
v Ferguson, this finding is amply supported
by modern authority. Any language in Plessy v
Ferguson contrary to this finding is rejected.

We conclude that in the field of public
education the doctrine of "separate but equal"
has no place. Separate educational facilities are
inherently unequal. Therefore, we hold that the

plaintiffs and others similarly situated for whom the actions have been brought are, by reason the segregation complained of, deprived of the equal protection of the laws guaranteed by the Fourteenth Amendment. This disposition makes unnecessary any discussion whether such segregation also violates the Due Process Clause of the Fourteenth Amendment.

Because these are class actions, because of the wide applicability of this decision, and because of the great variety of local conditions, the formulation of decrees in these cases presents problems of considerable complexity. On reargument, the consideration of appropriate relief was necessarily subordinates to the primary question—the constitutionality of segregation in public education. We have now announced that such segregation is a denial of the equal protection of the laws. In order that we may have the full assistance of the parties in formulation decrees, the cases will be restored in the docket, and the parties are requested to present further argument on questions 4 and 5 previously propounded by the Court for the reargument this Term. The Attorney General of the United States is again invited to participate. The Attorneys General of the states requiring or permitting segregation in public education will also be permitted to appear as amici ciriae upon request to do so by September 15, 1954, and submission or briefs by October 1, 1954.

IT IS SO ORDERED.

Following the court's order of May 17, 1954, the court issued an opinion and judgments regarding relief on May 31, 1955. This followed arguments before the court from April 11-14, 1955. John Harlan had replaced Robert Jackson on the court.

State attorney generals met with the Court and presented briefs which addressed relief.

BROWN ET AL. v. BOARD OF EDUCATION OF TOPEKA ET AL.
APPEAL FROM THE UNITED STATES DISTRICT COURT FOR THE DISTRICT OF KANSAS.

Reargued on the question of relief April 11-14, 1955—Opinion and judgments announced May 31, 1955.

1. Racial discrimination in public education is unconstitutional, 347 U.S. 483, 497, and all provisions of federal, state or local law requiring or permitting such discrimination must yield to this principle.

2. The judgments below (except that in the Delaware case) are reversed and the cases are remanded to the District Courts to take such proceedings and enter such orders and decrees consistent with this opinion as are necessary and proper to admit the parties to these cases to public schools on a racially nondiscriminatory basis with all deliberate speed.

    (a) School authorities have the primary responsibility for elucidating, assessing and solving the varied local school

problems which may require solution
fully implementing the governing constitutional principles.

(b) Courts will have to consider whether
the action of school authorities constitutes good faith implementation of the
governing constitutional principles.

(c) Because of their proximity to local conditions and the possible need for further hearings, the courts which originally heard these cases can best perform
this judicial appraisal.

(d) In fashioning and effectuating the
decrees, the courts will be guided by
equitable principles-characterized by a
practical flexibility in shaping remedies
and facility for adjusting and reconciling public and private needs.

(e) At stake is the personal interest of the
plaintiffs in admission to public schools
as soon as practicable on a nondiscriminatory basis.

(f) Courts of equity may properly take
into account the public interest in the
elimination in a systematic and effective manner of a variety of obstacles
in making the transition to school systems operated in accordance with the
constitutional principles enunciated in
347 U.S. 483, 497; but the vitality of
these constitutional principles cannot
be allowed to yield simply because of
disagreement with them.

(g) While giving weight to these public
and private considerations, the courts
will require that the defendants make

a prompt and reasonable start toward full compliance with the ruling of this Court.

(h) Once such a start has been made, the courts may find that additional time is necessary to carry out the ruling in an effective manner.

(i) The burden rests on the defendants to establish that additional time is necessary in the public interest and is consistent with good faith compliance at the earliest practicable date,

(j) The courts may consider problems related to administration, arising from the physical condition or the school plant, the school transportation system, personnel, revision of school districts and attendance areas into compact units to achieve a system of determining admission to the public schools on a nonracial basis, and revision of local laws and regulations which may be necessary in solving the foregoing problems.

(k) The courts will also consider the adequacy of any plans the defendants may propose to meet these problems and to effectuate a transition to a racially nondiscriminatory school system.

(l) During the period of transition, the courts will retain jurisdiction of these cases.

3. The judgment in the Delaware case, ordering the immediate admission of the plaintiffs to schools previously attended only by

white children, is affirmed on the basis of the principles stated by this court in its opinion, 347 U.S. 483; but the case is remanded to the Supreme Court of Delaware for such further proceedings as that Court may deem necessary in the light of this opinion. P. 301. 98 F. Supp. 797, 103 F. Supp. 920, 103 F. Supp. 337 and judgment in No, 4, reversed and remanded. 91 A. ed 137, affirmed and remanded.

MR CHIEF JUSTICE WARREN delivered the opinion of the Court.

These cases were decided on May 17, 1954. The opinions of that date declaring the fundamental principle that racial discrimination in public education is unconstitutional, are incorporated herein by reference. All provisions of federal, state, or local law requiring or permitting such discrimination must yield to this principle. There remains for consideration the manner in which relief is to be accorded.

Because these cases arose under different local conditions and their disposition will involve a variety of local problems, we requested further argument of the question of relief. In view of the nationwide importance of the decision, we invited the Attorney General of the United States and the Attorneys General of all states requiring or permitting racial discrimination in public education to present their views on that question. The parties, the United States, and the States of Florida, North Carolina, Arkansas, Oklahoma, Maryland, and Texas filed briefs and participated in the oral arguments.

Their presentations were informative and helpful to the Court in its consideration of the complexities arising from the transition to a system of public education freed of racial discrimination. The presentations also demonstrated that substantial steps to eliminate racial discrimination in public schools have already been taken, not only in some of the communities in which these cases arose, but in some of the states appearing as amici curiae, and in other states as well. Substantial progress has been made in the District of Columbia and in the communities in Kansas and Delaware involved in this litigation. The defendants in the cases coming to us from South Carolina and Virginia are awaiting the decision of this Court concerning relief.

Full implementation of these constitutional principles may require solution of varied local school problems. School authorities have the primary responsibility for elucidating, assessing, and solving these problems; courts will have to consider whether the action of school authorities constitutes good faith implementation of the governing constitutional principles. Because of their proximity to local conditions and the possible need for further hearings, the courts which originally heard these cases can best perform this judicial appraisal. Accordingly, we believe it appropriate to remand the cases to those courts.

In fashioning and effectuating the decrees, the courts will be guided by equitable principles. Traditionally, equity has been characterized by a practical flexibility in shaping its remedies and by a facility for adjusting and reconciling public and private needs. These cases call for the exercise of these traditional attributes of equity power. At stake is the personal interest of the plaintiffs in admission to public schools as soon as practicable on a nondiscriminatory basis. To effectuate this interest may call for elimination of a variety of obstacles in making the transition to school systems operated in accordance with the constitutional principles set forth in our May 17, 1954, decision. Courts of equity may properly take into account the public interest in the elimination of such obstacles in a systematic and effective manner. But it should go without saying that the vitality of these constitutional principles cannot be allowed to yield simply because of disagreement with them.

While giving weight to these public and private considerations, the courts will require that the defendants make a prompt and reasonable start toward full compliance with our May 17, 1954, ruling. Once such a start has been made, the courts may find that additional time is necessary to carry out the ruling in an effective manner. The burden rests upon the defendants to establish that such time is necessary in the public interest and is consistent with good faith compliance at the earliest practicable date. To that end, the courts may consider problems related to administration, arising from the physical condition of the school plant, the school transportation system, personnel, revision of school districts and attendance areas into compact units to achieve a system of determining admission to the public schools on a nonracial basis, and revision of local laws and regulations which may be necessary in solving the foregoing problems. They will also consider the adequacy of any plans the defendants may propose to meet these problems

and to effectuate a transition to a racially nondiscriminatory school system. During this period of
transition, the courts will retain jurisdiction of
these cases.

The judgments below, except that in the
Delaware case, are accordingly reversed and the
cases are remanded to the District Courts to
take such proceedings and enter such orders and
decrees consistent with this opinion as are necessary and proper to admit to public schools on a
racially nondiscriminatory basis with all deliberate speed the parties to these cases. The judgment
in the Delaware case—ordering the immediate
admission of the plaintiffs to schools previously
attended only by white children—is affirmed
on the basis of the principles stated in our May
17, 1954, opinion, but the case is remanded to
the Supreme Court of Delaware for such further
proceedings as that Court may deem necessary in
light of this opinion.

IT IS SO ORDERED.

Impact of *Brown*

So, even with the outlawing of *Plessey v. Ferguson*, schools did not integrate "with all deliberate speed" as required by *Brown v. Board of Education of Topeka, Kansas*, in 1954. The practice of the South became delay, delay, delay, resist, resist, resist. These practices were designed to give those who didn't want to integrate time to build and recruit white kids to form private academies all across the South. Many of these private academies continue to this day. The majority of public schools were not integrated until the 1970s. There are a number of practices today which keep our students separated in public schools.

The use of test scores keeps our students separated. Because tests are not "culture fair," white students often perform better than black students. Classes are often set up using test score results, often putting white students in "accelerated" or more "academic" classes than their black counterparts. This practice in some schools often put black students in "vocational" classes and white students in "academic" classes. According to an article in the *News & Observer* newspaper of Raleigh, North Carolina, April 12, 1992, "White, Black and Asian faces mix in the halls of Hunter Elementary, a downtown school seems the epitome of 1990s integration. But when the bell rings and children file into classrooms, Hunter appears to snap back to another decade—the segregated 1950s."

"Neighborhood" schools also keep our students separated. There is a great return to neighborhood schools. Certain housing, usually unaffordable by most blacks, are often established with schools being built for these more affluent neighborhoods. Busing is no longer used to integrate these types of schools.

The use of special education keeps our students separated. More black students are referred to special education than white students, especially black boys. Since integration, more and more areas of special education have been created. More and more psychological and social areas have been established. This has allowed teachers to make more referrals to special education. Since the number of black teachers has diminished significantly since integration, the increase in numbers of black students in special education was inevitable.

The two remarkable figures discussed in this segment were honored by a small rural county in South Carolina. The name of the county is Williamsburg.

During the year 1993, the town of Kingstree and the County of Williamsburg renamed two of their main highways in honor of Dr. Martin Luther King Jr. and Supreme Court Justice Thurgood Marshall. In addition to the renaming of the two highways, a local group, named the Williamsburg County Committee of 101, made a request to the Williamsburg County Council that two monuments honoring these two men be placed on the Williamsburg County Courthouse grounds. The request was granted, and the monuments were dedicated in August 1993.

The twenty-fifth anniversary of the establishment of the monuments was held on August 24–25, 2018, in Kingstree. One of the main speakers at the event was this writer.

25TH COMMEMORATIVE CELEBRATION
OF
Installation of Monuments
Honoring

The Late
DR. MARTIN LUTHER KING JR.

The Late
SUPREME COURT JUSTICE THURGOOD MARSHALL

Friday
AUGUST 24, 2018

Saturday
AUGUST 25, 2018

"Lifting the Veil of Ignorance" in a Southern predominantly black county through the activities of a locally established community organization—the Williamsburg County Committee of 101

DR. JAMES A. FRANKLIN SR.

THE WILLIAMSBURG COUNTY
COMMITTEE OF 101

(The Early Years)
(Written in Observance of the Twenty-Fifth Anniversary
of the King-Marshall Celebration, August 24, 2018)

The Williamsburg County Committee of 101 (also referred to as Committee of 101) was incorporated as a nonprofit corporation on January 25, 1993, by the State of South Carolina.

Prior to its formation, several activities and events had occurred that may have influenced the establishment of the organization. Before the 1980s, the position of superintendent of Williamsburg County School had been an elected position. The creation of the appointed position brought to the forefront the first black superintendent of schools. This began the transition from a white paternalistic type of atmosphere to one more black control. Later, a new type of black leadership was elected to the South Carolina House of Representatives from Williamsburg County.

Under the leadership of the new superintendent, it was determined that the county needed to consolidate some of its schools. We had too many high schools, and we still had two all-black schools, now more than ten years after the integration of schools. There was black and white resistance to these changes. As a part of the results of consolidation, computer laboratories were established in all high schools, and JROTC programs were implemented in the county. There were savings in staff and material costs; a greater variety of subjects were available for students, and the county ended the last vestiges of segregated schools.

Another practice, which was addressed during the administration of this new superintendent was the practice of salary alignments. If an employee of the Williamsburg County School District wanted to borrow from a local lending institution, his/her check was made out to the lending institution jointly with the name of the employee, as a condition to getting the loan. In essence, the employee's check had to be cashed and payment made to the lender before the employee could get the remainder of the check. Strangely enough, most of the opposition to getting rid of the salary assignment came from school district employees. It did not seem to matter that the employee's self-esteem, higher interest rates, and paternalistic practice had been affected by this practice.

Before this change, there was an alternative to local citizens getting money, and that was the prevalence of loan sharks. Loan sharks were lending money with a 25 percent return on their money. And it was not being taxed by the government because it was not reported.

In addressing these and other backward practices, the new black superintendent was negotiated to leave his position.

One of the most powerful political positions left for Williamsburg County representation was that of the South Carolina Senate seat. It was anticipated that a young former human resources manager for a prominent industry in the county and local businessman, who happened to be black would easily defeat the incumbent senator who happened to be white. This was not to be. The black candidate was defeated. After his defeat, the whispers of "house Negroes" and "slave mentality" began to creep into conversations.

Because of these and other events, a local retired county agent and schoolteacher decided that the people needed a *voice*. He established and published a newspaper by that same name. The legacy of the late James "Jim" Fitts is interwoven into the life of the Committee of 101. Although he worked for thirteen years with the public schools and for twenty years with the Clemson University Extension Service, Jim's greatest impact was made after he had retired. He represented much of the conscience of the black community in Williamsburg County.

Mr. Fitts started the *Voice* on January 15, 1987. It was the late Mr. Alvin "Al" White, who was often referred to as Mr. Fitts's closest associate, who wrote of Mr. Fitts in the first edition of the *Voice*: "One of his fondest memories of his accomplishments in the public schools was when he coached a special education student who won a district public speaking contest." Al went on to say, "Jim put together the *Voice* newspaper to wake up a sleeping giant in Williamsburg

County, Black People." Jim's famous words when he started the *Voice* were "Hellbent to Go!"

Jim's team at the *Voice* included Mr. Keith Hunter, sales/circulation manager; Mrs. Pearl Brown, treasurer; Mr. Alvin White and Mrs. Selma Conyers, news editors; Ms. Elma Walker, secretary; Rev. Granville Hicks, religious editor; and Mr. Ludrick Cooper, photographer.

Two of Hunter's most notable writings were "The Dream of Dr. King Lingers" and "Paul Murray, County's First Black Elected Official." Often, the *Voice* told us about news that we did not get from the mainstream media. For example, we learned that Dr. King was more recognized in foreign countries than in the United States. Not only did the State of Israel honor Dr. King with a special day on January 20, 1986, but that same country had named the Dr. Martin Luther King Jr. Memorial Forest in 1976. The twenty-thousand-tree forest is located in Galilee.

The number 101 was magic back in the day. When Mr. Fred Fulton organized the Williamsburg County Mass Choir to honor Dr. Martin Luther King Jr. in 1987, he had 101 members from twelve churches to sing at Mt. Zion United Methodist Church on January 18, 1987. Also, the number 101 was borrowed from South Carolina State University's Marching Band. The state marching band celebrated when it got 101 students to participate in the band. Although the number of members in the band exceeds 101, the university's band is known today as the Marching 101. The black community finally heeded Mr. Al White's note of "a sleeping giant" (also borrowed from a comment about the United States from the attack on Pearl Harbor), and the Williamsburg County Committee of 101 was born.

The Committee of 101 was started with five major purposes: (1) to award scholarships; (2) to promote better government; (3) to assist in voter registration and participation; (4) to advance the field of education through research, applied science, and community involvement; and (5) to make the community aware of social and educational issues which impact it. The signers as declarants and petitioners on the application for a state charter for the Committee of 101 were Mrs. W. Ann Bartelle, Mrs. Julia McFadden, Mr. Alex Chatman, and Dr. James A. Franklin Sr.

The official registry of the certificate of mailings for the state charter included the following: Ms. Patricia Blake, Mr. Harold Brunson, Mrs. Carrie Brock, Mrs. Alyce Bettard, Ms. Melloney Brown, Ms. Lorene Bradley, Mr. Laurie Alston, Mrs. Fannie Watson, Mrs. Abigail Webb, Mr. Irene Reed Singletary, Mrs. Vernell Starks, Mrs. Jennie Thompson, Mr. John Scott, Mrs. Altormeaze Shaw, Mrs. Louretha Young, Mr. Julius Wilson, Mr. Eddie Woods, Rev. Frankie White, Ms. Annie Williams, Ms. Queen Wallace, Mrs. Tirah Dukes, Mr. Benjamin Ervin, Mr. Calvin Faison, Mr. Jerry Dicks. Mr. and Mrs. Charles Douglas, Ms. Dorothy Bufkin, Mr. and Mrs. Mack Burgess, Ms. Rena Giles, Ms. Vernell Graham, Rev. Frankie Fulmore, Ms. Lila Fulton, Mr. James Fitts, Ms. Ellarine Franklin, Ms. Gladys Franklin, Mrs. Lillie McGill, Mr. William McIlwain, Mrs. Ethel Israel, Mr. Franklin McClary, Mrs. Dorothy Holeman, Mrs. Linda Huell, Rev. Keith Hunter, Mrs. Barbara Pendergrass, Mrs. Jeanette Pendergrass, Mr. and Mrs. Booker T. Pressley, Ms. Shirley McKnight, Mr. John Moore, Mr. and Mrs. Andy McKnight, Mr. Harrison McKnight Sr., and Mr. Paul McKnight.

The early leaders of Committee of 101 were Dr. James A. Franklin Sr. (president), Mr. Alex Chatman (vice president), Mrs. Hester Gadsden (secretary), and Mrs. Altormeaze Shaw (treasurer). The board of directors were Mrs. Veronica Alston, Attorney Ronnie Sabb, Mr. Stanley Pasley, Mr. Adam Johnson, Mrs. Regina McKnight, Mr. Alvin White, Mr. W. B. Wilson, and Mr. Joseph Brown. The Committee of 101 awarded scholarships to deserving high school seniors, one at each high school in 1995. The three winners were Gary Nesmith of C. E. Murray High School, Robin Cooper of Hemingway High School, and Paulette Henderson of Kingstree Senior High School. Six criteria were used for the selection of the scholarship winners: scholarship, financial need, years matriculated in a Williamsburg County High School, a writing assignment, principal's recommendation, and a personal interview. The Screening and Selection Committee for 1995 were Mr. Winfred Murdaugh,

Mrs. Emma Cooper, Mrs. Lillian Robinson, Mrs. Priscilla McClary, and Mrs. Angela Fulton.

A highlight of the work of Committee 101 was the King-Marshall Celebration, which was held August 20–21, 1993. The celebration included a memorial banquet, the dedication of streets, a parade, and the memorial dedication.

Leading up to the King-Marshall Celebration, the members of 101 discussed what other communities had done to honor Dr. Martin Luther King Jr. and Supreme Court Justice Thurgood Marshall. The greatness of Supreme Court Justice Thurgood Marshall had demonstrated throughout his career, going back to the Summerton case on school desegregation, which became a part of the *Brown* case. The *Brown v. the Board of Education of Topeka, Kansas* case outlawed the *Plessy v. Ferguson* case of 1896 (separate but equal) on school segregation. After 1954, in his role as a US circuit judge and the US solicitor general and during his tenure on the Supreme Court, Marshall proved to be one of America's greatest jurists and a strong proponent of the rule of law.

Dr. Martin Luther King Jr., a student of the great educator and orator Dr. Benjamin E. Mays, influenced civil rights more than any other single individual in modern history. This black preacher and activist held degrees from Morehouse College and Boston University. He founded the Southern Christian Leadership Conference. He led the successful Montgomery bus boycott, which lasted for 381 days. Like Mays, King was an outstanding orator and intellect who led and motivated black and white citizens to work for the inclusion of all people into the fabric of American life. He subjected his body to beatings and numerous jail times while being committed to the use of nonviolence in his protests against "man's inhumanity to man." His book *Why We Can't Wait* and his letter from a Birmingham jail brought new meanings to human dignity, citizenship, and the role of the clergy. This Nobel Peace Prize winner was a modern "drum major" for justice and equality, for which he gave the "ultimate sacrifice."

The Committee of 101 felt that it needed to do something in Williamsburg County. The committee decided to request of the town of Kingstree and the county of Williamsburg that streets be named for these great Americans and that two memorials be established on the courthouse grounds. The committee was very excited when permission was granted by these two governmental bodies.

All of this led up to the most memorable occasions in the history of Williamsburg County: *The King-Marshall Celebration of 1993.* The celebration included a memorial banquet, the dedication of street, a parade, and the memorial dedication. Greetings and congratulations came from all over America—President Bill Clinton, Supreme Court Justice Warren Burger, Congressman Jim Clyburn, Governor Carroll Campbell, SC Black Caucus Chairman Joe E. Brown, and numerous college presidents. Other celebrated participants were Vernon King, a nephew of Dr. King, Parade Marshall, and songstress Ms. Kimberly Allen, who reigned as the first black lady named Miss South Carolina.

As part of the celebration, the committee published a booklet entitled *King-Marshall: A Celebration.* The booklet was a tribute to the committee's honorees.

Although the *Voice* newspaper was no longer in existence when the Committee of 101 was established, another newspaper, the *Black River Gazette*, was started in 1995.

The Committee of 101 continued to be involved in community activism. The Old-Fashioned Days Festival was a major annual event. Most persons seemed to enjoy the event and did not see any part of it as offensive, but a significant number of black citizens saw the scooping up of horse waste by black men and black women dressed in plantation garb, riding on bales of hay and wagon "tailgates" as demeaning and insensitive for modern festivals. Reactions from committee members helped to influence the name change to Barbecue Festival.

Members of the Committee of 101 influenced a campaign to take place at Kingstree Senior High School to change the antiquated mascot of the boll weevil. Like the Old-Fashioned Days Festival, the mascot was changed from boll weevil to jaguar.

Another major issue that caused concern for Committee 101 was the move by Hemingway to leave Williamsburg County to be annexed into Florence County. Once the Petition had been signed by Hemingway with the Office of the Governor, the Committee 101 helped to influence the Williamsburg County School Board to fight this effort by the town of Hemingway to be annexed into a predominantly white county from a predominantly black county. Attorney Brenda Riddix Smalls was contacted to file a legal brief with the federal courts against the town of Hemingway and against the Office of the Governor. Ultimately, a three-judge federal panel ruled in favor of the school district, which barred the annexation.

When the school district decided that it needed a new school, a public group was started to generate support for a referendum to be presented to the voters for a new school. The public group was finally chaired by Attorney Ronnie Sab. Most of the citizens did not vote to approve the referendum. Members of the Committee of 101 knew of an option to build a new school. The option was lease purchase. Members of the committee presented this option to the school board. It was approved, and ultimately, a new school and stadium were built.

During the early years of the organization, there were other memorable events that were influenced by the Committee of 101:

- The Patriot's Day Parade Celebration was inaugurated on April 30, 1994.
- The writing of a proposal by committee members helped the Williamsburg-Lake City area to be named the Williamsburg-Lake City Enterprise Community by the United States Department of Agriculture.
- The school district was awarded $119,000 in school incentive money for academic excellence and was named an Incentive Award District by the State Department of Education.
- The Greeleyville Elementary School was named a National Blue Ribbon School with the school and school district being recognized by President Bill Clinton at the White House in Washington, DC.
- The Hurricane Andrew Relief Transfer Truck took a truckload of goods and financial contributions by some mem-

bers of the Committee of 101 and other school officials to Homestead, Florida, during the weekend of August 28, 1992.

At the time, Hurricane Andrew was the worst natural disaster in the United States, causing more than $30 million in damages and leaving more than eighty thousand persons without shelter. A reporter wrote, "Residents of South Florida had faced the fury of hell." Eight brave volunteers traveled to Homestead: Mr. William Anderson, Mr. James Bartelle, Ms. Irene Reed, Ms. Jacqueline Washington, Mr. Mack Burgess, Mr. Richard Saxon, Dr. James A. Franklin Sr., and truck owner and driver, Mr. Michael McKenzie.

Not only did the group carry the needed food and supplies to southern Florida, they helped to clear debris, fed the victims, and provided comfort to the homeless.

So you see, the Williamsburg County Committee of 101 was very involved in community activism. We are proud of the very important impact that the Committee had on improving the climate and conditions of Williamsburg County's citizens.

Touched by the Challenger Disaster

On January 28, 1986, the Space Shuttle Challenger blew up off the coast of Florida. On that fateful day, I lost a fraternity brother, Dr. Ronald E. McNair. We were both members of the Omega Psi Phi Fraternity, Inc.

Ronald graduated as valedictorian from Carver High School in Lake City, South Carolina, in 1967. He received his bachelor's degree in Physics from North Carolina A.&T. State University in 1971. After graduating from A.&T., Ronald attended M.I.T., where he received his Ph. D. Degree in Physics in 1976.

Dr. McNair was selected as an astronaut candidate in January on 1978. After his one year of training, he was selected as a Mission Specialist Astronaut, and was assigned to the Challenger. Ronald became the second African American Astronaut to fly in space on February 3, 1984. The successful flight lasted until February 11th.

After his successful mission, his fraternity held a reception for him near his hometown of Lake City in the town of Kingstree, South Carolina. The reception was held on Thursday, April 12, 1984, at 7:00 p.m. The location of the reception was 423 School Street.

At the reception, he talked about his journey from lake City, becoming better educated, and performed a variety of experiments and studies at home and abroad. Naturally, he talked of his training and mission as an astronaut. This was the most interesting and exciting. To say the least, we were, and still are, very proud of Dr. Ronald E. McNair. During his young life, he played a positive impact on his community, his state, and his country. We can't imagine what he would have accomplished, had he lived.

Ronald was also an accomplished saxophone player. He had planned to play and record during his last mission in space.

Photo and program for the Dr. Ronald E. McNair Reception in Kingstree, South Carolina. Ronald is in the center of the photo wearing a dark coat.

Dr. Ronald E. McNair is a native of Lake City, South Carolina where he graduated from Carver High School. He received the Bachelor of Science Degree from A & T State University, Greensboro, North Carolina and the Doctor of Philosophy Degree from the Massachusetts Institute of Technology (M.I.T.).

Presently Dr. McNair is an Astronaut with the National Aeronautic and Space Administration (NASA) of the United States Government. Dr. McNair made his first space mission in February aboard the Space Shuttle Challenger.

PROGRAMME

Presiding......Charles L. Johnson, Sr.

Remarks.........Columbus J. Giles, Sr.

Remarks..............Ernest R. Reeves

Presentation...Charles L. Johnson, Sr.

Presentation of Guest....Clyde A. Bess
Basileus
Delta RHO Chapter
Omega PSI PHI

Remarks..........Dr. Ronald E. McNair

Remarks.............James A. Franklin

Autographs/Pictures.........Dr. McNair

The Challenger disaster took Ronald and six of his colleague from us. NASA PHOTO

Killed in the Challenger disaster were: (Front row, l-r): Francis R. Scobee, Commander; Michael Smith, Pilot; and Ronald E. McNair, Mission Specialist. (Second row, l-r): Ellison Onizuka, Mission Specialist; Judith Resnik, Mission Specialist; Gregory Jarvis, Payload Specialist; and Christa McAuliffe, Payload Specialist, Teacher. Christa was to be the first teacher to fly into space. She left us with those famouse words: "I touch the futue. I teach."

A Patriotic Family and 9/11

MY FAMILY HAS always been strong patriotic Americans. Five of my eight brothers served in the United States Navy. Two of my brothers served in World War II: Edward Franklin and Robert Franklin. The ship on which they were traveling was bombed during the war, but they were not harmed. Another brother, John Thomas Franklin, served during the Korean War although he was not assigned to combat. My other two brothers, Joe Louis Franklin and Roosevelt Franklin, served after the Korean War. My nephew, Thaddeus Chamberlain, retired from the Navy. I have several other nephews and nieces who serve our country in the Navy. We are truly a Navy family.

On a personal note, I had the desire to go into the Navy in 1965. I applied, passed all written tests, passed all physical tests, and had selected the OTS (Officer Training Service) at San Diego, California; but at the eleventh hour, I was denied admission to OTS because the Navy said that my eyesight could not be corrected to 20/20. I was devastated. My goal was to be a line officer, with the hope that I would one day command my own ship. The response of my senior classmates was that this was discrimination; after all, these were the 1960s.

I was in high cotton at the time. I was the only one in my graduating major who made an A on the National Teachers Examination. This was the test that determined your salary as a teacher in South Carolina. I had told my classmates that this A would not be of benefit to me because I was going into the Navy as an officer.

As with all Americans, my family was saddened and angry with the events of 9/11. I have included my story.

GROUND ZERO VISITED
BEFORE THE DUST SETTLED

I remember the summer of terror of 2001. As I worked in the office with some students, we were summoned across the hall to a classroom where the news was being brought to the world of what had happened. As I watched the news, in shock and in disbelief, I stood there, motionless for about thirty minutes, until I thought, "Hey, my son is in Washington. I need to get in touch with him."

Less than one month earlier, I had taken my son to Washington to begin his first job out of Duke University Law School as an attorney with the Federal Trade Commission.

The next few hours were the longest of my life. I could not reach my son. The telephones were down. As I persisted, one operator tried to reroute the calls, but the lines that she found operating were jammed. I finally reached my son around 4:00 p.m. He had gone to work, but all government offices shut down, and all employees were sent home. He was okay! What a sigh of relief! The Pentagon was minutes away from where he lived and he worked on Pennsylvania Avenue, just a few blocks from the White House.

Since that day, he had always wanted to go to Ground Zero. When I went to visit him during the weekend after 9/11, he insisted that we go to New York.

After leaving work, at approximately 5:30 p.m. on Friday, I traveled most of the night and arrived at my son's apartment at 4:45 a.m., with a couple of stops along the way. After a short nap, we headed to the Big Apple.

When we arrived in New York City, we were lucky in that we got a parking space one block from Ground Zero.

A small cloud of dust greeted us as we arrived at the site.

Having traveled to the World Trade Center in July of that year, with my sister Juanita and three nieces, we never imagined that less than two months later, the towers would no longer stately gleam their beauty across the New York sky.

As we entered the viewing area, I could imagine the firemen, health care workers, police, and all the terrified persons running away from what must have been hell on earth as the first tower fell and then the second tower. There we were at that same site.

The towers, which we visited two months before that fateful day, were now gone. What is left is a huge hole in the ground, with several pieces of earth moving and excavation equipment on the hole's floor, and a temporary road down into this massive pit. There is not much to see now except the cross-section of what was an underground garage. Of course, the hole looked somewhat like a canyon.

Visitors were greeted by a huge metal cross, which was made from steel beams, which previously supported the massive towers.

The flag which once flew with its colors of red, white, and blue on a piece of heavy-duty equipment, has now faded, but the spirit of those almost three thousand who died on that fateful day seemed to surround us as we reflected on the trauma of 9/11.

As I reflected, I remembered that on that day, our differences didn't matter. Our beloved America had been attacked.

It seemed such a shame that something so big, something so majestic, and something that took so many years to build, could be brought down so fast.

I could imagine persons on the ninetieth floor watching the second plane as it approached the tower. With disbelief and fear, they must have thought, "My God, this is not happening."

Only a terrorist could have thought of such a demonic plot. Only a terrorist could have been brainwashed to think that he was being immortalized as an angel by taking the lives of thousands of innocent people, including his own.

My son took a camera. He took pictures, here, there, everywhere. As the shutter snapped, it broke the silence of a quiet solemn evening from a crowd, which was obviously involved in their own meditation. To get some clear pictures, without the wire as an obstruction, my son stood up on the curbing of the fence. The "Keep Off the Fence" signs did not sway his determination to capture the full view of Ground Zero.

There were two ways to view Ground Zero. One could view this giant hole from the ground level, or one could view it from three flights up inside a glass enclosure. This higher level diminished the feel of Ground Zero. We were closer on the ground with only the wire barrier separating us from what also looked like the results of a fifty-ton bomb.

The surrounding buildings looked as though they had been fire-bombed and damaged from flying bomb shrapnel, which had exploded nearby.

The Memorial Wall had flowers, flags, canvas, pictures, boards, and a host of other types of memorials. With the thousands of names and symbols on all these items, my son did find some small spaces for us to leave a thought, a sympathetic message, a symbol, or a prayer.

The countless pictures which I had seen on television were no match to the very moving experience of standing there and feeling the emotion of the immortalized Ground Zero.

The wind provided the occasional smell of the dust coming from below. But there were the men in white suits who were accompanied by a white truck, as they were providing a ventilation system for the persons working below. We realized that the dust that sometimes engulfed us may have been stirred by this system.

As we observed the others who also made the pilgrimage to Ground Zero, we could see the sadness, the fear, and yes, the anger in their eyes and on their faces. There were no "Be Quiet!" signs or "Noise is Prohibited!" signs. None were needed. The crowd seemed overwhelmed with shock and sadness.

There was no talking. Everyone just seemed to be in awe of the sight.

As we gazed over this massive cavity in the earth, I am sure that others were also saddened too, as the media had told us that some of the victims' remains were never to be found, and for those families, there will never be closure.

While we were mourning the victims, I am sure that countless persons in the crowd felt as I did. I wanted to know how to punish the sponsors of the invaders so that no foreign foe would bring this type of terror to our shores again—to Pennsylvania, to the Pentagon, and to this city, or to anywhere else in the USA.

I wondered, what have we done so cruel to cause anyone to hate us so much? Through foreign aid, we have shared our bounty with the world. Just a few blocks away stood the United Nations building, the basic code of which is in a direct contradiction of what happened to us on that September morning.

The USA bled that day! Ground Zero reminded us that the wound was still open. It also reminded us that this generation of US citizens may never heal from such a tragedy. Yes, it, too, will be another day, which will live in infamy.

One could only imagine the pain, the fear, and the horror of that day—the running, the screams, the fire, the smoke, and the floors falling on top of the other, carrying with them death and destruction.

One could only imagine standing in the place where victims jumped to their deaths. Oh, what a hallowed place, this Ground Zero!

After a few hours, we slowly walked away.

I am sure that everyone who visited the sight left a part of themselves behind. The sadness, the autographs, the pain, the anger, the tears, and the prayers—oh, but then there was the hope, the strength, the fortitude, the pride, and the determination, which invigorated us as we drove past the Empire State Building, which now had returned as King of the Skies in New York City.

We remember the victims and their families today, and we will remember the horrors of that day for as long as we shall live.

May God bless the United States of America!

Folkways and Mores Geared toward Blacks in the Old South

The Brown Paper Bag

In poor communities, there was a use for most things that we encountered. The use of the brown paper bag in our community received a lot of attention.

The brown paper bag became a hat on the female's head when it rained.

The brown paper bag became rollers to curl freshly pressed, or hot combed hair of females.

The brown paper bag became toilet paper in the outhouse.

The brown paper bag became a lunch bag for students to carry their lunch to school.

The brown paper bag became a bag to conceal the whiskey bought from the liquor store or from the bootlegger.

The brown paper bag was used to carry groceries from the grocery store.

The brown paper bag was used to light the fire in the fireplace or stove.

The brown paper bag was used to light the wick on the kerosene lamps.

The brown paper bag was used to light cigarettes, cigars, and smoking pipes.

The brown paper bag was starched and used to cover holes in the walls of poor people to keep the wind out during winter months.

The brown paper bag was used as a change purse by poor people.

The brown paper bag was used as a garbage bag in the houses of poor people.

Children would use the brown paper bag by blowing air into the bag, twisting the opening of the bag, now filled with air, and then hit the bottom of the bag creating a small "explosion." This activity was also used to play pranks on others.

Black Gravediggers

The gravediggers for McCain Funeral Home, Keown Funeral Home, and later Walker-Letman Funeral Home were all black men. During this time, graves were dug with picks and shovels. While it may sound simple, there was an art form to digging a grave, from location, size, depth, and width.

One odd thing about some of the South, black men dug the graves of white people but were not allowed to cover those graves. The rumor in my hometown was that blacks were not allowed to throw dirt on a white person's face.

This was in connection with "Don't look that white person in the eye," "Get off the street to let that white person pass," "Don't whistle at a white woman," and "You cannot drink a small Coke, they are for white people."

Negro Baseball League

In the South, we heard about the Negro Baseball League. No, they were not on television; however, they may have been on some local black-operated radio stations.

The black press may have made note of the Negro Leagues in their coverage. Nationally, we had the newspapers *Afro American* and the *Journal and Guide*, to name two such newspapers. *Ebony*, *Jet*, *Sepia*, and other black-oriented magazines may have covered the Negro Baseball League. Some of the teams were the Homestead Grays and the Kansas City Monarchs.

The players in the Negro League often used surplus or used bats and supplies, which were no longer needed by the white Major Leagues.

Snuff

It was not respectful for black women to smoke cigarettes, so a large number of black women dipped snuff. Snuff was a tobacco-based product, which came in small round silver cans. Ladies would take a pinch of the snuff from the can and place the snuff between the lower lip and the front teeth. Obviously, this created the need to spit because if they swallowed the juice from the snuff, it would make them sick. This created the need for a spit bucket. A spit bucket or spittoon was always nearby unless they were outdoors. The pleasure experienced by men who smoked or chewed tobacco seemed to be provided for the women who dipped snuff.

Old-fashioned snuff is not like today's smokeless tobacco or ground tobacco, which is sniffed through the nose. Snuff use evolved from snuff use through the nose to what it became in the black and poor communities—placing moist snuff between the lower lip and the front teeth. Usually, you could tell a snuff user by the bulge of the lower lip and the need for the person to spit.

Burying the Dead

Back in the day, prior to the early 1950s, there were no black-owned funeral homes in my hometown of McCormick. The G. P. McCain Funeral Home and the Keown Funeral Home buried both blacks and whites. The H. W. Walker family, a black family, moved to McCormick in the late 1940s / early 1950s. Mr. Walker, along with Mr. Herbert Letman, purchased the black service component from the McCain Funeral Home. They started the Walker-Letman Funeral Home. The Walker's brought the expertise, funeral director, and embalmer; however, Mr. Letman was a local black businessman who had land and logging holdings. The Walker's later bought out Mr. Letman, and the business became the Walker Funeral Home.

Uncle Toms

There were a lot of Uncle Toms in the Old South. An Uncle Tom was a sell-out person, a black person who thought that he/she could benefit from turning their backs on other black people. This person was labeled as a traitor or a backstabber, a black person who colluded with white people to undermine the success of another black person.

Common Sayings/Folkways in My Hometown of McCormick

The dying white man would say, "Lord, please don't take me, take a nigger."

"I know that's the truth because a white man said so."

The black mother would tell her child, "If you don't sit down, I will knock you into next week."

The black mother would tell her children, "It's storming outside. Be quiet. Sit in the corner away from the window. Let the Lord do his work."

"Don't walk under that ladder. You will have bad luck."

"Nigger, come here, let me place my feet on your stomach (to draw the infirmities from his body)."

"If a black cat crossed in front of you, you will have bad luck."

"If two of you are walking down the street and came up to a pole in the street or sidewalk, don't split the pole, or you will have bad luck. Both of you must walk on the same side of the pole."

"If a man visits you on New Year's Day, your family will have good luck."

"If you are telling the truth, cross your heart, and hope to die (if you aren't)."

"If you stomp your toe, turn around and spit."

"Get off the sidewalk if you are meeting a white woman."

"Never look a white man in his face. If you do, it is a sign of disrespect."

"Go out to the tree and get me a limb so that I can whip your behind."

"Always grin at the white man's jokes (whether funny or not)."

"They can order us to integrate, but they can't tell us what rooms to rent to blacks."

"They can order us to integrate our restaurants, but they can't tell us where to sit blacks."

"Never pass a white person driving on the highway."

"They can order us to integrate, but they can't tell us what rooms to rent to blacks."

"They can order us to integrate our restaurants, but they can't tell us where to sit blacks."

Mississippi was considered the worst state for blacks back in the day. Children would say "What has four eyes and can't see? Mississippi!" and "Mississippi! Mississippi! My eye—crooked letter, crooked letter, eye, crooked letter, crooked letter, eye, humpback, humpback, eye!"

Degrading names for Blacks on Food Items in
Sayings and in Publications of the Old South

Old Black Joe Black Eyed Peas
"Coon" when referring to black men
"Boy" when referring to black men
Little Black Joe Crowder Peas
Old Black Joe Grease
"Mammy" when referring to black women
"Girl" when referring to black women
Rastus Cream of Wheat
Aunt Jemima Pancake Mix
"Uncle Tom" when referring to black men who told of the activities
of black people
Uncle Ben's Rice
Old Black Joe Peas and Beans
Pictures of "niggers" eating watermelon
Nigger Hair Smoking Tobacco
Nigger Head Shrimp
"Niggering the land"
Ten Little Nigger Boys
"Chopped-up niggers"
"Last one in is a nigger"
"Sambo" and "Hambone"
"Jolly nigger banks"
Nigger Milk ("Niggers drink ink for milk")
"Ten thousand niggers in hell" ("Don't send me no more niggers.
They are trying to put my fire out.")

White Childhood Playmate
in Dorn's Alley

**Former Representative
Jennings Gary McAbee**

CHILDHOOD PLAYMATE OF A DIFFERENT HUE

IN MY HOMETOWN of McCormick, black and white boys played together until the white child approached the age of ten to twelve years of age. After that age, we never communicated with each other again. The next writing is a tribute to one of my white playmates, which was part of the eulogy of my departed friend, Representative Jennings Gary McAbee. (Note: Mr. McAbee served my home area as a member of the South Carolina General Assembly for many years.)

Jennings and I were playmates as children in Dorn's Alley, where I was born and grew up.

Dorn's Alley was owned by the Dorn families: M. G. and J. J. Dorn. Most of the residents of Dorn's Alley worked for the M. G. and J. J. Dorn Company. My father was no different. He worked at the planer, or sawmill, as they are called today. We lived in one of the company houses.

At any rate, Jennings's father managed the company's building supply store and warehouse, among other properties. Jennings would come to work with his father. He would quietly leave his father and come into Dorn's Alley. Our playmates were Duck Callaham, Bobby Holloway, Billy Crawford, George Mims, and of course, Jennings McAbee.

What I am about to tell you has reference to several summers in Dorn's Alley with Jennings.

Now, in Dorn's Alley, there were a number of old gold mines, which had been left opened and abandoned. Now, this was our playground. There were no basketball courts, no tennis courts, no volleyball courts, and no gym sets or swings. Now, there were the mines, woods, water holes, small branches of water, and vines.

Now, back in those days, the Tarzan movies were very popular. I think that you all know where I am going with this. We would pretend to be Tarzan, with the holler, shirts off, almost the whole nine yards—connect these large vines that we had gotten out of the woods to large tree limbs near the water, and swing across the bodies of water, and often falling in. That was one of Jennings's favorite. Another one was the making of our toys. Nowadays, you just go to any store and buy your toys.

Jennings and his buddies were craftsmen back then. We made pop guns, bows, and arrows, and one of Jennings favorite was the slingshot. As we were making our slingshots one day: using a tree limb with the proper fork, getting a heavy-duty rubber band, and a piece of leather. We proceeded to make our slingshots. Jennings left and said that he would be back in a few minutes. When he got back, he had a store-bought slingshot that he had gotten from Smith's Five-

and Ten-Cent Store. Now, you see why it was one of his favorites. I think that we laughed for the rest of the afternoon.

We had a place to meet, nowadays, you might call it a club-house, but it was a vacant room on the back of one of the company's warehouses. When it rained, we would meet in this room. It was located near the railroad tracks, which we would walk the rails to compete to see who could reach the coal chute, first, without falling off the rail.

Every Christmas, the Dorn Company would sponsor a fire-works display in Dorn's Alley and would give a gift to all the residents. Jennings would always put some fireworks to the side for him and his buddies in the alley to use for New Year's Day.

The last summer that we spent together had to do with some bicycles. None of us had bicycles in Dorn's Alley. So Jennings went out and bought three bicycles from the Western Auto Store. He had one of the employees of the company to bring the bicycles to the Alley on the back of a company truck. There was more excitement in Dorn's Alley than ever before. Brand-new bicycles! He left the bicycles in the Alley for us to take turns riding every day.

Someone in his family found out about the bicycles and thus ended Jennings's playtime in Dorn's Alley. These were great times in a segregated South, a time when countless black and white youth spent time together—if only adults had followed our example.

Jennings and I went our separate ways, he to Wofford and me to South Carolina State. We saw each other some thirty years later, he with a successful career as a public servant, and me with a career as an educator.

Among the notable positions he held in life, Jennings was trea-surer of the John de la Howe School Foundation and, he, like Ms. Betty Carol McKinney, was a strong supporter of the John de la Howe School.

Jennings was one of the warmest, one of the kindest, and one of the most caring human beings that I have ever known. I knew that he would turn out that way from those summers that we spent in Dorn's Alley.

Poems by the Author

POEMS BY THE AUTHOR

TEACHER, TEACHER

Teacher, teacher
I need you each school day
To know something of my community
Long, long, before the month of May.

Teacher, teacher
I need you each school day
To help me know of my responsibilities
And the importance of grade A.

Teacher, teacher
I need you each school day
I come in many colors
To study, to learn, and to play.

Teacher, teacher
I need you each school day
I have difficult needs and abilities
Which only you can show the way.

Teacher, teacher
I need you each school day
Sometimes it's hard for you to understand me
Because I don't know what to say.

Teacher, teacher
I need you each school day
Although I can't understand why
You can't teach me how to pray.

Teacher, teacher
I need you each school day
To help me develop my talents
For a job which grants good pay.

Teacher, teacher
I need you each school day
To teach me to have compassion
In a world which seems to have lost its way.

LOVE

Love flows down from the mountain
Like the mighty flow from a Niagara Fall
Put your hat under the flow
And spread love to those who call.

I LOVE YOU

I love you
More than you will ever know
More than the daisy loves sunlight
And more than the skier loves snow.

I love you
Like a baby loves milk
Like a monkey loves bananas
And like a plant loves silt.

ETERNITY

Eternity is an adventure
To beset each of us
Plan now for the journey
And it will be a great plus.

BEAUTY

There is beauty beyond the mighty skies
Beauty beyond the visions of the mighty dreamer
There is beauty beyond the vastness of space
Beauty created by the mighty redeemer.

TO BE

To be poor and black
In a world without feelings
To be ragged and Afro
In an environment of disenchantment
To be shoeless and colored
In an atmosphere of despair
To be naked and a spook
In a community of disenfranchisement
To be destitute and a boot
In a state of listlessness
...To be anything but
Is a challenge to the man of soot!

A MAN

A man of many colors
Who travels across the seas
Sharing good tidings
To everyone's glee.

POWERFUL WIND

There is a powerful wind
Which blows over the land
Causing many people
To clutch hand in hand.

SHE

She was as beautiful
As the setting sun
Her glow not so bright
But she had more fun.

A DAY

There is a day in the time of man
A day which preceded dissolution
There is a day in the time of man
A day which provided absolution.

TIME

Time has an endless quantity
That no man can purchase
Time has no motivation
Except a Godly purpose.

PURPOSE

My goal is but a never-ending interest
In the condition of my people
A purpose I have chosen
which I learned under Bethany's Steeple.

My Family

The blood of my people
Flows through the sands of time,
Like water seeping through the earth
And leaving life behind.

My people have trod the earth
Over its seven continents they walked,
Sowing their seed everywhere
Even in Haiti where beside Toussaint they fought.

My people are a family
Woven together in its pedigree,
Who have helped to build whole communities
In America and across the sea.

Our family is a unit of love
As strong as the sound of Gabriel's horn,
For in God you see
We are all of His firstborn.

Our family together must stay
As a knight in shining armor,
Guarding the queen's castle
During the hot and muggy days of summer.

The love and friendship our family shares
Must remain an ever-guiding light,
Showing those who follow behind us
A strength and togetherness for which we all would fight.

And when death touches the doorsteps
Of any member of our ranks,
May God take that member to heaven
And to Him we shall all give thanks.

Final Thoughts

The Crisis of Identity and Self-Esteem among Black Males

You put him in slavery for 244 years and called him your property.

You barbecued his dead body to strike fear in anyone who would dare to protest.

You celebrated his lynching with a "hanging party."

You demeaned his women and children.

You burned his churches.

You took his schools.

You clustered him in buildings, high and low, and riddled his self-esteem with "bullets" of frustration and despair.

You changed his education to meet state and national standards, standards unknown to him.

You imprisoned his brothers for long periods of time.

You changed laws to make him more human, but laws didn't change hearts, attitudes, and prejudices.

You took the lives of Goodman, Chaney, Schwerner, Kennedy, King, Smith, Hamilton, Middleton, Liuzzo, Till, Reeb, Evers, three little girls in an Alabama church, and other civil rights memorial icons; lynched Michael Donald in 1981; and killed nine churchgoers in Charleston in 2015, to show your disregard for human life.

You never accepted Lincoln's equality in his Gettysburg Address.

You seem to be directed from a statement in a modem popular movie "Keep the traffic in the dark people, the colored. They are animals anyway." or by the century-old US Supreme Court's *Dred Scott* decision.

For centuries, you have been insensitive to the needs and aspirations of the black male. This lack of sensitivity continues to this day by suspending him from school, by expelling him from school, by putting him in special education, by not hiring him, by saturating his communities with illegal substances, and by putting him on that other "plantation."

You continue to expand your hate groups for blacks across the United States.

ENOUGH SAID!

Franklin's Ten Observations for the Rearing of Children

1. Teach the children beginning with infancy.
2. Love the children immensely.
3. Lead the children by example.
4. Show the children the value of work.
5. Discipline the children.
6. Support the children for success.
7. Demonstrate for the children acceptable moral values to include respect.
8. Show the children the importance of service.
9. Expect the children to excel in school and in life.
10. Guide the children to their waiting stars.

Young people have all kinds of needs, among which the belongingness need is paramount. Young people want to be a part of something. This is because they all have self-esteem needs. They have a need to feel good about themselves, to feel that they have self-worth. These needs are going to be met through either constructive or destructive means.

More clubs and organizations should be made available for young people to join so that their needs can be met through constructive means. These groups should be attractive enough to cause young people to want to join them, and there should be enough activities to retain their involvement. Ultimately, this will lead to more constructive involvement when these young people become adults. As the Bible reads, "train a child in the way it should grow, so that when he is old, he will not depart from it."

A TRIBUTE

Countless persons have contributed to the welfare of African Americans in the South. In addition to those mentioned in this manuscript, I want to thank the black and white men, the black and white women, and the children who sacrificed, suffered, and died in order for black citizens to have a better way of life.

AFTERTHOUGHTS

"Only the educated are free."—Epictetus (c. A. D. 100).

The true purpose of education is to cherish and unfold the seeds of immortality already sewn within us, to develop to its fullest extent the capacities of all kind with which the God who has made us, has endowed us.

Education makes a people easy to lead, but difficult to drive; easy to govern, but impossible to enslave.

References

REFERENCES

Index Journal Newspaper, Greenwood, SC.

Burgess, John Phillip, *History of the NFA in South Carolina*, June 1956.

Edmonds, Bobby F., "The Making of McCormick County," Cedar Hill Unltd., 1000 Cedar Hill Road, McCormick, SC.

Paid Political Advertisements, *The McCormick Messenger*, June 3, 1954, pages 7–8.

"Dr. C. H. Workman to be Honored on Wednesday, August 13." *The McCormick Messenger*, McCormick, SC, August 7, 1958, page 1.

James Meredith, hired as advisor to Jesse Helms, Associated Press, 1989.

Ronnie Chavis, Vietnam Veterans Memorial, the Virtual Wall, Washington, DC

Cases Adjudged in the Supreme Court of the United States. Superintendent of Documents, US Government Printing Office, Washington, DC.

Mattison, James C., Tribute to Dr. W. S. Mims, Mims High School, McCormick, SC, 1967.

Mims, Thales, *Memories of My Early Childhood*, Abbeville, SC, 2002.

Johnson, W. D., AME president, Columbia, SC. 1905.

Jones, Jae, Harbison Agricultural College: Freedman College in Abbeville, SC, July 7, 2017.

Avery L. Daniels, coordinator of Historical Collection at South Carolina State University, Orangeburg, SC.

Dr. Gabe Buckman, former professor of agriculture, former itinerant teacher-trainer, and former state NFA advisor, South Carolina State College, Orangeburg, SC.

A Chronology of the New Farmers of America, Dr. Ernest Norris, professor of agricultural education, Prairie View A&M University (retired), Prairie View, Texas.

New Farmers of America Records, 1929–1965, Ruth Lilly Special Collections and Archives, IUPUI University, Indiana University Purdue University, Indianapolis, Indiana.

Mays Museum, Greenwood, SC.

New Farmers of America 26 National Convention, October 3–6, 1960, Municipal Auditorium, Atlanta, Georgia.

Guide for New Farmers of America, Office of Education, Department of Health, Education, and Welfare, Washington, DC, the French-Bray Printing Company, Baltimore, Maryland, 1963.

South Carolina Young Farmer and Future Farmer Magazine, SC Office of Vocational Education, Agriculture Section, Columbia, SC, volume 21, no. 4., Summer, 1970.

Gifted Program Teaching Black, White Children Division, Robertson Barrett, *The News and Observer*, Raleigh, NC, April 12, 1992, page 1a.

"SC County Mirrors Gulf Between Races in the South," Eric Harrison, November 28, 1993, *The Los Angeles Times*, Los Angeles, California, page 1.

SC Department of Archives and History, Declaration and Petition Records. Columbia, SC.

"Carolina Town Seeks A Brighter—Some Say Whiter—Future," Helene Cooper, December 10, 1993, *The Wall Street Journal*, New York, NY, page 1.

"Classes at Cades Imbalanced by Race," Lisa Greene, *The State Newspaper*, April 4, 1992, page 1.

Associated Press, *The State Newspaper*, Friday, July 14, 2006, Columbia, South Carolina, page 5b.

The Mims High School Hornet, volume I, no. 1, Monday, May 22, 1961, McCormick, SC, page 1.

Bottoms contributors: Malinda Franklin Jennings, Amy Wilkerson, Barbara Sibert, Catherine Wilkerson, Shirley Callaham, Jackie Rodgers, Jeanette Reid, and H. W. Walker.

"Mississippi's Incredible Month: The Demise of the Sovereignty Commission and of Unprofessional Leadership at the Mississippi State Penitentiary," November 1973. Christopher P. Lehman, *The Journal of Mississippi History*, "Trying to Paper It Over," *Time*, September 4, 1964, pp. 31–32.

"The Jackson State Killings," 1970, Samuel Momodu, Tim Spofford, BlackPast.org, pp. 1–2.

"The Bulldog" Yearbook, 1963, 1964, 1965, South Carolina State College, Orangeburg, South Carolina.

About the Author

The author is from the South. He graduated from Mims High School in McCormick, South Carolina. He holds three degrees from South Carolina State College in Orangeburg, South Carolina. While at South Carolina State, he was arrested and jailed for participation in civil rights demonstrations. One of his favorite sayings is "The South would not have been so volatile during the civil rights years had it only listened to its children." Although this is his first book, he has authored several articles, the most popular of which was "Ground Zero Visited, Before the Dust Settled." His most rewarding job was that of being a teacher. He has worked at every level of school administration: assistant principal, elementary school principal, middle school principal, high school principal, assistant superintendent, and superintendent. He is most proud of the opportunities he had to help to mold the minds and experiences of young black males in a society that is most often not fair to them. He has four children. He resides in Columbia, South Carolina.

CPSIA information can be obtained
at www.ICGtesting.com
Printed in the USA
JSHW032259020521
14226JS00001B/3

9 781662 409417